Building
A New
Society

Building a New Society

The 25th Congress of the Communist Party of the Soviet Union

Edited by

Jessica Smith, David Laibman
and
Marilyn Bechtel

A New World Review Collection

NWR Publications, Inc.
New York, N.Y.

NWR Publications, Inc.
156 Fifth Avenue
New York, N.Y. 10010
1977

Library of Congress Catalog Card Number:
76-15478
ISBN: 0-916972-00-3
Printed in the U.S.A.

 209

CONTENTS

FOREWORD

The editors of NEW WORLD REVIEW consider it a privilege to present this report of the proceedings of the 25th Congress of the Communist Party of the Soviet Union. Part of the material was first published as a special enlarged issue of the magazine (May-June 1976). Fortunately we are able to give much fuller coverage in this book, more than half of which is devoted to additional material.

The main reports to the Congress by CPSU General Secretary Leonid Brezhnev and Chairman of the USSR Council of Ministers Alexey Kosygin, together with the speeches of the delegates, cover practically every facet of life in the Soviet Union — the road traversed, the road ahead. Achievements of the 1971-1975 plan are recorded with justified pride. Problems, shortcomings and errors are faced frankly. Ways to overcome them and reach still higher goals are set forth in the guidelines for the Tenth Five-Year Plan, 1976-80. Watchword of this new plan is quality and efficiency with stress on the application of the newest scientific and technological achievements in all phases of economic development.

One is struck above all by the pervasive emphasis on the quality of life itself, on the constant striving for higher standards of living and culture to insure *the well-being of the people* — words appearing more often than any others in the guidelines for the new plan adopted by the Congress.

The reports and discussions at the Congress vividly depict the quality of Soviet life: The absence of exploitation of the many for the profits of the few; the distribution of the profits of state enterprises for the needs of the workers; the creative work available for every person, of all races and both sexes, the young and strong, the old and still ablebodied; the free and ever expanding educational system, medical help and hospital beds without cost available for all the people, and numerous other free services and social insurance benefits in all the republics, in all parts of the land.

They tell too of the stable prices, the low rents, the free or low cost vacations; the hundred different peoples of various colors and cultures and traditions living together in true brotherhood and mutual help; the new plans in agriculture for land improvement, specialization, inter-farm collective and state farm cooperation, agro-industrial integration — bringing still greater progress in

7

narrowing the gap between city and country and that between manual and mental labor.

In short, we get a picture of the way of life of the world's first socialist society in the period of its maturity — a society based on the socialist principle of people giving "according to their abilities," and receiving "according to their work," while building toward a communist society in which people still give according to their abilities but receive "according to their *needs*."

We have laid special emphasis, as did the Congress itself, on the close involvement of all the people in decision making on all matters affecting their lives. This comes out clearly in the pre-Congress discussions. The plans to be considered are made available, through trade unions, youth and other mass organizations, to the whole people, who work over them and send in many thousands of suggestions which are considered before the final draft is submitted to the Congress and later to the Supreme Soviet of the USSR.

There can be no doubt that word of how all this is done, how a non-crisis society is achieved, is of vital importance to the people of the United States beset by the evils of unemployment, inflation, racism, repression and burdened by the biggest military budget in history.

Most vital of all for the rest of the world is the program of the 25th Congress for the Peace, Freedom and Independence of the Peoples, carrying forward the struggle for implementing the sweeping, all-inclusive peace program of the 24th Congress. Who could disagree with this program that calls for ending the arms race, reaching a new US-USSR agreement on limiting strategic arms, ending *all* nuclear weapons tests, banning chemical, weather and all terror weapons, convening a World Disarmament Conference, strengthening detente everywhere. Added to these are a draft treaty abolishing force in international relations, continuing the struggle to end all colonialism and racism, to eliminate all discrimination in trade and inequality in international economic relations.

We have done our best to present a true, comprehensive picture of the Congress. For those who wish to go further, we shall provide what help and guidance we can on access to original sources and complete texts.

Space limitations have compelled us to condense the Brezhnev and Kosygin reports by more than half, while striving to retain all essential ideas and facts. The language is as close to the original as abridgement permits. Direct quotation is indicated.

All the Soviet delegates opened their discussion of the main reports with warm expressions of gratitude to the Communist Party and the Soviet Government and to Leonid Brezhnev personally. Here we retained only excerpts reflecting various phases of Soviet life and experience and representing different national areas. Because of space limitations we have given only the most significant excerpts from the foreign guests' speeches.

Selections, condensations and editing have been done by the editors of NEW

WORLD REVIEW — Marilyn Bechtel, Associate Editor of NWR during the preparation of the manuscript and Editor-elect as of January, 1977; David Laibman, Assistant Editor; and Jessica Smith, Editor at the time of the preparation of this volume and slated to become Chairperson of the Editorial Board.

Our special thanks are due to all those who have contributed articles and statements not part of the Congress proceedings. And our warm appreciation to Novosti Press Agency for furnishing official texts and translations of the main reports and many of the speeches of Soviet delegates and guests from abroad.

THE EDITORS

Part One: The Congress' Impact

1

MARK SOLOMON

The 25th Soviet Party Congress And the US People

If one were to insist that study and analysis of the substance and spirit of the historic 25th Congress of the Communist Party of the Soviet Union was vitally important to the aspirations of the people of the United States, one would perhaps be met with a questioning if not hostile response. But that is the truth of the matter—a truth that becomes more compelling with the passage of time.

Anti-Sovietism and anti-communism remain the cutting edge of reaction. Nearly every policy in both the domestic and foreign spheres that undermines the welfare of the US people is justified on anti-Soviet and anti-communist grounds. Red-baiting is at the core of infamous Senate Bill 1, which revives a broad-gauged attack upon individual liberties. A reorchestrated "Soviet threat" remains the stock-in-trade of the militarists and their political allies who are seeking to impose an unbearable $112.7 billion military budget on a society dangerously weakened by neglect of its human services. Unemployment, inflation, deteriorating housing and health care continue to plague the nation as growing numbers particularly among minorities, youth and the elderly face a despairingly hard present and a grim future. While the hope for peace is shared by more and more Americans, the Reagans, Jacksons and Wallaces revive the ugly voices of the past to smear a changing world with the

PROFESSOR MARK SOLOMON is Associate Professor of History at Simmons College in Boston. His special interests include American intellectual and cultural history, labor history, Afro-American history, and Third World studies. In 1972-1973 he was a Visiting Lecturer in Humanities at Massachusetts Institute of Technology and in 1974 was a Harvard Fellow in Ethnic Studies. In 1973 and 1974 he lectured at the Institute for United States Studies of the Academy of Sciences in Moscow. A delegate to the World Congress of Peace Forces in Moscow in 1973, Dr. Solomon has since served on its Continuing Liaison Committee.

charge of communist "expansionism," to revile the revolutionary tide in southern Africa, to pressure an already right-wing president even further to the right, into scuttling the hope for progress this year in the SALT II nuclear limitation talks. Punctuating the presidential campaign is a new demon of the right called the "dollar gap" in military spending, which *The New York Times* (March 14, 1976) admits "may turn out to be as much a myth as the 'missile gap' of 16 years ago." While the scandalously wasteful B-1 bomber is approved by the House of Representatives, the President surrenders to the ultra-right by not only dropping the word, detente, but more importantly, capitulating to a narrowing of its scope and undermining of its most dynamic and hopeful elements.

It is to the credit of the majority of the US people that they have not abandoned the vision of a peaceful, better world based on coexistence and cooperation among nations. Despite the heavier drumbeats of anti-communism—despite a Secretary of State who clings to the myopic idea of Soviet "expansionism," despite a cascade of attacks upon the internal life and policies of the Soviet Union including the calculated creation of a picture of a repressive, inhumane society, despite growing physical assaults on Soviet representatives in the United States—the present realities and future potentialities of detente endure.

But the cause of peace and coexistence must continue to survive the crescendo of anti-Sovietism. It is more essential than ever to cut through the layers of propaganda, to separate truth and falsehood about Soviet society, in order to lead our own nation away from the relentless rationalizations for a corporate-garrison state and toward the path of peaceful competition in the effort to create a better life.

No better vehicle exists to probe and test the realities of Soviet life as they affect this country than the historic 25th Congress of the CPSU. Here was an event which absorbed and reflected every current within the vastness of Soviet life; here was the culmination of an unprecedented involvement of the Soviet people in decision making; here was the most sensitive barometer of the successes, shortcomings and prospects of the Soviet Union at home and abroad; here was the frankest forum of the great cross-section of Soviet leadership. There is no better place to explore the political values and cultural soul of Soviet society, to assess its motives and intentions as it hovers in the 59th year of socialism upon the threshhold of a communist society. There is no better context to explore the interior dialogue among the Soviet people. For the Congress is the assemblage of the vanguard of Soviet society charged with the major responsibility for synthesizing policies and leading the nation toward the achievement of concrete domestic goals and international policies. The magnitude of the Congress' responsibilities requires clarity, searching self-criticism, openness, and a political and psychological posture which itself becomes a model for the nation's goals. And finally, no better event exists to compare the claims of cold warriors about the USSR against the claims of Soviet leaders themselves. And there is no better place to begin than with the report of General Secretary Leonid Brezhnev.

Reverberating through the report is an unyielding commitment to achieve "a turn from cold war to peaceful coexistence of states with different social systems, a turn from explosive tensions to detente and normal mutually beneficial cooperation." Nowhere in the address is a suggestion of adherence to the arrogance of power, to the fetishism of atomic bombs and nuclear diplomacy, or to the ugly and precarious balance of terror doctrine. While there is pride in the growth of the strength and influence of the world's socialist states—especially the achievement of independence and national unity by the brave people of Vietnam, the independence won by Laos and Cambodia and the steady progress of socialist Cuba—the "spirit of true equality" among socialist states and their commitment to world peace is emphasized. While the political-military alliance embodied in the Warsaw Treaty is affirmed "as long as the NATO bloc continues to exist and as long as militarist elements continue their arms drive," the Brezhnev report also stresses the Soviet Union's firm opposition "to the world's division into . . . military blocs and to the arms race." In fact, the USSR has repeatedly called for dismantling the Warsaw Pact and NATO simultaneously, beginning with their military forces. Economic relations among socialist states are discussed in terms of mutually beneficial trade and common efforts to solve greater needs in energy, fuel and basic primary materials.

Dramatic changes in the developing countries are of growing significance to all who do not wish to experience more Vietnams. In southern Africa, the growing investments of US-based multinational corporations and deepening US strategic and military involvement in the racist Republic of South Africa are putting the US on a collision course with southern African liberation movements determined to control their own resources. The success of the MPLA in establishing the Republic of Angola with the help—requested by them—of the Soviet Union and Cuba, has rekindled cold war threats against those nations. Soviet and Cuban support to Angola had become a pretext for an escalating US military involvement until Congress stepped in. Thus, Brezhnev's comments on these issues have special importance. He emphasized that the Soviet Union has supported and will continue to support peoples fighting for national independence and, "in so doing . . . does not look for advantages, does not hunt for concessions, does not seek political domination, or exact military bases." That explicit declaration, backed by a concrete record, demolishes the fiction of Soviet "imperialist expansion" and provides the basis for evaluating the threats to peace in developing countries. Angola is a striking illustration of the dynamic relationship between detente and national independence. The efforts of multinationals and militarists to control the resources of emerging nations creates the seedbed of neocolonialism and war. On the other hand, support for independence strengthens world peace by forcing respect for sovereignty and indigenous control of wealth.

War clouds and intense human suffering continue to underscore the situation in the Middle East. And in no other region has Soviet policy come under sharper attack. The Soviet Union has been accused of undermining the sovereignty of Israel, of contributing to the arms race in the region, of seeking to gain a foothold for its own undefined interests. In that light, the authoritative forum of the 25th Congress provides an excellent basis to measure those claims against official Soviet policy. The Brezhnev report reaffirms Soviet efforts to establish good relations with the states of the region, its adherence to the principle of inviolable borders, and its support for eliminating the consequences of Israeli aggression. In contrast, US policy stresses access to oil, cultivation of reactionary Arab states through saturation with armaments, implacable hostility to Arab socialism and Palestinian aspirations, growing ambivalence toward Israel as Washington seeks to use that nation as a military buffer against radical change in the Middle East while attempting to buy off Egypt and other states. The Soviet call for a reconvening of the Geneva Conference thus becomes the greatest hope for the inseparable goals of stability for Israel and realization of Palestinian rights. Everyone concerned with peace should seriously consider this fact, as well as the Soviet offer to participate in a search for a solution to the arms race in the region within the context of advancing an overall settlement.

The foreign policy review at the 25th Congress persistently reflects a passion for normalized relations, inviolable borders, and encouragement of steps away from interventions and foreign military bases. While the press in our country heralds new US military pacts with Greece, Turkey, and Spain, the Brezhnev report speaks warmly of the achievements of the All-European conference at Helsinki and the building of cooperation in science, economy and culture between states of differing social systems.

Advances in peaceful relations between the United States and the Soviet Union are singled out for special attention. Agreements relating to the prevention of nuclear war and growing exchanges on political, technological, and cultural levels are heralded. It is vital for Americans to grasp the thrust of the Congress' views on the future direction of American-Soviet relations. The arms race and its main motive—an alleged Soviet threat —is castigated. Brezhnev speaks with sensitivity of the tragic social consequences of larger military budgets while allocations for social needs are reduced, and while the technology of new weapons development goes forward. "There is no Soviet threat either in the West or in the East. The Soviet Union has not the slightest intention of attacking anyone . . . does not increase its military budget, and far from reducing, is steadily augmenting allocations for the people's well-being."

The jaded political observer will counter that these are just words and that the realities of international power relations require deeds. In this regard, the Brezhnev report reemphasizes many proposals which are probably unfamiliar to a majority of US people. Stressing that "general and complete disarmament was and remains our ultimate goal," the report calls for convening a World Disarmament Conference. The international convention banning and destroying bacteriological weapons, based on an initiative from the socialist states, is underlined as an historic example of what can be achieved. The sphere of coverage of the Treaty on the Non-Proliferation of Nuclear Weapons is expanding. On current strategic arms limitations talks with the United States, Brezhnev says: ". . . we have persistently and repeatedly offered the United States not to stop at just limiting the existing types of strategic weapons. We thought it would be possible to go farther. Specifically, we suggested banning the development of new, still more destructive weapons systems, in particular the new Trident submarines carrying ballistic missiles and the new strategic B-1 bombers in the United States, and similar systems in the USSR. Deplorably, these proposals were not accepted by the US side. But we have not withdrawn them." Here is an offer that no sane and honest person can refuse—an opportunity to test Soviet and US intentions in the crucible of negotiations, which would have the most direct bearing on the welfare of the US people. In Asia, the Soviets have proposed a ban on military bases in the hitherto peaceful Indian Ocean. Similarly the socialist states have offered concrete proposals to reduce the levels of Soviet and US armed forces in Europe this year. Where in our nation's press have such proposals, which hold out the promise of alleviating the arms burden upon the US people, been publicized? Where have we been informed that the USSR "now offer(s) to conclude a world treaty on the non-use of force in international relations, to promote a new Soviet-American agreement on limiting and reducing strategic armaments, and conclude international treaties on universal and complete termination of nuclear weapons tests, on banning and destroying chemical weapons, on banning development of new types and systems of mass annihilation weapons, and also banning modification of the natural environment for military and other hostile purposes"?

Predictably, professional and academic Soviet baiters (cf. Adam Ulam, "The Smug Russians," *New Republic*, March 27, 1976) disdainfully and cruelly ignore the 25th Congress proposals relating to the needs of the world's peoples for disarmament, independence and development. Reworking the tired demonology of anti-Sovietism, Adam Ulam proclaims that detente is "a kind of soporific drug administered to the West while it goes through internal political convulsions . . . and economic crises." It may not matter to Ulam, but millions of people would gladly accept the "drug" of arms reduction, normalized relations, and attention to grievously neglected social and human problems in the United States.

Another recent theme of cold war revivalists is Soviet support for the anti-colonial struggles of emerging nations. The report is explicit on this controversial issue. Brezhnev contends that detente does not abolish the laws of social struggle and does not imply a communist-capitalist reconciliation. At the heart of history is the inevitable tide of national and social revolution. Strict observance of non-intervention in the internal affairs of other states can only serve democracy and the movement for national independence. Not only does the world's democratic majority have nothing to fear from detente, but detente's underlying principle of respect for sovereignty is a foundation for peaceful social change. Those forces that dread the historic movement toward freedom seek to reverse its processes and thus are drawn to interfere in the internal affairs of nations. One need only recall the observation of *The New York Times'* journalist Seymour Hersch that Soviet and Cuban assistance to the Angolan MPLA was largely in response to a massive intervention by the United States, South Africa and Zaire in the internal affairs of the emerging Angolan nation.

The theme of independence and mutual respect also arises in regard to relations among Communist parties. Brezhnev briskly obliterates again the lingering, weary myth of "orders from Moscow"—the idea of a world Communist apparatus directed from the Soviet Union. While the Soviet leader speaks warmly of the growth of Communist parties throughout the world, expresses anger at the persecutions of Communists in Chile, Paraguay, Uruguay, South Africa, Indonesia, Brazil and other countries, and speaks of the existence of a common internationalist perspective among Marxist-Leninists, he reiterates "the inviolate standards of equality and respect for the independence of each party."

Finally, we come to the internal dynamics of Soviet society. This question is of great importance to us because the picture of Soviet life promoted with a deafening din in the US media pollutes the environment of cooperation, kindles hatred and anti-Sovietism and thus again encourages distrust and the deadening repetition of military spending and cold war psychoses which have paralyzed our nation for more than thirty years. Following the media, one would believe that the Soviet Union is obsessed with failing agriculture and shady grain deals with the US, dissenting intellectuals, persecution of Jews and chaotic economic and social services. But the report vividly reflects a profoundly different society which is deeply and energetically absorbed in raising the living standards of the people, in elevating their cultural and economic levels, in promoting a politics which broadens participation in the exciting journey to the creation of the world's first advanced communist society. The picture of the efforts of millions that emerges is a striking antithesis to the menacing, expansionist, repressive social system pictured in much of the US media.

Consider for a moment the addresses of even the most liberal political figures in the US—giving only grudging assent to the principle of normalized and constructive US-Soviet relations, uttering Cassandra-like wails over the exhaustion of our natural resources, warning of the "return" of scarcity economy to our society and projecting an unpromising future. The report to the Congress, in a contrast that will be disquieting for some, speaks of improved housing for 56 million people over the past five years; increases in wages, in pensions and scholarship grants; improvement of the quality of rural life and technological upgrading of agriculture; 9,300,000 graduates of vocational and technical schools plus more than nine million specialists with higher or secondary degrees flowing into a society that has room for every one of them; new plans to satisfy the nation's energy needs; new enterprises from the commissioning of factories to space flights to the creation of new residential districts.

These achievements are not catalogued with smugness and complacency. "We have not always worked in the manner required by our own decisions," Brezhnev admits. This manifestly self-critical spirit would look like ill-fitting raiment if adopted by the average US political leader. The report admits that "we have not yet put an end to breaches of planning, technological and labor discipline." A pledge is made to work toward the elimination of mismanagement and carelessness which retards material and cultural advances towards a communist society. A "determined struggle against obtuseness and red tape" is called for; the need for improvement in the quality of consumer goods is stressed as a major part of the movement to achieve a historic transformation. Satisfying the needs and desires of the Soviet people is considered a serious matter and high political priority. Methods must be refined, Brezhnev says, to allow the consumer "broad possibilities for influencing production" and to promote "democratic principles and local initiatives" in order to curb delays, losses, poor decisions, and superfluous bureaucracy.

Some people in our commodity-saturated society may find this concern either trivial or misplaced. Such an attitude, aside from its insensitivity to the first socialist society's inheritance of a backward economy, two cataclysmic wars, relentless external pressures—ignores the simple fact that the 25th Congress' emphasis upon upgrading the quality and quantity of consumer goods provides a solid foundation for the realization of the fundamental needs of both the US and Soviet people. For it is in the very struggle to improve material and cultural conditions that the basis for peace and the healthiest competition between systems can be located. The Tenth Five-Year Plan goals should be a signal that both the internal momentum of Soviet life and the urgent needs of people in the US require the end of the arms race and peaceful use of the precious resources of both our nations. We should look upon the projections of the Tenth Five-Year Plan as a basis for setting the world upon that desperately needed but elusive path of peaceful competition.

The 25th Congress stresses the need for "an effective system of material and moral incentives" to best serve the people. This emphasis avoids the spurious pure "moral incentive" approach which often, intentionally or not, loses touch with the basic objective of serving the people's needs and substitutes a manipulative "consciousness" for a better life. On the other hand, the Congress rejects the pure "material incentive" approach which can lose sight of the collectivist spirit and the need to build a society that is as psychologically and morally uplifting as it is materially productive.

In contrast to the intense ideological pounding of *The New York Times* and other media—the torrent of books and articles which hysterically paint an ugly and despairing picture of Soviet life—the report of the General Secretary creates an entirely opposite view of the concentrated energies and values of Soviet society and its people. The large working class majority of the CPSU membership is a source of pride as is the growth of party membership among collective farmers, teachers, technical workers and artists, women, young people, ethnic minorities. For those who are told that the political culture of Soviet life is framed in secrecy (a hypocritical charge in the light of Watergate and other revelations) the forceful expression of open links between ruling party and people is significant: "The Party has no secrets from the people. It has a vital concern in having all the Soviet people know about its undertakings and plans, and in having them express their own views on these matters." Thus, letters and messages from people to responsible leaders are stressed as effective means of assuring growing involvement of the people in shaping of policies.

Indeed, the report places strong emphasis on the very moral and democratic issues which have been trumpeted in this country to create an anti-Soviet atmosphere. From the authoritative platform of the Congress a plea is made to Party leaders to deepen their responsibilities as organizers and inspirers of the masses, to reject subjectivism and reinvigorate criticism and self-criticism. "Trust and respect for people should go hand in hand with a high exactingness towards those responsible for assignments." The value of criticism, Brezhnev stresses, lies in its sincerity, constructiveness, and readiness to instantly overcome mistakes and shortcomings within the framework of people's control. The modern leader, he says, must have well-grounded competence, initiative, humane commitment, and must be thoughtful and considerate towards others: "He who has lost his ability to make a critical assessment of his activity, he who has lost touch with the masses, who breeds toadies and bootlickers, and who has lost the trust of the Communists cannot be a Party leader.''

Thus, the building of a communist society is to be based on the people's awareness, involvement and commitment— on the concept that "our state is a state of the whole people, expressing the interests and the will of the whole people.'' This necessitates a partisan ideological battle against chauvinism and nationalism, for peace and internationalism, for a socialist morality ranged against "acquisitiveness, proprietary tendencies, hooliganism, red tape and indifference to one's fellow humans. . .'' It is undoubtedly difficult for many in the US, nurtured in a psychological climate of strained individualism and competitiveness to grasp this ethos which seeks the realization of individual potential within the context of a collective emphasis on the common good and commitment to the social, rather than individual solution of human problems. Our national culture has always been strained by the contradiction between our communitarian and individualist tendencies. It is difficult for Americans to grasp this collectivist outlook because we are constantly fed the view that societal commitments are violations of "individual human freedom.''

The General Secretary's remarks on the relationship between social commitment and free choice are particularly challenging. It is suggested to Soviet educators that young people need to augment their knowledge of facts with an ability to find their bearings—to seek the most promising individual fulfillment within an education which integrates individual desires with social commitment. In the arts, the issue of "socialist realism" emerges again with considerable emphasis. This too is a difficult issue for Americans who have been acculturated to believe that artistic expression at the core is a deeply personal matter involving only the imagination of the artist—and his ability to sell his work. The report again stresses the belief that the artist does not live and work in a vacuum. The artist too has a profound responsibility to assist in the effort to create a qualitatively advanced civilization. But the report also seeks to synthesize the unique gifts and the autonomy of the artist with the needs of society. Ranging over the potential of great themes involving material and ethical conflicts, the struggle for peace and internationalism, the General Secretary attacks the production of drab, lifeless, mediocre works, which reflect rote and dogma rather than the flesh and blood of human beings. Art is perceived as not merely the province of the professional, but the property of an entire people manifested in thousands of theater, literary, dance and other groups. The Party approaches artistic issues in terms of respect for the artist, assistance to the creative quest and insistence upon the highest attainable human-cultural standards: "If some functionary happens to take the oversimplified approach and tries to resolve by fiat matters relating to aesthetic creativity and diversity of form and individuality of style, the Party does not ignore such cases and helps to rectify the situation.''

In the end one comes to the inescapable ethic of an emerging communist society which cannot separate individual liberation from society's struggle against exploitation, scarcity and individualism. The controversial issue of legal rights and responsibilities of citizens is dealt with in this context. Is the need to "tighten up discipline and enhance the responsibility of citizens" a violation of democracy? "Democracy is inconceivable without discipline and a sound public order. It is a responsible approach by every citizen to his duties and to the people's interests that constitutes the only reliable basis for the fullest embodiment of the principles of socialist democracy and the true freedom for the individual." A society built on the welfare of the whole community must, in turn, constantly broaden the base of democratic participation: ". . . socialism is impossible without a steady development of democracy."

The realization of the fullest humanistic potential of a socialist state requires both a "discipline" in terms of directing individual energies toward the creation of a better life for all and an increasing emphasis upon individual democratic rights and democratic participation as the ultimate guarantee of people's rule. We find ourselves daily in the midst of extensive media glorification of some Soviet citizens who have chosen a path away from the dialectical interplay between individual autonomy and social responsibility. It is healthy to cut through the propaganda drive surrounding Soviet emigres to consider that many who have not been able to integrate personal ambition with social responsibility, who have capitulated to the marketplace, will find themselves within a capitalist ethic which increasingly displays contempt for anything other than mean-spirited marketability. Growing numbers of Americans will be drawn to a consideration of the class, moral and ethical issues contrasted in the future development of capitalist and socialist societies. This is as it should be, not because the details of the Soviet experience or any other experience are applicable to America (our differing history and culture will stimulate our own path) but because with peace we can hopefully be inspired to embark on the most important journey to freedom in human history.

The section of the Brezhnev report which deals with foreign economic relations alone—the vast increase in Soviet trade with other nations over the last five years, and the promise of much more—is enough to capture the attention of millions of Americans in urgent need of jobs and security. That aspect of the thinking of the 25th Party Congress, like every other aspect, is subject to testing and verification through concrete relations. There is no need for either implacable hostility or mindless apologetics.

The most vital need is for the American people to recognize their own interests that flow from the proceedings of the historic 25th Congress—to study the Congress from the focus of that interest and to seize the opportunities offered by it to put an end to the scourge of the arms race, joblessness and material and spiritual injustice within our own society.   □

2

JOHN PITTMAN

The Marxist-Leninist Party
In the Soviet Union

We are pleased to present to our readers the following account of the CPSU and its role, written in the perspective of Marxist-Leninist theory. The author is well equipped by experience to propound this view and the insights it affords into the crucial area of leadership in socialist societies, as Editor of the English-language edition of World Marxist Review.

A prominent feature of the 25th Congress of the Communist Party of the Soviet Union was the Party's all-encompassing, all-pervading guidance in planning and implementing developed socialism's progress to communism. This was demonstrable evidence of the Marxist-Leninist Party's historically established role of political, ideological and organizational leadership for socialist and communist construction. It was manifest in the *Report of the CPSU Central Committee* delivered by General Secretary Leonid Brezhnev, the *Guidelines for the Development of the National Economy for 1976-1980*, delivered by Chairman A. N. Kosygin, in the reports of other Party officials and the speeches of delegates, and in the pre-Congress discussions involving millions of people, both Party members and non-Party.

All this was a forceful reminder that the CPSU is the Party of Lenin, founder of the world's first socialist state, and the trail-blazing, pioneering Party with the longest and most varied experience in building socialism. It added authority to the answers which the 25th Congress gave to old and new questions concerning the role of the Marxist-Leninist Party in the epoch of the transition from capitalism to socialism, questions which persist among peoples of the non-socialist world, especially in countries of developed capitalism and particularly in the United States.

One question has to do with the relevance in general of the Marxist-Leninist

JOHN PITTMAN grew up in the Black ghetto of Atlanta, Georgia, was educated at Morehouse College in Atlanta and the University of California in Berkeley. A journalist all his life, mainly for the Black and working class press, he was accredited to the founding meeting of the United Nations and many sessions of the General Assembly. Formerly co-editor of the *Daily World*, he is now a member of the editorial staff of *World Marxist Review* and living in Czechoslovakia.

Party. This is an old question which Marx, Engels and Lenin answered many times in many volumes of their writings, but it is said that they wrote for other times and other conditions and their ideas are no longer applicable. Essentially, those who hold this view reject fundamental Marxist-Leninist tenets, particularly the concept of the working class as the class which is capable of doing away with the old society based on exploitation and building a new society free of all exploitation, and which must do this because it cannot free itself without freeing all working people from exploitation.

Variations of this general question of the Party's relevance, apply specifically to the CPSU. One asks why the Party is necessary at the present stage of development of Soviet society, when ideology is said to be no longer relevant for the fulfillment of social functions. The Party's continued "politicizing" in the spheres of the economy, culture, the arts and social relations, it is said, interferes with the free development of society.

This question betrays, on the part of those who sincerely seek an answer, a misconception of the nature of socialism and the Party's role in its development. It fails to take into account that socialism and communism do not develop spontaneously, but must be built according to scientific principles of social development. Although Soviet society is presently in the stage of advanced or developed socialism, that is, the second stage of the socialist phase of communism, its further advance to communism requires both the creation of the productive forces capable of replacing distribution according to work with distribution according to need, and the further development of communist production and social relations. Hence, the Party's theoretical, ideological, political and organizational role is not only still necessary, but has been considerably enhanced by the new tasks arising from the growing complexity of Soviet society in its progress to communism.

The same question is raised, however, by capitalist ideologists for purposes far from enlightenment. From accusations of "ideological indoctrination" and "politicizing" by the Party, they proceed to equate the Party's political and ideological guidance with the total political control of fascist regimes, and employ the cold war "totalitarian" stereotype to characterize it. Basically, this is a denial of the existence of socialist democracy in the Soviet Union and the Party's democratizing role.

Such a position flies in the face of elementary common sense. Quite apart from subjective considerations, such as the expressed intentions of Party leaders and the motives of the founders of scientific socialism, the constant improvement and extension of democracy is an objective law of socialist development. Today it is no more possible to mobilize the forces required for building the foundations of communism without the extensive participation of the population than it was possible in 1917 to capture state power without the support of the broadest masses among the peasants, workers and soldiers.

Some who pursue this line of attack, either from ignorance or hypocrisy or both, question the very principle of party leadership of the state and society, as if political parties were not natural instruments of class rule institutionalized by historical practice, but an invention only of Communists. Yet, the selection, formation and direction of the government by the political vanguard of the ruling class, the most conscious and able champions of its interests, is a fundamental reality of class society, notwithstanding efforts by capitalist ideologists to conceal this fact. Long before Marx and Engels founded the League of Communists in 1847 and the First International in 1864, the principle of party leadership had been established in the politics of many countries. Marxist-Leninists, therefore, have always stressed that the party of the working class is the most conscious, politically active and organized part of the working class, its vanguard, whose leadership is a fundamental principle of socialist revolution and communist construction.

T he view that ideology is no longer relevant for the completion of advanced socialism's tasks in the spheres of the economy, culture, the arts and social relations thrives on misconceptions of the nature of ideology and its role in the contemporary struggle of the two systems. Such misconceptions also underlie doubts concerning democracy in the Soviet Union, which are implanted by imperialist psychological war in relation to the treatment of so-called "dissidents," as well as criticisms of this treatment from some of the USSR's friends and sympathizers.

Feeding such misconceptions is the erroneous idea that imperialism, defeated militarily, politically and economically in recent confrontations with socialism, has abandoned its war aims and aggressive designs against the Soviet Union and other socialist countries. Although the turn to detente gives some plausibility to this view, it in no way accords with the realities of the imperialist arms race and obstruction of the practical implementation of the principles of peaceful coexistence. The importance attached by capitalist politicians and propagandists to the so-called "Third Basket," or "freedom of information," in the talks before the Helsinki Conference, and the zeal and resources which they devote to disseminating their views on this question, make clear their high assessment of the weapon of ideological subversion.

In present-day conditions of the unprecedented intensity of the ideological struggle, what is at stake for the developed socialist society of the Soviet Union is the foundation of a new, well-rounded, harmonious human being through materialization of the communist world outlook. The prospects of socialist development to communism depend on the transmutation of ideas of collectivism, internationalism, labor as life's prime want, respect for human dignity, and the intolerance of all forms of human oppression into the feelings, thoughts, motives and, above all, the habits of Soviet people. Living and working in a socialist society, it is true, inculcates socialist and communist ideas, since social consciousness is ultimately determined by social being. But the ordinary consciousness derived from sensory impressions received in socialist society is not yet the communist consciousness instilled by ideology, which grows through conscious activity in accordance with a system of views and ideas.

It should not be forgotten that Soviet power is not yet 60 years old, hardly sufficient time to uproot habits formed in the course of millenia of exploitative societies and implant habits for an altogether different way of life, based on a absence of exploitation, hardly sufficient time for communist ideology to become the material force required for administering a communist society. This is unavoidably a protracted process, for socialism, even in its advanced stage, is "still stamped with the birthmarks of the old society from whose womb it emerges," as Marx expressed it. And, in the words of Lenin, "the force of habit in millions or tens of millions is a most formidable force."

Anyone in the non-socialist world engaged in efforts to change racist and male supremacist habits of thought and action among the population should have no difficulty in understanding that the CPSU must continue its work of safeguarding and elaborating the ideology of socialism and communism in all spheres of the life of society. For ideology influences the development of the economy, culture, art, morality and social relations, and reactionary ideas may exert a powerful negative influence on any of these spheres of activity. This, in effect, could impair the progress that embraces all aspects of social activity— the political, economic, social and spiritual. And this is the real objective of imperialist pyschological warfare and the attacks of revisionists.

Delivering the report of the CPSU Central Committee to the 24th Congress in 1971, Brezhnev said that "the leading role of the Communist Party . . . is one of the fundamental questions of the revolutionary movement and the building of a new society. Today it has become the pivot of the struggle between Marxist-Leninists and representatives of various forms of revisionism." At the 25th Congress five years later, he said: ". . . the ideological contest between the two systems is becoming ever more acute, and imperialist propaganda ever more subtle. There is no room for neutralism or compromise in the struggle between the two ideologies. Here there is a need for constant political vigilance, active, efficient and convincing propaganda, and timely rebuffs to hostile ideological subversion."

Adopting the Central Committee's report, the Congress specified the ways by which the Party has discharged its responsibilities and will continue to discharge them in the coming period. First place was given to Marxist-Leninist theory, the validity of which has been proven in the revolutionary struggle of the working class and of all the other working people, and in the practical activity of the Communists. This has been the basis of the CPSU's efforts in education as in all of its other activities. Examples were cited of successful efforts by the Central Committee to improve the Marxist-Leninist education of Communists in Tashkent, Byelorussia and in the profession of journalists. But, said Brezhnev, "at the present stage in the country's development, the need for further creative development of theory, far from diminishing, has, in fact, been growing."

The stress given by the 25th Congress to the necessity for more intensive efforts to defend and elaborate Marxism-Leninism is in conformity with the Leninist tenet that without revolutionary theory there can be no revolutionary practice. Progress to communism is impossible without knowledge of the laws, tendencies and motive forces of social development which have been scientifically substantiated in practice, that is, in the revolutionary struggles of the working people. Marxism-Leninism, continuously enriched by generalizations of practice, combines this knowledge with the wealth of ideas produced by humankind and the newest data provided by science. Guided by Marxism-Leninism, this most advanced science of social development, the CPSU is enabled to project a program of communist construction which is a basic ingredient of its leadership role in Soviet society.

Brezhnev explained the CPSU's stand on the defense of Marxism-Leninism in connection with "differences of opinion and approach to some questions which may arise" from time to time among Communists of different countries, and which "hostile propaganda has repeatedly sensationalized." He said "Marxist-Leninists approach such questions from internationalist positions, concerned about strengthening the unity of the whole movement, and discuss the emerging problems in a true comradely spirit in the framework of the immutable standards of equality and respect for the independence of each Party." But he ruled out "compromise on matters of principle" and "reconciliation with views and actions contrary to the communist ideology," because "a concession to opportunism may sometimes yield a temporary advantage, but will ultimately do damage to the Party." He emphasized the importance of proletarian internationalism today, saying that to renounce it "is to deprive Communist parties and the working-class movement in general of a mighty and tested weapon." The class enemy, he pointed out, "actively coordinates its anti-communist activities on an international scale."

The 25th Congress listed some of the new ideological tasks to be solved on the basis of Marxism-Leninism. These include political enlightenment of the population, because "the mass-scale study of Marxism-Leninism is a most important feature of the development of social consciousness at the present stage"; enhancement of the theoretical level of the Party, promotion of both the patriotic and internationalist education of the masses; the economic, labor and moral education of the working people through "further improvement of the whole system of general education, secondary schools in the first place"; raising the ideological level, coordination and efficiency of the mass media; further intensification of the activity of all creative intellectuals in the sphere of culture. The Party's all-embracing ideological guidance is manifest in the scope and variety of these tasks.

Another essential element of the CPSU's leadership role is its guidance of state and public or mass organizations, its political and organizing, functions. Of these it can be said that no other aspect of the CPSU's leadership has been subjected to more attacks from imperialist and revisionist ideologists, or to more criticism from Soviet friends and well-wishers. The main theme of the propaganda of imperialist and revisionist sources, and also of much of the well-intentioned if ill-founded criticism, is that the Party usurps the functions of the state and mass organizations and governs the country by administrative methods.

An extreme version of this charge views the CPSU as ruling by police-state measures ("totalitarianism") against the interests and opposition of the masses, which is said to be mainly passive but is represented by the "dissidents." And a variation, to which many who are not ill-disposed towards the Soviet Union subscribe, belabors the theme of deformations in Soviet society during the period of Stalin's leadership and contends that no change has occurred since then. Indeed, imperialist and revisionist propagandists try to convince the peoples that the restrictions on democracy under Stalin are the essential and permanent characteristics of socialism in the Soviet Union.

None of these charges and criticisms is valid. Their falsity is rooted both in a metaphysical approach to socialism, viewing it not as a developing process but as fixed and static, and in the ignoring or belittling of what is really inherent and essential in socialism and exaggerating the mistakes and transitory aberrations that have been overcome or are in the process of being overcome. The "exposure" of mistakes and such transitory phenomena requires no "investigative reporting"; they are continuously proclaimed by Party leaders and publicized by the Soviet mass media in accordance with Lenin's thesis that the mark of a serious political party is its frank admission of mistakes and shortcomings and its intentions and plans to overcome them.

Actually, the separation of Party functions of political-ideological and organizational leadership from the administrative functions of the state and governmental apparatus and from the educational and economic functions of mass organizations has been clearly defined in Soviet theory and practice. Today the principle is incorporated in the rules of the CPSU. And practice is the proof: the universal method of the Party's guidance of state, public and economic organizations is that Communists accept the Party's line and can strive to obtain its acceptance and implementation by the non-Party organizations in which they work. This is the general and predominant practice, a method not of dictation but of persuasion and political struggle.

Departures from this practice are exceptions and not the rule. They are brought to light and corrected through the process of criticism and self-criticism, an obligatory and permanent principle of Party life. Such departures arise as a result of circumstances which engender a temporary enhancement of centralization, such as arose following the fascist invasion of the Soviet Union, or in consequence of errors made in the attempt to resolve non-antagonistic contradictions in socialist development.

The correction of serious errors and crimes committed in the period of Stalin's leadership is evidence of the inherent, essential tendency of socialist development in the Soviet Union and the Party's practice of self-correction. It cannot be ignored or discounted that the Central Committee itself exposed the errors and crimes and undertook their correction, that the 20th Congress took measures to restore and strengthen the Leninist norms of Party life, and that, despite the harm and setbacks suffered by the Party and the country, socialist construction triumphantly registered new gains, and the Party not only retained the confidence of the masses but was able to enhance its leadership role.

"The experience of past years has convincingly shown that the surmounting of the consequences of the personality cult and also of subjectivist errors," said Brezhnev in the Central Committee report to the 24th Congress, "has favorably affected the general political and, above all, the ideological situation in the country." And at the 25th Congress Brezhnev said: "The Party has always displayed a highly principled approach, standing up for these principles and combating any breaches of them. In this context, the decisions of the 20th Party Congress, whose twentieth anniversary now falls due, were highly important."

In adopting the Central Committee report delivered by Brezhnev, the 25th Congress gave its endorsement to his call for "raising the level of Party guidance of economic and cultural development, the education of our men and women, and improvement of organizational and political work among the masses." This, as he developed it, means concretely that primary Party branches should exert more influence on raising the effectiveness of production, accelerating scientific and technical progress, and improving the education and working and living conditions of the people. It means concretely that they should enhance an exacting, critical approach to all matters, including an objective evaluation of every aspect of the activity of organizations and individuals, with no liberalism towards shortcomings or to those who allow them. It means concretely an enhancement of the control and verification of adopted decisions, a key aspect of organizational work.

Brezhnev reported the Party's work during the period since the 24th Congress to promote the all-round development of the activity of state agencies and mass organizations and to stimulate their initiative. These, with the Soviets and their 2.2 million deputies and 25 million volunteer assistants, are the main vehicles for expanding the participation of the masses in administering and controlling all the affairs of society, a precondition for communist self-administration which is to replace the state in the phase of mature communism. Brezhnev singled out for comment the 107-million-member trade unions, the 35-million-member Young Communist League (Komsomol), and organizations of Soviet women. In other sections of the report, he took account of the activities of many other non-Party organizations of the masses which reflect the prevalence and steady growth of collectivism in Soviet society.

Brezhnev called on the trade unions to organize their work more fully to conform with their rights and the degree of their responsibility. He noted that recently the trade unions' role in collective farms has been growing, and said that questions needing resolution pertained to the structure of trade unions to conform more fully with the structure of management, the forms and methods of trade union activity in production associations, and the powers of governing bodies of sectoral trade unions. He urged the Komsomol to keep alive the fervor of the young and their conscious participation in communist construction. And he said the Party considers it to be its duty to improve the conditions of women as workers, mothers, educators of children, and housewives.

In concluding this summary of the attributes of the CPSU's leadership role in building the material and social bases of communism, it would be a serious omission to leave out consideration of its unifying force in promoting the social homogeneity of Soviet society. There is quite visible evidence of its achievements in harmonizing the still contradictory interests of different non-antagonistic classes and strata. Owing to its planned and consistent guidance, the process which Marx envisioned as the consummation of socialism's development is steadily advancing—the elimination of differences between town and country and between manual and mental labor.

Outstanding, too, is the role of the Party in carrying out the Leninist national policy of equality and friendship of all the 100 peoples making up the multinational Soviet Union. This was pointed out by Brezhnev in his report on the 50th anniversary of the formation of the Union of Soviet Socialist Republics in a gala joint meeting of the Party and Government, December 21, 1972. He said: "the very logic of the struggle for socialism demanded the formation of a united multinational socialist state," and "the establishment of such a state required the Party's organizing role, correct policy and purposeful activity."

The Party has played a leading role in the extra economic attention given from the beginning by the central government to the most backward and primitive areas, exploited as colonies in tsarist days, and bringing them up to the level of the more developed republics. This has fostered both equality and friendship and true internationalism in bringing workers of many nationalities together in the great new projects already in operation or being built in these areas. Friendship and economic development have both been furthered in the mighty demonstrations of mutual aid shown in such examples as the great flow of people and material aid which helped rebuild Tashkent into a shining modern city after the great earthquake of 1966.

Through the Party's sensitive understanding of the need of all peoples to treasure and continue certain of the customs handed down by their forbears, Party policy and practice, fully shared in by each nationality, has led to a beautiful flowering of all the arts in the formerly oppressed areas. Written languages where none had been known before have led to a rich growth of national literature. Use of their native language in school and daily and official life, with Russian universally used as a second language, has made possible a rich exchange of all the arts, constant intercommunication and intermarriage among all the Soviet peoples. All of this has meant that along with the preserving and growth of the best of their national characteristics, while discarding the old and oppressive, a process is taking place of blending peoples of diverse national and cultural backgrounds into what is clearly emerging as one Soviet people.

All Soviet peoples are beneficiaries of this policy. But most of all, perhaps, the formerly enslaved women of Soviet Central Asia, now active in every sphere of life and holding high official positions in Party and government. The role of these many peoples could be seen in the delegates of many nationalities at the Congress, and their integral part in pre- and post-Congress discussions.

Finally, such a summary must take into account the profoundly democratic and humanistic content of the CPSU's guidance of policies in home and foreign affairs. This is especially manifest in the care it gives and the measures it proposes for improving the material and spiritual conditions of the population, and for creating the "new socialist human being." The abolition of human exploitation was itself a deed of such democratic and humanistic magnitude as had not previously occurred in the many millenia of social development. Now the CPSU's efforts to universalize this experience can be seen in its program for promoting the security of other countries through preventing a new World War by the consolidation of detente and the achievement of universal disarmament. It can be seen in its comradely relations with other Marxist-Leninist Parties, in its mutually beneficial cooperation with other socialist countries, and in its persistent implacable struggle against the remnants of colonialism, racism and all forms of oppression and exploitation.

These policies of the CPSU and its Central Committee also won the whole-hearted approval and full endorsement of the 25th Congress. □

3

VASSILY STEPANOV

The CPSU's Guiding Role In Soviet Society

Nearly all countries are governed by political parties representing the interests of one or another social class.

Only one party, the Communist Party of the Soviet Union (CPSU) exists in the USSR. The CPSU's leading role was established during the early stages of development of Soviet society, and is legally fixed in the Soviet Constitution, which designates the Party as the leading core of all Soviet public and state organizations.

A look at the CPSU's history is helpful for an understanding of its past and present role in Soviet society. At the beginning of this century, the Russian Communists led by Vladimir Ilyich Lenin created their Party as a party of the working class, based on Marxism-Leninism. Their program provided for the complete abolition of private property, of exploitation, poverty and unemployment. To accomplish this, they set the following goals: the overthrow of tsarist autocracy through the efforts of the working class allied with the peasantry and all working people, and removal of capitalists and their political parties from the government; winning of state power by the working class with the aim of building a socialist and then a classless communist society.

Other political parties of prerevolutionary Russia either openly defended or compromised with tsarism and capitalism. In the course of the struggles which led up to the Russian Revolution, it became obvious that the majority of the working people trusted the Communist Party and was ready to follow it as the only political authority in the battle against capitalism.

When in October 1917 the working class allied with the peasantry and all working people and led by the CPSU carried out the socialist revolution, the Soviet people became pioneers in establishing the world's first socialist state.

Though the Communists had a majority in the highest body of state power, elected democratically after the Revolution and thus had the right to form a one-party cabinet, they sought to cooperate with other democratic forces. At the very moment of the Revolution, they entered an alliance with the petty

VASSILY STEPANOV, a journalist, is a member of the Editorial Board of *Kommunist*, the CPSU's main theoretical organ.

bourgeois peasantry by adopting the entire agrarian program of their party, the Socialist-Revolutionary Party, without alteration.

The SRs, who were a fairly influential force, were in fact divided into two parties, the Right and Left Socialist-Revolutionaries. Immediately after the Revolution the Communists proposed that the Left SRs participate in formation of the Soviet Government. After a delay, the Left SRs accepted, and eleven Communists and seven Left Socialist-Revolutionaries were included in the government. This two-party system survived for several months. However, the Socialist-Revolutionaries opposed ratification of the peace treaty of Brest-Litovsk with Germany, and resigned from the Council of People's Commissars in March 1918. On July 6, they attempted an armed revolt against Soviet power, assassinating Ambassador Mirbach, the German envoy in Moscow, and wounding several embassy officers. They seized several leading Communists including Felix Dzerzhinsky, occupied the Central Telegraph Office and tried to disrupt other government operations. By the afternoon of July 7, Soviet forces had overcome the rebellion.

Lenin characterized the revolt as "senseless and criminal folly," "a mad attempt of the Left Socialist-Revolutionaries to embroil us in war by assassinating Mirbach," and called it an adventure which placed Russia "within an ace of doom." These open actions of the Left SRs against the people, and the subsequent attempt on Lenin's life by the Socialist-Revolutionary terrorist Fanny Kaplan, ended any possibility of cooperation between the Communists and the SRs.

During the Civil War and intervention (1918-1920), all the leaders of the petty bourgeois parties supported the White Guards and the foreign invaders seeking the overthrow of the Soviet Government. Naturally, the great majority of the people, including the peasants, rejected them. The petty-bourgeois parties thus were not "destroyed" or "dissolved" by the Communists, as some Western historians assert. Rather, according to the Left Socialist-Revolutionary leader M. Spiridonova, "The Socialist-Revolutionaries were utterly destroyed . . . by their previous conciliatory policy."

During this time, the Communist Party consistently expressed the interests of the working class and all working people, and won the sympathies of more people with every new step of the Revolution. As the civil war and intervention were defeated, and the process of building socialism got under way, the social structure of Soviet society changed radically. The former ruling classes of capitalists and landowners disappeared; the workers, collective farmers, and the intellectuals allied with them remained. Both farmers and intellectuals were won to the ideological and political positions of the working class. Soviet power spread throughout the length and breadth of what is now the Union of Soviet Socialist Republics, with its 100 different peoples. Thus, there emerged a new entity, the Soviet people, comprising diverse nations, friendly classes and social groups, united in a single state and joined by common goals and interests, and adhering to a common ideology — Marxism-Leninism. Socialism has engendered a new historic community of nations that has no precedent in any multinational state.

In the new conditions the CPSU became a party of the entire people. It retained, however, its proletarian class character and has remained a party of the working class, socially and ideologically.

The vanguard role in socialist society belongs to the working people as the most numerous and most disciplined and organized class. Workers hold key positions in all branches of social production; 58 per cent of those now joining the Party are workers.

Not a single question of nationwide importance pertaining to Soviet domestic or foreign policy remains outside the responsibility of the Communist Party. It maps out plans for the country's economic and cultural development, organizes the people's efforts to fulfill them and has a decisive impact on the country's whole social life.

The CPSU guides Soviet society by democratic methods. A voluntary political organization, the Party is not vested with state power; it does not issue laws or decrees. Neither an administrative nor a paramilitary organization, it does not employ methods of command.

It influences the masses through persuasion, education, example and practical advice. It introduces into society an atmosphere of collectivism and comradely relations, respect for the human being, a principled and exacting attitude to one's work and fidelity to communist ideals.

Lenin's Party guides society first and foremost through its collectively elaborated Marxist-Leninist policy, by convincing the people of its correctness and organizing people for its implementation. The Party always carries on its work in the open, before the eyes of all the people, from whom it has nothing to conceal.

The Party guides the work of state and public organizations through the communist cadres employed therein and the vast contingents of non-Party people. It does not substitute for any of these organizations, nor interfere in their day-to-day work, but promotes their initiative and independent action.

Organs of state power — Soviets of Working People's Deputies — are elected by the people and number more than two million deputies. They also draw into their work 30 million active citizens who contribute their efforts on a strictly voluntary basis. The Soviets discuss and reach decisions on hundreds of thousands of questions dealing with the work of industrial, agricultural, transport, building, communications, trade, public health, educational, social security, and other organizations.

More than 107 million people are united into trade unions which embrace nearly all workers who comprise over 60 per cent of the gainfully employed Soviet population. The trade unions' task is to see that industrial management is conducted along democratic lines, that the working people are active in their work and politically, that labor protection laws are observed and the workers' social rights ensured, and that living conditions of factory and office workers are improved.

Standing production conferences at plants and factories are a major form of drawing factory and office workers into production management. More than 130 thousand such conferences function in the Soviet Union. Their members (more than five million) are chiefly rank-and-file workers, and they enlist the services of scores of millions of others.

Thirty-five million young people are Komsomol (YCL) members. Today many young people, with YCL members in the lead, help build gigantic projects such as the Baikal-Amur Railway and the Kama Auto Works.

These and other mass organizations and associations of working people embrace practically the entire adult population and take an active part in state management.

Like every socioeconomic system, socialist society has different stages or periods: socialism in process of construction, and mature or developed socialism, as now exists. Both represent the same mode of production, production relations and sociopolitical organization. Advanced socialism is distinguished by more developed economic, sociopolitical, ideological and other forms, the high consciousness and organized character of the people and the gigantic scope of their creative activity.

In the Soviet Union all industrial and many agricultural facilities (state farms), financial institutions, trade, means of communication and transport, the building industry, the housing resources, public buildings, medical services and public education are managed by the state. To ensure the development of these, to organize the supplying of the population with all the essentials including food, clothes and housing, to plan effectively, to coordinate the development of separate branches and the entire national economy, there must be an authoritative political organization having at its disposal all the available information on the state of the country's economy and culture and the people's requirements, one that can outline a clear perspective of national economic development.

Only a Communist Party having an excellent command of the methods and theory of Marxism-Leninism and well aware of its goals and the ways to achieve them is capable of organizing and carrying out the entire theoretical, ideological and educational work and solving the numerous practical problems that come up in the process of socialism's transformation into communism.

The success of building communism depends not only on internal conditions and the people's desire to attain that goal as soon as possible. One must always take into account the constantly changing world situation, the continuing struggle between socialism and capitalism. In the complex international situation only the Communist Party is capable of working out and implementing a foreign policy whose object is to preserve and consolidate world peace. It has enormous experience of struggle against world imperialism and conducting a flexible foreign policy. Considerable success has been achieved in the last few years by the CPSU's foreign policy as the result of implementing the Peace Program of the 24th CPSU Congress and reducing international tensions.

At the 25th CPSU Congress Soviet Communists declared the defense of proletarian internationalism and the strengthening of the international solidarity of the working class their sacred duty, and called upon all adherents of Marxism-Leninism to continue to work for that. This is particularly urgent today when the world reactionary and anticommunist forces are closing their ranks.

With the development of the socialist system the Communist Party also grows in size and strength. Today it numbers 15.5 million members who form a tremendous contingent of builders of a communist society. The Party is a mighty, highly organized sociopolitical organism, extremely flexible and in a state of constant development. It includes 390,000 primary branches, among them 150,000 branches at enterprises in industry, construction, transport and communications, on collective and state farms and other production units. Through them the Party translates its policy into life, influences all sections of the population and forges unbreakable links with the people.

The Soviet Communist Party is international not only as regards its world outlook and policy but also in its composition which represents more than 100 nationalities of the Soviet Union. All have equal rights as members of a single organization and are equally responsible to it for their actions. The CPSU includes 15 Communist Parties of the Union Republics. All of them form a single organism, and have a common program and rules. Thus in practice the Leninist Party personifies the inviolable friendship of the Soviet peoples united, of their own free will, in a single state.

Democratic centralism, worked out by Lenin and developed and verified in practical work, is the basic organizational principle of the Communist Party. It means the electiveness of all leading Party bodies from top to bottom, accountability to their organizations and to higher bodies, equally firm Party discipline for all members, subordination of the minority to the majority, and the mandatory nature, for lower bodies, of decisions issued by higher bodies.

The 25th Congress made a point of the need to develop all the aspects of inner-Party democracy and criticism and self-criticism. The Congress set all Party and state cadres the task of persistently and systematically mastering the Leninist style of work, which means a creative and scientific approach to all social processes, and is incompatible with subjectivism. It further implies a high degree of exactingness with respect to oneself and to others, and rules out any complacency and any manifestations of bureaucracy and formalism.

In the past thirty years CPSU membership has increased nearly threefold. In the last five-year period alone more than 2.5 million new members have been admitted, 80 per cent of whom are engaged in material production.

In the last five years 40,000 persons have been trained for executive work in the Party's educational institutions alone, and 240,000 Party and government workers have taken retraining courses. Life, however, continues to make new demands. The Party cannot tolerate cadres who have lost the ability to make a critical assessment of their activities, lost touch with the masses, who no longer have the trust of the Communists. The 25th CPSU Congress has outlined a whole range of measures to improve the training of leading Party cadres in this respect.

Party organizations attach great importance both to the political enlightenment of leading Party cadres and of all Communists and non-Party people. Twenty million persons, including over seven million non-Party people, are studying after work in the Party educational system. Thirty-six million are studying in the system of economic education which provides training in economic management and promotes the spread of advanced experience, the application of scientific and technological achievements in production and the improvement of labor organization in industrial and agricultural enterprises.

Schoolchildren and students are learning the fundamentals of political and theoretical knowledge in schools and higher educational establishments. These fundamentals are widely popularized through the mass media: press, radio and TV. Mass-scale study of Marxist-Leninist theory is a major feature in the development of social consciousness, in cultivating in Soviet people high moral and progressive ideas, and in the all-round development, both physical and mental, of the new Soviet human being.

In their work Soviet Communists proceed from the general laws of social development, including the building of socialism and and communism. At the present stage in the country's development the need for further creative elaboration of Marxist-Leninist theory, far from diminishing, is in fact growing.

The 25th CPSU Congress, having outlined the further program for the building of communism and defined the basic lines of the five-year economic development plan of the Soviet Union for 1976-1980, showed once again that the Leninist Party is brimming with vital force and creative energy; that it is confident in the victory of communism, and is firmly resolved to bring the great cause of building a communist society to its triumphant fulfillment. □

Part Two: The Proceedings

4

Leonid Brezhnev

General Secretary of the
CPSU Central Committee

Report of the CPSU Central Committee and the Immediate Tasks of the Party in Home and Foreign Policy, February 24, 1976

The version we are bringing our readers of General Secretary Leonid Brezhnev's report to the 25th CPSU Congress is as complete as possible within our space limitations. We have sought throughout to adhere as closely as possible to Brezhnev's own words, without editorial comment, and have in fact condensed, rather than simply summarized, retaining all of Secretary Brezhnev's essential points. Exact quotations of his words, without condensation, have been set either within quotation marks or in easily identifiable form.

The five years since the 24th Congress of the Communist Party of the Soviet Union has been a period of events and undertakings of truly immense significance. The world is changing before our very eyes and changing for the better. Our people, our Party are active participants in these changes.

Following the Leninist course set by the 24th Congress of assuring a considerable rise in the people's living standard and cultural level, we can confidently assert that the course we chose was correct. The Soviet people are better off materially and richer spiritually.

In fulfilling our Peace Program, everything possible has been done to assure peaceful construction in our country and the fraternal socialist countries, to assure peace and security for all peoples. The foreign policy of the land of Soviets enjoys the respect and support of many millions of people all over the world. And we shall continue this policy with redoubled energy, working to bridle the forces of war and aggression, to consolidate world peace and assure the people's right to freedom, independence and social progress.

I. The World Situation and the International Activity of the CPSU

Friendship and Cooperation with Socialist Countries

Our foreign policy has to reckon with the state of affairs in every part of the globe. But naturally, closest to our minds and hearts is that part of the world where communist ideals are embodied in practice. These ideals are freedom from exploitation and oppression, full power of the working people, development of socialist democracy, flowering of culture and increase in the well-being of the broad masses, equality and fraternity of all peoples and nationalities.

The ties between socialist states are becoming ever closer with the flowering of each socialist nation and the strengthening of their sovereignty, and elements of community are increasing. There is a gradual levelling up of their development. This process of growing together of socialist countries is now operating quite definitely as an objective law.

Of course much depends on the policy of the ruling parties and their ability to safeguard unity, combat isolation and national exclusiveness, to honor the common international tasks and to act jointly in performing them.

First among the major tasks fulfilled through unity, solidarity and mutual support, is the victory of the Vietnamese people. Imperialism failed to destroy a socialist state by armed force and to crush a national liberation revolution. The Soviet people take pride in having given considerable aid to Vietnam in its struggle against the imperialist invaders. The Vietnamese people are now working arduously to restore their country and are building a socialist future. It was a glorious victory, and will be inscribed forever in the history of the people's struggle for freedom and socialism. Our ardent fraternal greetings to them and to Laos and Cambodia who won freedom in the wake of Vietnam and to all the working people of Southeast Asia to whom new horizons have been opened by Vietnam's victory.

Largely to the concerted efforts of socialist states must be credited the worldwide recognition of the sovereignty of the German Democratic Republic, its entry into the UN, and the international confirmation of the inviolability of the Western frontiers of the GDR, Poland and Czechoslovakia. Conditions have been created for a stable peace in Europe.

Despite US imperialism's policy of diplomatic and economic blockade, Cuba's international situation has improved and her prestige heightened. The recent Communist Party Congress, the program and Constitution adopted, show the steady progress of the first socialist state in the Western hemisphere.

No matter what problems arise in its relations with socialist countries the CPSU believes that they must be resolved in the spirit of strengthening friendship, unity and cooperation. That is how we shape our relations with the fraternal socialist states—Bulgaria, Hungary, Vietnam, the German Democratic Republic, the Korean People's Democratic Republic, Cuba, Mongolia, Poland, Romania, Czechoslovakia and Yugoslavia. The guiding force of our relations is the indissoluble militant alliance of *the Communist parties of socialist countries*, the identity of their world outlook and aims. The leaders of the Communist parties of the socialist community maintain constant contact, regular multilateral and bilateral meetings, and there are deep, varied and systematic contacts between thousands upon thousands of fighters for the common cause, builders of socialism and communism, which add to our common strength:

On the whole, complete unity and fruitful cooperation are the hallmark of our relations with most parties of the socialist countries. A few parties, as we know, have particular views on a number of questions, but the overall tendency is unquestionably characterized by a growing cohesion of socialist countries. We value this tendency highly, and shall, as before, promote it in every way. This requires joint efforts by the fraternal parties on the basis of the tested principles of Marxism-Leninism, socialist internationalism, equality and comradely cooperation.

We are firmly against the world's division into opposing military blocs and the arms race. But as long as the NATO bloc continues to exist and the militarists continue their arms drive, our country and the other signatories of the Warsaw Treaty will continue to strengthen this political-military alliance.

The socialist community has become the world's most dynamic force. In the past five years the industry of its member countries has grown four times as swiftly as that of the developed capitalist states. In 1975 the industrial output of our community was more than double that of the Common Market countries.

The Party Central Committee has devoted unremitting attention to *economic cooperation* with these socialist states. In this connection it attaches special importance to the long-term program of socialist economic integration adopted jointly with other CMEA (Council for Mutual Economic Assistance) countries in 1971. This means joint development of natural resources for common benefit, joint construction of large industrial complexes and long-term planning of cooperation between enterprises and whole industries. Trade among CMEA countries has more than doubled in five years, reaching 26 billion rubles annually.

In addition to strengthening the material base of the socialist community, ideological cooperation with parties of fraternal countries has expanded substantially in recent years, as well as cooperation in spreading the truth about socialism through mass information media in the present ideological confrontation of two social systems.

Relations with China, of course, are a special and separate question. The policy of its present leaders is openly directed against the majority of the socialist states. More, it merges directly with the position of the world's most extreme reaction—from the militarists and enemies of detente in the Western countries to the racists of South Africa and the fascist rulers of Chile. This policy is not only entirely alien to socialist principles and ideals, but has also, in effect, become an important aid to imperialism in its struggle against socialism.

Peking's frantic attempts to torpedo detente, to obstruct disarmament, to breed suspicion and hostility between states, its efforts to provoke a world war and reap whatever advantages may accrue, create a great danger for all peace-loving peoples. This policy conducted by Peking is deeply opposed to the interests of all peoples. We shall continue to repulse this incendiary policy and to protect the interests of the Soviet state, the socialist community, and the world communist movement. It is far from enough to say that Maoist ideology and policy are incompatible with Marxist-Leninist teaching; they are directly hostile to it.

In its relations with China, our Party firmly adheres to the course charted by the 24th Congress. This course has been proved correct by facts. We shall continue principled and irreconcilable struggle against Maoism.

At the same time, we should like to repeat once again that in our relations with China, as with other countries, we adhere firmly to the principles of equality, respect for sovereignty and territorial integrity, non-interference in each other's internal affairs, and non-use of force. In short, we are prepared to normalize relations with China in accordance with the principles of peaceful coexistence. Furthermore, we can say with assurance that if Peking returns to a policy truly based on Marxism-Leninism, if it abandons its hostile policy towards the socialist countries and takes the road of cooperation and solidarity with the socialist world, there will be an appropriate response from our side and opportunities will open for development of good relations between the USSR and the People's Republic of China consonant with the principles of socialist internationalism. The matter rests with the Chinese side.

Greater Cooperation with the Liberated Countries

Soviet ties with countries liberated from colonial dependence have multiplied and strengthened and their political content has been enriched. Far reaching, progressive changes are taking place in these countries such as nationalization of industries and foreign enterprises, to assure the young states' effective control of their own resources and development of their own personnel, abolition of feudal land ownership, increasing intensity of different forms of the class struggle.

Progressive changes have taken place in the economic and political life of the socialist-oriented Arab, African and Asian countries, while other countries have followed the capitalist road. Efforts to undermine the social and political

gains of the Egyptian revolution and the recent rightist campaign against the
Indira Gandhi government, indicate reactionary pressures against socialist
aims. Or take the People's Republic of Angola:

As soon as it was born, this progressive state became an object of foreign intervention,
the handiwork of imperialism and South African racists, the mortal enemies of independent
Africa, and also of those who undertook the unseemly role of their henchmen. That
was why Angola's struggle for independence was supported by the world's progressive
forces, and the success of this struggle testified once again that nothing can crush the
peoples' aspirations to freedom . . .

The Soviet Union does not interfere in the internal affairs of other countries and
peoples. It is an immutable principle of our Leninist foreign policy to respect the sacred
right of every people, every country, to choose its own way of development. But we do
not conceal our views. In the developing countries as everywhere else, we are on the side
of the forces of progress, democracy and national independence and regard them as
friends and comrades in struggle . . .

The Soviet Union does not look for advantages, does not hunt for concessions, does
not seek political domination, or exact military bases.

The influence of states only recently colonies or semi-colonies has grown
considerably. Their political activity is apparent in the non-alignment movement, the Organization of African Unity and several economic associations.
With the present correlation of world class forces these countries are able to
resist imperialist diktat.

From the rostrum of our Congress we again emphasize that the Soviet Union supports
the legitimate aspirations of young states, their determination to put an end to all
imperialist exploitation, and to take full charge of their own national wealth.

As for the Arab countries, good mutual understanding has arisen between us
and Syria and we act in concert on many international problems. The Treaty of
Friendship with Iraq is an important development, and cooperation with
Algeria and South Yemen is deepening. Significant steps have been taken in
Soviet-Libyan ties. Friendly contacts with the Palestine Liberation Organization have intensified. While certain forces attempt to undermine Soviet-
Egyptian relations, we consider that the Treaty of Friendship and Cooperation
between the USSR and Egypt constitutes a long-term basis of our relations in
the interests not only of our countries but of the entire Arab world.

However, "certain forces are making persistent efforts to undermine
Soviet-Egyptian relations."*

---

*On March 14 President Anwar el-Sadat called on the Egyptian People's Assembly to
abrogate immediately the Soviet-Egyptian Treaty of Friendship and Cooperation. The
move was interpreted as intended to clear the way for the purchase of arms in the United

The Soviet Union has consistently supported the Arab people's struggle to eliminate the consequences of Israeli aggression, to build up the strength of the countries opposing the aggressor, Egypt, Syria and Iraq, to aid the Arab political struggle both within the United Nations and outside it.

The danger of new hostilities in the Middle East will persist as long as Israeli armies remain in occupied territories; as long as the hundreds of thousands of Palestinians driven from their land are deprived of their legitimate rights and live in appalling conditions; as long as the Arab people of Palestine are denied the possibility of creating their national state. For Middle East peace to be lasting, the security of all the states of the region, their right to independent existence and development must also be guaranteed:

As co-chairman of the Geneva Conference, the USSR is prepared to cooperate in all efforts to reach an effective settlement. We are prepared to participate in international guarantees of the security and inviolability of the frontiers of all Middle East countries either in the UN framework or on some other basis. Incidentally, it is our opinion that Britain and France, too, could participate in such guarantees along with the USSR and USA. . .

We are for creating conditions that would facilitate the development of our relations with all Middle East countries. We have no prejudices against any of them. Finally, we are also prepared to participate in a search for a solution to such a problem as ending the arms race in this region. But it stands to reason that this must be tied in closely with a general settlement in the Middle East. To take up the problem before such a settlement is reached would place the aggressor on a par with his victims.

In the period under review the Central Committee has devoted much attention to normal and wherever possible also friendly relations with Asian states. Close political and economic cooperation with India has been our constant policy, now risen to a new level with the treaty of peace, friendship and cooperation. We are in solidarity with India's peace-loving foreign policy and wish her complete success in the efforts of her progressive forces to solve the country's difficult socioeconomic problems. We welcomed the termination of the India-Pakistan armed conflict in 1971.

We have recently extended the almost half-century old treaty of neutrality and nonaggression with our good neighbor Afghanistan. Cooperation with Turkey is gradually spreading from the economic to the political sphere.

We shall also continue our active participation in the search to consolidate peace and security on the Asian continent, both through bilateral and multilat-

States and Western Europe (*New York Times,* March 16). An official statement made public by TASS denounced the action declaring that responsibility for abrogation of the treaty "rests entirely with the Egyptian side."

eral contacts. We have repeatedly set forth our readiness to heed any proposals prompted by a concern for lasting peace and security in Asia and for assuring them by collective effort.

Much has been done to further friendly ties with the African states in this period which is witnessing the final phase of the end of the colonial system. We have supported such heroic struggles for independence as those of the peoples of Guinea Bissau and the Cape Verde Islands, Mozambique and Angola, whose victory we acclaim, and with whom we have warm and friendly interstate relations. Long-time friendly ties with the Republic of Guinea and the People's Republic of the Congo have grown closer; ties with the Somali Democratic Republic are strengthened by the new friendship treaty; good relations with Nigeria have expanded.

Relations with Capitalist States

Struggle to consolidate the principles of peaceful coexistence, to assure lasting peace, to reduce and in a longer term to eliminate the danger of another world war has been, and remains, the main element of our policy towards the capitalist states. Considerable progress has been achieved in this.

The change from cold war and confrontation to detente was primarily due to the new correlation of world forces. An important role in convincing people of the necessity of this was played by the Peace Program of the 24th CPSU Congress which mapped out a realistic way to replace the cold war with peaceful cooperation, following Lenin's precepts from the very beginning of Soviet power that peaceful coexistence is "the only correct way out of the difficulties, chaos and danger of wars" *(Collected Works*, Russian edition, Vol. 33, p. 357). Concrete examples of our Party's implementation of this Peace Program follow:

Changes toward detente and a more durable peace are especially tangible in Europe, where socialist positions and the impact of the agreed policy of the socialist states are at their strongest.

The cooperation of the Soviet Union and other socialist countries with France have developed through Summit meetings first with de Gaulle, then with Presidents Pompidou and D'Estaing. Positions drew closer on a number of foreign-political questions and diverse ties and contacts developed. Relations with France are broadly supported by the French people and most political parties; we value them and are prepared to extend areas of accord and cooperation.

Relations with the FRG have been normalized on the basis of the 1970 treaty recognizing postwar frontiers; the FRG is a major partner in our mutually beneficial business cooperation with the West. The four-power agreement of 1971 and other agreements and understandings have relieved former tensions. All sides, however, must show true respect for these agreements, which unfortunately is not being done. We shall insist on strict and complete observance. The USSR favors a tranquil and normal life for West Berlin.

Relations with Britain and Italy may be described as positive. We want to develop and enrich our good-neighbor relations with Finland and our ties with Scandinavian countries, Austria, Belgium and other West European states. Restoration of relations with Portugal and improved relations with Greece were a reflection of the welcome changes in the continent's political climate.

Early convocation of the European Security Conference urged by the 24th Congress was realized with the coming together of 33 European States joined by the US and Canada, and the Final Act signed at the Summit level in Helsinki last August, which collectively reaffirmed the inviolability of existing frontiers. Perspectives for peaceful all-European cooperation have been outlined in economy, science, technology, culture, information and development of contacts between people, certain military aspects and other measures to promote mutual confidence between states. Thus favorable conditions have been created for safeguarding peace on the entire continent, the essential thing being to translate all the principles and understandings reached at Helsinki into practical deeds. This the Soviet Union is doing and will continue to do.

But negative aspects cannot be overlooked. The Cyprus problem remains a complex and dangerous source of tension. Consideration for the rights and interests of both communities, unconditional respect for the independence, sovereignty and territorial integrity of Cyprus and prohibition of any attempts to impose outside solutions should pave the way to a peaceful settlement.

Influential circles reluctant to abandon the cold war policy remain in some European states. Right-wing pressures affect certain aspects of Bonn's policy. A large section of the mass media continues to distort Soviet policies and incite hostility toward the socialist countries. Certain quarters are trying to use the Final Act adopted at Helsinki as a screen for interfering in the internal affairs of the socialist countries and for anti-communist demagogy. Much effort is still essential to make detente irreversible. "Before us, comrades, is the great aim of making lasting peace the way of life for all the European peoples."

Comrades, the turn for the better in our relations with the United States, the biggest power of the capitalist world, has, of course, been decisive in reducing the danger of another world war and in consolidating peace. This has beyond question contributed to the improvement of the international climate in general, and that of Europe in particular. Acting in complete accord with the guidelines set by the 24th Congress, we have devoted very great attention to the objective of improving relations with the United States.

As a result of negotiations with President Nixon in Moscow and Washington, and later of the meetings with President Ford in Vladivostok and Helsinki, important and fundamental mutual understanding has been reached between the leaders of the Soviet Union and the United States on the necessity of developing peaceful, equal relations between the two countries. This is reflected in a whole system of Soviet-US treaties, agreements and other documents. Unquestionably the most important of these are "The Basic Principles of Mutual Relations between the Union of Soviet Socialist Republics and the United States of America," the Agreement on the Prevention of Nuclear War, and the series of strategic arms limitation treaties and agreements. What is the main significance of these documents?

In all, they have laid a solid political and legal foundation for greater mutually beneficial cooperation between the USSR and the USA in line with the principles of peaceful coexistence. To a certain extent they have lessened the danger of nuclear war. Precisely in this we see the main result of the development of Soviet-US relations in the past five years.

There are good prospects for our relations with the United States in the future as well—to the extent to which they will continue to develop on this jointly created realistic basis and when, given the obvious difference between the class nature of the two states and between their ideologies, there is a firm intention to settle differences and disputes not by force, not by threats or saber rattling, but by peaceful political means.

In recent years our relations with the United States have been developing in many areas. There is a frequent exchange of delegations, including parliamentary, and cultural exchanges have become more active. Many Soviet-US agreements have been concluded, envisaging expansion of mutually beneficial cooperation in various economic, scientific, technical and cultural areas. Most of them have already come into force and are being put into practice to the obvious benefit of both sides, and, more important still, of mutual understanding between the Soviet and US peoples.

Secretary Brezhnev then spoke of the serious threats to detente emanating from certain circles in the United States and the necessity of opposing them, and reiterated Soviet determination to adhere to the course of improving US-USSR relations in the interests of both peoples and the peace of the world:

The essentially positive development of Soviet-US relations in recent years is, however, complicated by a number of serious factors. Influential forces in the US, that have no interest either in improving relations with the Soviet Union or in international detente as a whole, are trying to impair it. They portray the policy of the Soviet Union in a false light and refer to an imaginary "Soviet threat" to urge a new intensification of the arms race in the USA and in NATO. We may recall that there have also been attempts to interfere in our internal affairs in connection with the adoption by the USA of discriminatory measures in the field of trade. Naturally we could not and will not suffer that sort of thing. That is not the kind of language one can use with the Soviet Union. By now, I think, this is clear to all.

It is no secret that some of the difficulties stem from those aspects of Washington's policy which jeopardize the freedom and independence of peoples and constitute gross interference in their internal affairs by siding with the forces of oppression and reaction. We have opposed and will continue to oppose such actions. At the same time I want to emphasize once more that the Soviet Union is firmly determined to follow the line of further improving Soviet-US relations in strict accordance with the letter and spirit of the agreements reached, in the interests of both peoples and peace on earth.

Our relations with Canada are ever richer in content and prospect. Ties with Latin America have expanded. We support their striving for fuller economic and political independence, and a greater international role.

Relations with Japan are generally positive. Trade, business and cultural ties have expanded. However, in relation to a peace settlement, certain quarters are trying—sometimes with direct incitement from without, to present groundless and unlawful claims. We are working for good neighborly and friendly relations and hope Japan will not be pushed from this road by those eager to reap advantage from Soviet-Japanese differences.

Cultural exchanges with other countries have increased about 50 per cent in the last few years as a result of detente.

Efforts to End the Arms Race and Promote Disarmament

These vital points on our Peace Program remain a principal trend of our foreign policy, and are more essential than ever. Mankind is weary of sitting on a mountain of arms, yet the race becomes more intense, spurred by aggressive imperialist groups. They invoke the so-called "Soviet threat" to acquire larger military budgets, reducing allocations for social needs, to develop new types of deadly weapons and to justify NATO's military activities.

The Soviet Union has not the slightest intention of attacking anyone. The Soviet Union does not need war. The Soviet Union does not increase its military budget, and far from reducing, is steadily increasing allocations for improving the people's well-being. Our country is consistently and staunchly fighting for peace, and making one concrete proposal after another aimed at arms reduction and disarmament.

Our Party calls on all countries, all peoples, to end the perilous arms race. "General and complete disarmament has been and remains our ultimate goal in this field." In the meantime we are taking separate steps along the road.

The international convention banning bacteriological weapons, initiated by the USSR, the first real disarmament measure in history, has entered into force. More states have become party to the Non-Proliferation of Nuclear Weapons Treaty. The USSR is prepared to cooperate in further effective measures to prevent the spread of nuclear weapons over this whole planet.

In current SALT talks we are trying to carry out the 1974 Vladivostok accord and prevent the opening of a new channel for the arms race. We have repeatedly proposed to the United States to go farther than limiting existing types of strategic weapons; reaching agreement, for example, on banning new, still more destructive systems, in particular the new Trident submarines carrying ballistic missiles and the new strategic B-1 bombers in the United States, and similar systems in the USSR. Regrettably these proposals were not accepted by the US side. But we have not withdrawn them. How beneficial their implementation would be for strengthening mutual confidence! Both sides would be able to save considerable resources and use them for productive purposes, for improving people's life.

Let me add one more thing. Of late, pronouncements have been proliferating in many countries against any of the powers setting up military bases in the region of the Indian Ocean. We are in sympathy with those pronouncements. The Soviet Union has never had, and has no intention now, of building military bases in the Indian Ocean. We càll on the United States to. take the same stand.

The time must come when other nuclear powers will join in strategic arms limitation. Those who refuse bear a heavy responsibility before the world's peoples.

We are gratified that the UN General Assembly has, on our initiative, adopted a number of resolutions on restraining the arms race and banning new types of mass annihilation weapons. The task is to have these resolutions implemented. This is impeded by reluctance of a number of major states to end the arms race and by opponents of detente and disarmament who still have considerable resources and are highly active:

Though imperialism's possibilities for aggressive action are now considerably reduced, its nature remains the same. That is why the peace loving forces must be highly vigilant. Energetic actions and unity of all the forces of peace and goodwill are essential.

Therefore, special importance attaches to the proposal submitted by the vast majority of UN member countries to convene a World Disarmament Conference.

Political detente needs to be backed up by military detente. Our Peace Program called for reduction of armed forces and armaments in Central Europe. After over two years of negotiations the NATO countries are still trying to secure unilateral military advantages. They demand concessions prejudicial to the socialist countries while refusing any similar concessions to the other side.

The socialist states have recently submitted new proposals in order to get the talks off the ground. For a start, a reduction of only Soviet and US troops this year, with reduction of forces of other states in the negotiations only in the second stage, 1977-78. We have also made concrete proposals on reduction by both sides of the number of tanks, nuclear-weapons-carrying planes and missile launchers and the ammunition required for them—all on the basis of preserving the present equilibrium. We hope the response will make actual measures for reducing armed forces and armaments possible.

The 24th Congress proclaimed the objective that "renunciation of the use and threat of force must become the rule in settling international disputed questions. . ." This principle is reflected in bilateral treaties concluded by the USSR and included in the Final Act of the European Security Conference:

To make the danger of war recede still farther and to create favorable conditions for progress towards disarmament, we now offer to conclude a world treaty on the non-use of force in international relations. Its participants, naturally including the nuclear powers, would undertake to refrain from using all types of weapons, including nuclear, in settling disputes that may arise. The Soviet Union is prepared to join other states in examining steps leading to the implementation of this proposal.

A great role and responsibility devolve on the mass movement to consolidate peace.

Milestones in the growth of this movement have been the World Congress of Peace Forces in Moscow, the Brussels Assembly of Representatives of Public Opinion for European Security, and the World Congress of Women in Berlin. Our Party and the Soviet people took an active part in all these events. We shall continue great efforts to draw broad popular masses into the work of consolidating peace. And in our foreign policy we shall seek new forms of cooperation between states of different social systems and new ways leading to disarmament. "We shall continually increase our efforts in the struggle for lasting peace."

The following section, containing the Party Congress' concrete program for peace, point by point, is printed in bold face type for emphasis, with the 1971 peace program of the 24th Congress following, for comparison purposes.

Program of Further Struggle for Peace, Freedom and Independence of the Peoples

The Party's Central Committee considers that *further struggle for peace and international cooperation and for freedom and independence of the peoples require first of all fulfillment of the following vital tasks:*

While steadily strengthening their unity and expanding all-round cooperation in building the new society, the fraternal socialist states must augment their joint active contribution to the consolidation of peace:

• Work for ending the expanding arms race, which is endangering peace, and for transition to reducing the accumulated stockpiles of arms, for disarmament. To this end:

a. Do everything to complete the preparation of a new Soviet-US agreement on limiting and reducing strategic armaments, and international treaties on universal and complete termination of nuclear weapon tests, on banning and destroying chemical weapons, on banning development of new types and systems of mass annihilation weapons, and also banning modification of the natural environment for military or other hostile purposes.

b. Launch new efforts to activate negotiations on the reduction of armed forces and armaments in Central Europe. Following agreement on the first concrete steps in this direction, continue to promote military detente in the region in subsequent years.

c. Work for a switch from the present continuous growth of military expenditures of many states to their systematic reduction.

d. Assure the earliest possible convocation of a World Disarmament Conference.

• Concentrate the efforts of peace-loving states on eliminating the remaining seats of war, first and foremost in implementing a just and durable settlement in the Middle East. In connection with such a settlement the states concerned should examine the question of helping to end the arms race in the Middle East.

• Do everything to deepen international detente, to embody it in concrete forms of mutually beneficial cooperation between states. Work vigorously for the full implementation of the Final Act of the European Conference, and for greater peaceful cooperation in Europe. In accordance with the principles of peaceful coexistence continue consistently to develop relations of long-term mutually beneficial cooperation in various fields—political, economic, scientific, cultural—with the United States, France, the FRG, Britain, Italy, Canada, and also Japan and other capitalist countries.

• Work for ensuring Asian security based on joint efforts by the states of that continent.

• Work for a treaty on the non-use of force in international relations.

• Consider as crucial the international task of completely eliminating all vestiges of the system of colonial oppression, infringement of the equality and independence of peoples, and all seats of colonialism and racism.

• Work for eliminating discrimination and all artificial barriers in international trade, and all manifestations of inequality, diktat and exploitation in international economic relations.

Peace Program of 24th
CPSU Congress
(in condensed form)

• *First:* To eliminate the hotbeds of war in Southeast Asia and in the Middle East and to promote a political settlement in these areas on the basis of respect for the legitimate rights of the states and peoples subjected to aggression.

To rebuff, firmly and immediately, all acts of aggression and international lawlessness. For this, full use must also be made of UN possibilities.

Repudiation of the threat or use of force in settling differences must become a law of international life. For its part, the Soviet Union suggests that the countries which accept this approach conclude appropriate bilateral or regional treaties.

• *Second:* To proceed from the final recognition of the territorial changes that took place in Europe as a result of the Second World War. To bring about a radical turn towards detente and peace on the continent. To ensure the convocation of an all-European conference.

To do everything to ensure collective security in Europe. We reaffirm the readiness expressed jointly by the member countries of the defensive Warsaw Treaty to simultaneously annul this treaty and that of NATO or—as a first step—to dismantle their military organizations.

• *Third:* To conclude treaties banning nuclear, chemical and bacteriological weapons.

To work for an end to the testing of nuclear weapons, including underground tests, by everyone and everywhere. To promote the creation of nuclear-free zones in various part of the world.

We stand for the nuclear disarmament of all states in the possession of nuclear weapons, and for the convocation for that purpose of a conference of the five nuclear powers—the USSR, the United States, the People's Republic of China, France and Britain.

• *Fourth:* To invigorate the struggle to halt the race in all types of weapons. We favor the convocation of a world conference to consider all aspects of disarmament.

We stand for the dismantling of foreign military bases. We stand for a reduction of armed forces and armaments in areas where military confrontation is especially dangerous, above all in Central Europe.

We consider it advisable to work out measures that would reduce the likelihood of accidental or deliberately fabricated armed incidents that could lead to international crises and war.

The Soviet Union is prepared to negotiate agreements to cut military expenditures, above all by the major powers.

• *Fifth:* The UN decisions to end the remnants of colonial rule must be carried out in full. Manifestations of racism and apartheid must be universally condemned and boycotted.

• *Sixth:* The Soviet Union is prepared for mutually advantageous cooperation in every sphere with other interested states. Our country is prepared to work with other states on such common problems as the preservation of the environment, the development of power and other natural resources, the development of transport and communications, the prevention and eradication of the most dangerous and widespread diseases, and the exploration and development of outer space and the world ocean.

●

As we see it, fulfillment of these main tasks is essential at present in the interests of peace and the security of peoples and the progress of mankind. We consider these proposals an organic projection and development of the peace program advanced by our 24th Congress, *a program of further struggle for peace and international cooperation and for the freedom and independence of the peoples.* We shall direct our foreign-policy efforts toward achieving these tasks, and shall cooperate in this with other peace-loving states. We are confident these aims will be received with understanding and win the wholehearted support of all the peace-loving progressive forces, and all honest people on earth.

The CPSU and the World Revolutionary Process

In this epoch of radical social change socialism's positions are expanding and growing stronger. The development of the world revolutionary process is signified in the victories of the national liberation movement, the intensification of the class struggle of the working people against monopoly oppression and exploitation, the steady growth of the scale of the revolutionary-democratic, anti-imperialist movement. We are witnessing what Lenin wrote about: "As man's history-making activity grows broader and deeper, the size of that mass of the population which is the conscious maker of history is bound to increase." *(Collected Works,* Vol. 2, p. 524, Russian edition).

Socialism is now the main direction of mankind's social progress. Its power of attraction has become still greater against the background of the crisis in the capitalist countries. The developments of recent years bear out convincingly the conclusions of the Party's 24th Congress that "the general crisis of capitalism is continuing to deepen." The crisis has spread to all the main centers of world economy. All the methods of economic regulation applied to stimulate economic growth could not remove the contradictions of the highly developed state-monopoly economy that emerged in the postwar period. The sharp cutback in the economy and the growing unemployment in most of the capitalist countries intertwine with such serious convulsions of the capitalist world economy as the money, energy and raw materials crises. Impelled by growing military expenditures, inflation has reached dimensions unprecedented in peacetime,

Inter-imperialist rivalries and discord in the Common Market and NATO have sharpened, and the greater power of the international monopolies has made the competitive struggle still more ruthless. The nature of imperialism is such that each endeavors to impose his will at the expense of others. The myth that present-day capitalism is able to avert crises has collapsed. Promises of a "welfare state" have failed. A heavy burden has fallen on the masses. The rising cost of living is inexorably reducing people's incomes. Even according to official UN figures over 15 million people in the developed capitalist countries have been flung out of factories and offices. In addition millions are compelled to work a short day or two or three days a week. The working class retaliates. The strike wave has risen to its highest level in several decades. The strength and prestige of the working class have increased. Trade unions shift leftward, and unity of workers with other democratic forces grows and becomes stronger.

The politico-ideological crisis of bourgeois society has grown more acute. Corruption even at the top is increasingly open. The crime rate rises, and debasement of culture continues. Communists are far from predicting an "automatic collapse." Capitalism still has considerable reserves, but it is a society without a future.

Powerful blows were struck by the revolutions in Chile and Portugal in the past five years, the revolutionary liberation forces in Peru achieved important success, the fascist military government in Greece fell, and the Franco regime in Spain began to totter. The Portuguese revolution wiped out one of the last fascist regimes of our time, causing collapse of the last of the colonial empires. While the anti-fascist revolution opened the way for the emergence of political forces of a motley, often contradictory nature, one thing is absolutely clear:

The people of Portugal are for laying dependable foundations for the country's democratic development, for social progress.

The Soviet Union is categorically opposed to all interference in Portugal's internal affairs. Like any other people, the people of Portugal have a right to take the road of their own choice. Permit me from this rostrum to express the wholehearted solidarity of the Soviet Communists, of all Soviet people, with the revolutionary people of Portugal, its Communists, and all democrats.

The revolution in Chile strikingly expressed its people's ardent desire for liberation from the oppression and exploitation of their own bourgeoisie and foreign monopolies. It was headed by people of great honesty and humanism. The conspiracy of Chilean reaction, "planned and paid for—as is now well known—by foreign imperialism," drenched the country in blood. Tens of thousands of working people were killed, mortally tortured or imprisoned, in a dark night of terror. But this temporary defeat does not detract from the significance and historic importance of the Chilean revolution:

The Chilean tragedy has by no means invalidated the communist thesis about the possibility of different ways of revolution, including the peaceful way, if the necessary conditions for it exist. But it has been a forceful reminder that a revolution must know how to defend itself. It is a lesson in vigilance against present-day fascism and the intrigues of foreign reaction, and a call for greater international solidarity with all those who take the road of freedom and progress. Here, at our Congress, on behalf of all Soviet people, we again demand "Freedom for Luis Corvalan, freedom for all prisoners of the fascist junta!"

Recent experience has shown that imperialism will stop at nothing, discarding all semblance of democracy, if a serious threat arises to the domination of monopoly capital. It tramples on all legality, resorts to slander, duplicity, economic blockade, sabotage, starvation, bribes, threats, terrorism, assassination and fascist-style pogroms—all these and worse horrors are in its armory. But such efforts are doomed to failure. "The cause of freedom and progress is inconquerable."

The growth of the influence of Communist parties in the capitalist world, their numerical development by nearly a million (400,000 in Western Europe), and increased votes in elections, is an auspicious development. This bears out the conclusions of the 1969 Meeting of Communist Parties. Communists of different countries follow each other's work with interest:

Differences of opinion and approach may arise among them from time to time. Hostile propaganda has repeatedly sensationalized this. But Marxist-Leninists approach such questions from internationalist positions, concerned with strengthening the unity of the whole movement, and discuss the emerging problems in a true comradely spirit in the framework of the immutable standards of equality and respect for the independence of each party. Certainly there can be no question of compromise on matters of principle, of reconciliation with views and actions contrary to communist ideology. This is ruled out. Doubly so because both Right and ultra-Left revisionism is by no means idle, and struggle for the Marxist-Leninist principles of the Communist movement and against attempts to distort or undermine them is still the common task of all.

A deep understanding of the laws of Marxism-Leninism, collectively formulated at international conferences of fraternal parties, and reliance on these laws in combination with a creative approach and with consideration for the concrete conditions of each separate country, have been and remain a distinct feature of Communists. "And we can say this with assurance: a concession to opportunism may sometimes yield a temporary advantage, but will ultimately do damage to the Party."

Proletarian internationalism is one of the main principles of Marxism-Leninism. There are, unfortunately, some people who openly suggest renouncing internationalism:

But as we see it, to renounce proletarian internationalism is to deprive Communist Parties and the working class movement in general of a mighty and tested weapon. It would work in favor of the class enemy who, by the way, actively coordinates its anti-communist activities on an international scale. We, Soviet Communists, consider defense of proletarian internationalism the sacred duty of every Marxist-Leninist.

In the period under review our Party has extended its ties with the fraternal parties. There has been an extensive exchange of delegations, and important inter-Party and regional conferences on political and theoretical problems. Many parties are calling for a new world Conference of Communist and Workers' Parties. The CPSU supports this idea in principle, but when and how it is held must be decided by common consent.

Sending greetings to fighters for the working people's cause and prisoners and martyrs in many countries, Brezhnev proposed that a monument be erected in Moscow to the heroes of the world communist and working class movement.

We have continued to extend our ties with *progressive non-Communist parties*—revolutionary-democratic and also left-socialists, and have expanded our contacts with socialist and social-democratic parties in a number of countries. We will continue to work in this direction, while combating anti-communist and anti-Soviet trends among them which play into the hands of reaction. There can be no ideological convergence between scientific communism and reformism. But we can be and are united with Social Democrats conscious of their responsibility for peace.

With detente a reality, the question of how it influences the class struggle often arises both in the international working class movement and among its opponents.

Some bourgeois leaders raise a howl over the solidarity of Soviet Communists, the Soviet people, with the struggle of other peoples for freedom and progress. This is either naivete or a deliberate befuddling of minds. Detente and peaceful coexistence have to do with interstate relations. This means above all that conflicts between countries are not to be settled by war, by the use or threat of force. Detente cannot abolish or alter the laws of the class struggle. No one should expect that detente will cause Communists to reconcile themselves with capitalist exploitation or that monopolists will become revolutionists. On the other hand, strict observance of the principle of non-interference in the affairs of other states and respect for their independence and sovereignty is one of the essential conditions of detente.

We make no secret of the fact that we see detente as the way to create more favorable conditions for peaceful socialist and communist construction. This only confirms that socialism and peace are indissoluble.

As for the ultra-leftist assertion that peaceful coexistence is the next thing to "helping capitalism" and "freezing the socio-political status quo," our reply is this: every revolution is above all a natural result of the given society's internal development. Life itself has refuted the inventions about "freezing of the status quo." Suffice it to recall the far-reaching revolutionary changes in the world in recent years.

That is how things stand with respect to the relationship between detente and the class struggle. Faithful to the revolutionary cause, we Soviet Communists are fighting and will continue to fight for peace, the greatest of all boons for all peoples and an essential condition for the progress of humanity in our time.

II. Results of the Five-Year Period and the Main Objectives of the Party's Economic Policy

Section II of Leonid Brezhnev's report is entitled "Results of the Five-Year Period and the Main Objectives of the Party's Economic Policy." Brezhnev emphasized that the Ninth Five-Year Plan topped all preceding ones in its increase in industrial output (43 per cent), capital investment and new measures to raise living standards; the USSR now leads the world in production of vital items such as steel, oil, mineral fertilizers, coal, iron ore, cement and others. Discussing the fundamental features of the Tenth Five-Year Plan, 1976-80, the General Secretary pointed out that it was drawn up with guidelines up to 1990 in mind and estimated that in the next 15 years the country would roughly double the material and financial resources of the previous 15. Continued rise of the people's living and cultural standards and well-being is envisaged. Brezhnev described the new plan as "a five-year plan of efficiency and quality." He spoke bluntly of continuing shortcomings that must be eliminated.

This is all material of the utmost importance, and an integral part of the report as a whole. For reasons of space, however, and because the factual material is largely duplicated in the report of Premier Alexey Kosygin that follows, it is not possible to include it here. The sections of Part II dealing with agriculture, consumers' goods and foreign economic relations follow.

Further Promotion of Agriculture as a Task of the Whole People

The Party has two related aims in agriculture, first, to secure an adequate supply and reserves of food and primary agricultural materials; second, steady progress in levelling up material, cultural and everyday conditions of life in town and countryside.

Objective historical reasons have prevented large investments in agriculture until recently. Of 320 billion rubles invested in agriculture under Soviet power, 213 billion were invested during the past two five-year periods, concentrated in three main areas. *Mechanization:* In this decade collective and state farms received over three million tractors, 900,000 harvester combines, 1,800,000 trucks and special purpose vehicles and billions of rubles worth of other farm machinery. Power per worker has doubled. *Land Improvement:* 6,400,000 hectares of irrigated land and over 8,000,000 hectares of drained land were cultivated. *Chemicalization:* a more than 180 per cent increase in the use of fertilizers, over 100 per cent increase in use of plant protection chemicals. All this has meant 40 per cent increase in grain yield, a rise of 58 per cent in labor productivity and nearly 25 per cent growth in farm products per capita despite a population growth of 23 million. Much remains to be done; 41 billion rubles more is to be invested in the new five-year plan than in the last. That will mean millions of tons more fertilizers, comprehensive mechanization of grain farming and a higher level in livestock, a vast increase in reclamation including large scale improvement in the Non-Black Soil Zone, large new irrigation systems in Central Asia and Kazakhstan as well as in the South and Southeast of the European part of the country.

Grain production is to be increased 14-17 per cent as against the last five-year plan and all other crops must be increased. Increased livestock farming means more fodder crops, improved lands and pastures. Much has been accomplished, but there are still cases of negligence toward the land and inefficient use of machinery and fertilizers.

Experience shows that specialization and concentration of production on the basis of interfarm cooperation and agro-industrial integration open up great possibilities for rapid growth of production.

Among urgent problems before us is development of seed selection and growing; good pedigree livestock; more rational use of mineral fertilizers; more sophisticated machinery and more of it; improved training of agricultural personnel; improvement of organization and management of agricultural production and coordination with the industries that serve its needs. Finally:

We builders of communism must approach agriculture from yet another angle, that of protecting the natural environment. This is a problem that confronts not only industry. The labor of the farmer and the livestock breeder essentially involves the utilization of nature, our natural environment, for the satisfaction of man's requirements.

One can leave in one's wake barren, lifeless expanses inimical to man. The history of mankind knows many such examples. But comrades, it is possible and necessary to improve nature, to help it unfold its vital forces more fully. There is a simple expression, "flowering region," which everyone knows. This is the name given to lands where people's knowledge, experience, attachment and love for nature have indeed worked miracles. This is our socialist way. Consequently, we must regard agriculture as a huge, constantly operating mechanism of protecting and cultivating living natural resources. And nature will repay it a hundredfold.

The Party regards the further development of agriculture as a key task of the state and people. All branches of the economy must make a worthy contribution to its fulfillment. (Italics added.)

Increasing Consumer Goods; Improving Trade and Services for the People

A rise in the people's living standard is inseparable from an ever fuller satisfaction of their demand for the most diverse goods and services. That is why along with rapid growth of agriculture the Party attaches such great significance to the industries known as Group B (light and food industry— Group A is heavy industry). Nearly a thousand new light and food industry enterprises have been built in the last five years. There has been a substantial increase in foodstuffs, everyday goods, household appliances and durables for the people. Yet the situation in Group B industries is not satisfactory. This is not only because planned targets could not be reached due to shortage of primary agriculture materials resulting from crop failures. While the 24th Congress called for a fundamental change in both quantity of goods and services, we still have not learned to promote Group B at a faster rate while insuring a high rate of growth in heavy industry.

Our central planning and economic organs have shown inadequate concern for light, food and service industries; far from everybody has been able to surmount the attitude that consumer goods are secondary and ancillary. We must be more demanding that ministers in charge commission new capacities on schedule and provide Group B industries with efficient equipment and high quality primary materials. Annual plans must provide for an accelerated growth of these industries along with improvement in quality and range of products. Last year we produced nearly 700 million pairs of shoes, three pairs per person, but the demand was not satisfied due to shortage of high quality, modern footwear. The same was true in many other branches. Executives in heavy industry who fail to carry out commitments for consumer goods will be disciplined: To the 40 million workers in service, consumer and food industries, I would like to say: "Comrades, in many ways the well-being and mood of the Soviet people depend on you, on your work. Work better, with more initiative, emulating foremost workers. The Party calls upon you to do this, and expects this of you."

Development of Foreign Economic Relations

The growing importance of foreign economic relations is a direct result of the growth of our economy, far-reaching changes in the world and success of the policy of peace and detente. Economic ties have strengthened the might and cohesion of the socialist community of countries. They have aided the progressive economic growth of the developing states and broadened the material basis of peaceful coexistence with the capitalist states. The Soviet Union and other socialist countries cannot hold aloof from such global problems as primary materials and energy, eradication of the most dangerous and widespread diseases, environmental protection, space exploration and utilization of the resources of the World Ocean.

During the Ninth Five-Year Plan the volume of foreign trade increased from 22 to 51 billion rubles. Complete sets of equipment were imported for nearly 2,000 projects, especially in the light, chemical, automotive and food industries. Our exports consisted mainly of machines and equipment including atomic reactors, power generators, aircraft and machine tools. We took part in building hundreds of industrial projects abroad.

A substantial increase in foreign trade is planned for the tenth five-year period. While our main foreign trade is with the socialist world, we shall enhance our foreign trade structure and balance with the capitalist world, increase the share in exports of the manufacturing industry and enlarge output of goods in demand in foreign markets. We also have in mind new forms of foreign economic ties under which we are granted credits, equipment and licenses to build new enterprises, belonging entirely to our state, in cooperation with foreign firms, and we pay for this with part of the output of these or other enterprises. Such arrangements require a high degree of responsibility in bringing capacities up to their rated level and producing high-quality products on schedule.

Our foreign economic policy is coordinated with the fraternal countries. Acting in the spirit of the Final Act of the Conference on Security and Cooperation in Europe, the Council for Mutual Economic Assistance (CMEA) has offered to establish official relations with the European Economic Community.

Secretary Brezhnev here raised very sharply the question of the necessity of improvement in economic planning, improving the organizational structure and methods of management and more skillful use of economic incentives and levers which are also discussed in the Kosygin report.

III. The Party in the Conditions of Developed Socialism

The results of the past five-year period provide convincing evidence that the Communist Party of the Soviet Union has been following the Leninist line. It has lived up to its role of political leader of the working class, of all the working people, of the whole people. The Party has once again demonstrated the power of its scientific prevision and the realism of its policy, and its capability of directing the energy of the masses towards the fulfillment of the tasks of communist construction.

The Party's Further Development. Questions of Cadre Policy

Since the 24th Congress, nearly 2.6 million men and women have been admitted into the CPSU. The Party now has 15,694,000 members. Of them 41.6 per cent are workers, 13.9 per cent collective farmers, nearly 20 per cent work in the technical fields, and over 24 per cent as workers in science, literature, the arts, education, public health, management and the military spheres.

Under developed socialism, when the Communist Party has become a party of the whole people, it has in no sense lost its class character. The CPSU has been and remains a party of the working class. We are deeply pleased with the fact that 58 per cent of those now joining the Party are workers. This is natural and is a reflection of the leading role of the working class in the life of society.

In the period under review more than 11 per cent of those joining the Party were collective farmers, in line with further consolidating the alliance of the working class and the peasantry. Almost 80 per cent of those joining are engaged in the sphere of material production, the decisive sphere of social life. The percentage of specialists in the national economy, the professions and the arts who are Party members has grown substantially. The Soviet intelligentsia plays an important role in the scientific and cultural revolution, raising the people's cultural standards and in all aspects of communist construction. More than two-thirds of new Party members come from the Komsomol, showing that the Party's vital forces are inexhaustible. In the past 30 years, CPSU membership has tripled.

The Party seeks not numerical growth, not members concerned with obtaining advantages, but those who work selflessly for the benefit of communism. Thus a scrupulous approach to all-around testing of political qualities and capabilities is required. The exchange of Party cards meant dropping 347,000 members who failed to live up to the high requirements of Party membership. Communists have become more exacting of each other throughout our organization. Smooth and purposeful Party functioning can be achieved only through unfailing application of the Leninist rules of Party life and principles of Party

leadership and the principle of democratic centralism. The consistent development of inner-Party democracy, in which the October 1964 Plenary meeting
and subsequent Congresses played a key role, continues to be the basis for the
development of the Party. Pre-Congress reports and election meetings were
attended by over 94 per cent of the Communists and through extensive coverage
in press, radio and television involved the whole people. The Party has no
secrets from the people. It is vitally interested in having all the Soviet people
know about its undertakings and express their own views.

Letters from the working people are an important link between the Party and
the masses. They are growing steadily. The most important are taken into
account in drafting decisions and laws. Many were used in preparing for the
present Congress.

The Party attaches great importance to all levels of Party organization. The
extent of Party guidance directly depends on how much vigor and initiative is
displayed by primary Party branches, helping to combine the Party's policy
with the vital creativity of the masses. Central Committee decisions emphasize
that the primary Party branches must exert an even more active influence on
raising effectiveness of production and accelerating scientific and technical
progress, creating concerted effort, educating our people and improving their
working and living conditions.

The Party's guiding and mobilizing role is not an abstract conception. It is
life itself. In difficult times like 1972 the people were rallied by Party organizations. Workers from the cities, Soviet Army men and students took part in a real
battle for the grain harvest side by side with the collective and state farmers.

The *Leninist style of work* is an important condition for success in the Party's
leadership. The Leninist style is a creative and scientific approach in all social processes,
one which eschews subjectivism. It implies a high degree of exactingness with respect to
oneself and to others, rules out any self-complacency, and is opposed to any manifestations of red tape and formalism.

On self criticism. With the growth in the scale and complexity of the tasks
that face us, an exacting, critical approach to all matters acquires particular
importance. The substance of self-criticism is that every aspect of this or that
organization or individual should be given an objective evaluation. Shortcomings should be subjected to all-round analysis in order to eliminate them. There
should be no liberalism toward shortcomings or those who allow them. Trust
and respect for people should go hand in hand with a high exactingness. Every
instance of incorrect response to criticism must evoke a sharp and swift
response from party organs. The value of self-criticism is determined by its
sincerity, and a readiness instantly to start correction of mistakes and shortcomings.

Checking up on fulfillment of decisions is a key aspect of organizational work. This is the duty of every Party and government worker and every Party organ. Important work is done in this by the Party Control Committee, and better use should be made of the potentialities of the people's control.

Cadre policy. In the past few years many young and promising comrades who have shown themselves good and capable organizers in practical work have been promoted to leading posts.

The modern leader must organically combine the Party approach and well-grounded competence, a sense of high discipline and initiative and creative approach to his work. At the same time the leader must take account of the sociopolitical and educational aspects, be sensitive to the needs and requirements of people and set an example in work and everyday life.

He who has lost his ability to make a critical assessment of his activity, who has lost touch with the masses, who breeds toadies and bootlickers, and who has lost the trust of the people cannot be a Party leader.

The Party's Work in the Field of Ideological Education

In the period under review, a major aspect of all our work has been the ideological education of our people, and the problems arising in the molding of the new man, a worthy builder of communism.

Marxism-Leninism is the only reliable base for formulating the right strategy. At the present stage in the country's development, the need for further creative elaboration of theory has been growing:

In-depth research into questions relating to the development trends of our society and its productive forces is highly necessary. This applies, for instance, to the character and content of labor under developed socialism and to changes in the social structure. Improvement of distribution according to work, the combination of moral and material incentives, the socialist way of life and the development of our multinational culture— all this requires a pooling of the efforts of scientists working in various fields. There is also need for a further study of the problems relating to the development of our state system, and the forms and methods of our educational and ideological work. In this context, much attention should be given to the study of public opinion.

Soviet scientists should not lose sight of the problems of the environment and population growth which have recently assumed such a serious aspect. Improvement of the socialist use of natural resources and the formulation of an effective demographic policy are an important task.

The importance has been steadily growing of scientific research into the cardinal problems of world development and international relations, the revolutionary process, the interaction and unity of its various streams, the relationship between the struggle for democracy and the struggle for socialism, and the contest of forces on the main issue of our day, the issue of war and peace.

The tasks facing our social science can, apparently, be fulfilled only if there is the closest connection with life. Scholastic theorizing will merely act as a brake on our advance. Connection with practice can alone make science more effective.

The task of establishing a creative atmosphere in scientific work remains as important as ever. It goes without saying that the creative comparison of views should proceed on the basis of our Marxist-Leninist ideological platform.

The people's growing awareness of the fact that they are better informed makes greater demands on all our work among the masses. The positive changes in world affairs and detente create favorable opportunities for the broad spread of socialist ideas. But, on the other hand, the ideological contest between the systems is becoming ever more acute, and imperialist propaganda ever more subtle.

On socialist emulation. Here the current upswing is a graphic result of the close *combination of political and labor education.* The whole country has responded to the splendid movement for adopting supplementary plans exceeding the set targets. We are all happy to see how deeply the Leninist ideas of socialist emulation have taken hold. We take pride in the fact that Communists are in the forefront of emulation. Our common militant slogan is to do our utmost to develop still further socialist emulation and the movement for a communist attitude to work.

Communist education implies constant perfection of the public education and vocational training system. It is obvious that there is need for further and serious improvement in the whole system of general education, secondary schools in the first place. In modern conditions, when the volume of knowledge a person needs tends sharply and rapidly to increase, it is no longer possible to rely mainly on the assimilation of a definite sum of facts. It is important to develop in a young person the ability to augment his knowledge independently and to find his bearings in the torrent of scientific and political information. Much remains to be done in this field.

An extensive system of education in economics was set up on the basis of decisions of the 24th Congress. More than 42 million people have already taken advantage of it; 36 million are studying at the present time. We should see to it that this type of education promotes to the utmost throughout the country the spread of advanced experience in labor organization and the application of scientific and technical achievements in production.*

---

* Following a decision of the 24th CPSU Congress, the Central Committee, in September 1971, passed a decree ''On Improving the Education of the Working People in Economics.'' Since then a large network of formal and informal courses for school-children, workers, students and managers has been established. Special schools, courses and seminars have been established through such organizations as *Znanie,* Scientific and Technical Societies, the All-Union Society of Inventors and Innovators, People's Universities, Party schools and at large industrial establishments. Textbooks and materials for regular schools have been revised to include more material on economics. Content of the various forms in which knowledge of economics is disseminated is adapted to the needs of the various groups involved.

Moral education to create a constructive attitude to life, and a conscious approach to one's duty to society, is also necessary. We have achieved a great deal in improving the Soviet people's material welfare. We shall continue consistently to pursue this task. But it is necessary that the growth of material opportunities should be constantly accompanied by a growth in our people's ideological, moral and cultural level. Otherwise we may have relapses into the philistine, petty-bourgeois mentality.

The higher the level of our society's development, the more intolerable are departures from socialist rules of morality. Acquisitiveness, proprietary tendencies, hooliganism, red tape and indifference to one's fellow humans run against the very grain of our system. In combating such phenomena there is need to make full use of the opinion of the working collective, criticism in the press, methods of persuasion and the force of law—all the instruments at our disposal.

On literature and art. The period since the last Congress has seen further intensification of the activity of all creative intellectuals, who have been making an ever more tangible contribution to the creation of a communist society. This positive and vivifying process has naturally been reflected in new works of socialist realism which respond more frequently and more deeply to the basic and essential ideas which animate the country. The "production topic" has acquired a truly aesthetic form. The Great Patriotic War has been dealt with in truthful and impressive works and through the miraculous effect of art the younger generation feels involved in the exploits of its fathers. In the topic of morality, moral quests, there have been some failures, but achievements have been greater. Our writers and artists seek to bring out the best human qualities like firmness of principle, honesty and depth of emotion, always in line with the sound and solid principles of our communist morality.

Another source of inspiration for our artists, writers and poets has been the important and lofty topic of the struggle for peace, for the liberation of the peoples, and the international solidarity of the working people in the struggle. The intellectuals engaged in the arts have become more exacting with respect to their own and each other's works, and drab and mediocre stories and plays, to say nothing of ideological mistakes, are being duly assessed without regard for personalities.

The spreading movement in which our theaters and the literary and art journals give encouragement and guidance in artistic matters to workers at factories and collective farms, and on construction projects such as the Baikal-Amur Railway and the Kama Motor Works, should be welcomed without any reservations. Amateur art groups, literary associations and people's theaters are directed by experienced masters. Thus an invigorating process is under way in which, on the one hand, art is being enriched with a knowledge of life and, on the other, millions upon millions of working people are being introduced to cultural values.

The Party approach to questions of literature and art combines tact with respect to intellectuals working in the arts, assistance in their creative quest, and a principled stand. If some officials take an oversimplified approach and try to resolve matters relating to aesthetic creativity and diversity of form and individuality of style by issuing decrees, the Party does not ignore such cases and helps to rectify the situation.

Soviet writers, artists, composers and workers of the stage, screen and television, all those whose talents and skills serve the people and the cause of communism, deserve our deep gratitude. We are happy to see a young generation of creative intellectuals emerging on the scene with ever greater confidence. Talented works of literature and art are part of the national heritage.

Party Guidance of State and Social Organizations

The Party and the Central Committee start in all things from the premise that a developed socialist society has been built in our country and is gradually growing into a communist society, from the premise that our state is a state of the whole people, expressing the interests and the will of the whole people. We have always started from the premise that we now have a fully shaped new historical community, the Soviet people, based on the solid alliance of the working class, the peasantry and the intelligentsia and on the friendship of all the big and small nations of our country.

The Party devotes attention to the *work of the Soviets*. In accordance with proposals of the 24th Congress we have enhanced the role of deputies who now take the initiative in raising many important matters. Laws have also been adopted extending the rights and material capabilities of rural, village, district and city Soviets, as a result of which their work has now acquired a new dimension.

We have constantly dealt with *improvement of our legislation and consolidation of socialist law and order*. In this a vigorous role has been played by the standing commissions of the USSR Supreme Soviet.

Legal provisions now encompass matters like protection of the environment, including bodies of water, the earth, air and so on, where more purposeful work may be accomplished. Much more must be done to improve legal regulation of economic activity. Constant attention must continue to be given to the activity of the militia, the procurator's office, the courts and the organs of justice. The state security organs carry on all their work under the Party's guidance, in the light of the interests of the people and the state, with the support of the broad masses of working people, and with strict observance of constitutional rules and socialist legality. Our Party will continue to see that the armed forces of the Soviet Union are provided with all the necessary means for standing guard over the Soviet people's labor and acting as a bulwark of world peace.

Our social organizations are one of the important channels through which citizens are enabled to participate in running the affairs of society. The work of our trade unions, with over 107 million members, furthers the exercise of democracy in production. The trade unions have the task above all of protecting the rights and interests of the working people. Because of this it is their duty to show concern for boosting production. With the reestablishment of the sectoral management of industry, the concentration of production has been growing and production associations are being set up. However this has not yet been duly reflected in the life of the trade unions. Their structure in production needs to accord more fully with the structure of management.

The role of the trade unions on the collective farms has been growing. We must help make them more of a mass organization capable of both boosting agricultural production and improving the collective farmers' working and living conditions.

Youth. The 35-million-strong army of Komsomol members has always tackled tasks set by the Party with enthusiasm. In the last five-year period more than half a million young men and women have been involved in 670 high priority construction projects, such as the Baikal-Amur Railway and 1,200 land-improvement and rural construction projects in the Non-Black Soil Zone of the RSFSR. Through student building teams they have done work worth roughly five billion rubles.

The labor glory of the Komsomol is firmly established and through the Komsomol young people are actively brought into conscious participation in communist construction. Our task is to keep their fervor alive and make sure it is not dimmed by encounters with formalism and a bureaucratic approach to educational work.

Women. In many ways our homeland owes its achievements and victories to our women's dedication and talents. In the fulfillment of the important tasks our Congress will outline for the future, our fine women will undoubtedly make a great contribution in every sphere. Our Party displays constant concern for women, improving their condition as participants in the labor process, as mothers and educators of children and as housewives.

Critics abroad frequently seek to distort the meaning of the measures taken by the Soviet state for consolidating our legality and law and order. Democracy is inconceivable without discipline and sound public order. Let us recall Lenin's idea that everything is moral in our society that serves the interests of communist construction. Similarly, we can say that for us the democratic is that which serves the people's interests, the interests of communist construction. We reject everything that runs counter to these interests.

We know not only from theory but from long years of practice that genuine democracy is impossible without socialism, and that socialism is impossible without a steady development of democracy. We see the improvement of our socialist democracy as consisting above all in a steady effort to ensure ever fuller participation by the working people in running all the affairs of society, in further developing the democratic principles of our state system and in creating the conditions for the all-round flourishing of the individual.

Socialism is a dynamically developing society. A great deal has been done. And the time has now come to sum up what has been accomplished. That is our premise in preparing the draft of a new *Constitution of the USSR*. This work is being done thoroughly, without any haste, so as to consider every problem with the greatest possible precision, and then to place the draft for discussion by the whole people.

The Constitution will give a detailed definition of the principles governing the management of the national economy. At the same time it will reflect the role of the state in the spiritual life of society and in ensuring the conditions for the development of science, education and culture, thereby emphasizing the humanistic character of the socialist state, which sets itself the goal of building communism in the interests of the working people, in the interests of the people as a whole. One of the basic features of the draft of the new Constitution will be further consolidation and development of socialist democracy.

It is envisaged that draft all-Union laws are to be submitted for discussion by the whole people. Such discussion is already our practice, but it remains to be given legal expression.

We have created a new society, a society the like of which mankind has never known before. It is a society with a crisis-free, steadily growing economy, mature socialist relations and genuine freedom. It is a society governed by the scientific materialist world outlook. It is a society of firm confidence in the future, of radiant communist prospects. Before it lie boundless horizons of further all-round progress.

The atmosphere of genuine collectivism and comradeship, cohesion and the friendship of all big and small nations in the country, which gain in strength from day to day, and the moral health which makes us strong and steadfast—these are the radiant facets of our way of life, these are the great gains of socialism that have become the very lifeblood of our reality.

Finally, there is the new Soviet person, the most important product of the past 60 years. A person who having gone through all trials, has changed beyond recognition, combining ideological conviction and tremendous vital energy, culture, knowledge and the ability to use them. This is a person who, while an ardent patriot, has been and will always remain a consistent internationalist.

In the eyes of the peoples of the whole world, the Land of Soviets is by right regarded as the bulwark of peace. We will continue to do all we can to safeguard and consolidate peace, to rid mankind of new destructive wars.

Indeed we are aware that not all the problems have yet been solved. We have a better knowledge than all our critics of our shortcomings, and are aware of the difficulties. And we have been successfully overcoming them. We know and see the ways leading to the further development and improvement of our society.

The Soviet people wholeheartedly support the Party's domestic and foreign policies. This augments the Party's strength and serves as an inexhaustible source of energy.

And the Communists, for their part, are aware that the people who have entrusted them with the country's leadership, are a people of exceptional industry, courage, stamina, a people of generous spirit, talent and intellect, who will not flinch in time of ordeal. They are responsive to the joys and sorrows of other peoples, always prepared to help them in their struggle for justice, freedom and social progress. The Soviet people are a truly great and heroic people.

"Comrades, the Soviet country and our people have travelled a difficult but glorious path. I think that every one of us Communists, asked whether he would choose any other path, would say no. Our path is the path of truth, the path of freedom, it is the path of the people's happiness." □

5

Alexey Kosygin

Chairman of the USSR
Council of Ministers

Basic Orientations of Economic Development of the USSR for 1976-1980
Report Delivered March 1, 1976

Extended summary

Alexey Kosygin's report to the Congress, March 1, had as its overall purpose presentation for adoption of the Central Committee's draft "Basic Orientations," which are to guide the formulation of the specific directives and targets of the Tenth Five-Year Plan. The general report, delivered by L. I. Brezhnev, examined, in Kosygin's words, the "radical and urgent problems" of the present stage, and defined the main "long-term directions" of the CPSU's domestic and foreign policy. In line with these directions, the "Basic Orientations" draft "sets out a full-scale program for the further construction of the material and technical basis of communism in our country."

The draft had already been widely discussed in the Party, at meetings of working people, in the press, a "truly nationwide discussion of the various aspects of our economic and social policy . . . in which the working people expressed their views on an extensive range of complicated and vital questions of communist construction. . . . . This is a vivid and convincing example of the effectiveness of socialist democracy, and one of its basic advantages over bourgeois democracy. Such a discussion is altogether inconceivable in any country of the capitalist world even if only because of the limited class character of bourgeois democracy and the lack of political and socioeconomic purposes uniting the whole of society." The discussions focused on problems, on eliminating shortcomings in the organization of production, the development of technology. Mr. Kosygin specifically mentioned agriculture and consumer goods as areas of major concern in the discussions; "critical remarks were also made on individual aspects of planning, organization of capital construction and material and technical supplies." All proposals are to be closely considered when the new five-year plan is elaborated.

Results of the Ninth Five-Year Plan

The main socioeconomic targets of the last five-year period have been achieved; "the orientation and character of our economic development has been in complete accord with the fundamental guidelines and Directives of the 24th Congress of the CPSU." The absolute increment of industrial output, capital investments, and appropriations for the people's welfare exceeded any preceding five-year plan, and in that sense "the Ninth Five-Year Plan period has been the best five-year period in our country's history." As compared with the eighth plan period (1966-1970), national income in absolute terms for the entire ninth plan period was 34 per cent higher, and a larger share, some 80 per cent, went to raising people's welfare. Industrial output was 45 per cent higher; agricultural output, 13 per cent; capital investments, 42 per cent; social consumption funds allotments, 43 per cent; cash incomes of the population, 42 per cent. The "people's labor exploits" reflected in these figures amount "to a great political triumph."

The *social program* charted by the 24th Congress set the task of raising the welfare of the entire population, while concentrating especially on the lowest brackets. In 1971-75, average monthly cash wages rose by 20 per cent, to 146 rubles; with payments from social funds included, to 198 rubles per month. In the same period collective farmers' income went up by 25 per cent. Minimum wages, and rates for the middle brackets, were increased, along with wages for workers in the non-productive (*i.e.*, service) sphere. Pensions, scholarships and stipends were raised. Retail trade increased by 36 per cent, with stable prices, and even faster increases for meat, meat products, eggs, automobiles. Eleven million new housing units, 544 million square meters, were built, which helped improve housing conditions for 56 million people; this represents a move "in the main to the distribution of new housing according to the one-flat-one-family principle." Also completed "in the main" was the transition to universal secondary ten-year education.

In production, the plan brought about improved quality indicators, and a raising of the role of labor productivity in the increment of national income. Industrial output increased 43 per cent over 1970, "in accordance with the Directives of the Party's 24th Congress." Heavy industry targets have been surpassed, with 1975 production of 491 million tons of oil, 289 billion cubic meters of gas, 701 million tons of coal, 1.038 billion kwh of electric power, 141 million tons of steel, 90 million tons of mineral fertilizer, 122 million tons of cement. Heavy engineering industry increased 73 per cent, farm machinery, 78 per cent, means of automation 90 per cent, computers 330 per cent—these figures showing a qualitative improvement in production not seen in the aggregate growth rates. Consumer goods output rose 37 per cent; items of cultural and everyday use and household appliances, 60 per cent.

Agriculture was the focus of a comprehensive development program, and 131 billion rubles, more than one quarter of total investments, were earmarked for that sector. Despite extremely adverse weather, output rose by 13 per cent averaged over the entire period; "however, by and large, the output of farm produce fell short of the five-year plan target, and this could not help affecting the growth rate of the food and light industries." Technical indices for the countryside show enormous change: almost all collective and state farms are now electrified, with power consumption 250 per cent greater than in 1965, and total machine capacity in the same period increased by 80 per cent. Cultural facilities, household appliances, etc., gradually approach the level of the cities; the level of education of the rural population is rising. These changes "cannot be measured solely by statistics. . . . They mirror the qualitatively new stage in the development of socialist production, the beginning for which was laid by Lenin's cooperative plan."

In the capital construction field, the total investments of more than 500 billion rubles resulted in the renewal of nearly 43 per cent of the fixed production assets; the renewal rate for agriculture was 56 per cent. The stock of fixed capital increased by half during the period, with a labor productivity increase of almost a quarter. However, Mr. Kosygin notes, "we have been unable fully to solve a number of problems and remove some bottlenecks in the national economy." In capital construction, some plans were fulfilled 60-80 per cent, with investments scattered among innumerable projects, a result of government departments "investing in new projects rather than making fuller use of operating fixed assets and consistently pursuing a policy of intensifying production."

Mr. Kosygin gave summary figures covering the competition with industrialized capitalist countries. In 1971-75, USSR industrial output grew at an average annual rate of 7.4 per cent, while the USA and Common Market countries together averaged 1.2 per cent. The USSR leads the world in production of iron, manganese and chromium ore, coal, cement, potassium salts, phosphate primary materials, tractors, locomotives, cotton, wool, flax; steel, oil and mineral fertilizers; the last three items having joined the list in the recent period. Contrasting the socialist experience with the "grave economic crisis," the "organic disease of the capitalist system," Mr. Kosygin claimed that "the socialist world gives the answer to the basic questions of social development." The recent and forthcoming congresses of the fraternal parties of the socialist countries "eloquently show that the socialist community has clear prospects for development based on the steady growth of its planned economy. We announce our aims and creative plans, our policy for many years in advance publicly, to the whole world, because all our plans meet the interests of the broad masses of the working people, the interests of peace and social progress. We have solved and shall solve our problems, whatever their magnitude, in the interests of society as a whole, and we are confident in the success of the great cause of communism.''

The Tenth Five-Year Plan: Socioeconomic Tasks

The core formulation of the tasks of the Tenth Five-Year Plan is taken from the "Basic Orientations" document: *"The cardinal task of the five-year period is consistently to implement the Communist Party's line towards promoting the people's living standard and cultural level on the basis of a dynamic and balanced development of social production and enhancement of its efficiency, the acceleration of the scientific and technological progress, the growth of labor productivity and the utmost improvement of the quality of the work in every sector of the national economy."* The new plan is a new stage in socio-economic development, and in the "development of socialist social relations and the Soviet way of life, and also in assuring our country's security."

In the past, attention was devoted to raising the role of the "intensivity factors" in economic growth; in the present period, "this will acquire cardinal significance." "The main thing now is to effect a decisive turn to more efficient use of the mighty technical and production potential created in our country." The high output of materials is not adequate, if those materials are not effectively used; so "quality indicators"—lower per unit consumption of materials and fuel, higher quality of final outputs—now have "determining significance" in the plan.

Turning to income and consumption policy, Mr. Kosygin stressed that remuneration according to labor remains the principal way of raising people's income, and accounts for about three quarters of the increment in income; the goal is to raise the stimulating role of workers' and collective farmers' incomes, make them depend on the end results and efficiency of production. Average wages and salaries are to rise 16-18 per cent in the coming five-year period. Collective farm incomes are to rise 24-27 per cent, and payments from social consumption funds will rise 28-30 per cent; all of this marks a steady trend toward greater social equality, especially between city and countryside. Improvements are planned in maternity leaves and grants, pensions, the tax system, disability pensions, etc.

Trade turnover will increase 27-29 per cent; "the real security of incomes is guaranteed by maintaining stable state retail prices for basic consumer items, and reducing the prices of some types of goods as the necessary conditions are secured and commodity stocks built up." Housing construction will continue at about the same pace as before (huge by capitalist standards), but quality is to be improved, especially as regards amenities, support services, etc. While most new housing will be built by the state, some cooperative and private housing, especially in the rural areas, will be encouraged.

"The humanism of our system . . . is always, even in hard times, strikingly manifested in the concern shown for the working conditions, health and the educational and cultural standards of Soviet people." The course of automation, gradually eliminating unattractive manual labor, will be continued. The "role of social factors in expanding production" will be substantially higher in the new five-year period. In the fields of health, education, spiritual and cultural requirements, the emphasis will be on the fullest satisfaction of the Soviet people's needs; while this is the *purpose* of the plan, it is *simultaneously* "an important premise for the further growth of production and its efficiency." The quality of life—including "a creative and constructive environment and a sound social-psychological climate in the collective"—is not only a goal, but also a necessary factor with a "beneficial effect on the results of production."

Industrial output in 1976-1980 is to grow by 35-39 per cent, with heavy industry (group A) 38-42 per cent and light or consumer industry (group B) 30-32 per cent. Mr. Kosygin points out that a one per cent increase at the current level means a more than 40 per cent larger absolute increment than a one per cent increase starting from the 1970 level. The priority growth of heavy industry does *not* mean any let-up in the expansion of consumer goods; in fact, consumption will rise to 27-29 per cent of 1975, while the accumulation or investment portion of national income will rise by 17-23 per cent. This indicates that large increases in productivity and efficiency are to result from the heavy industry outlays. The rise in the share of consumption, also, "is convincing evidence of our socialist state's policy for peace."

The plan envisions a planned rise in the share of investments devoted to agriculture, with major efforts aimed at intensification, land improvement, specialization and concentration of agricultural production. New construction, in all sectors, should be oriented toward technical reequipment and reconstruction of existing enterprises, instead of the proliferation of new installations, often only slowly put into operation. Along with improvement in the use of raw materials, there will be major efforts toward development of new sources, so that the ratio of proved deposits to the rate of extraction will grow.

Mr. Kosygin then outlined what he termed a "coherent technical policy," based on the need for the scientific and technological revolution to be "organically tied in with the advantages of the socialist economic system." In the production of instruments of labor, emphasis is on switching from production of individual machines to machine *systems,* covering the whole technological process. Technologies which reduce the total number of operations—*i.e.,* furnaceless metallurgy, spindleless spinning and shuttleless weaving— will be promoted. Stepped-up development of atomic energetics, hydroelectric power stations, thermal electric power stations, production of high-grade steels, increased use of aluminum, titanium, polymers, synthetic materials, all these are specially stressed aspects of the production plan. Reserves will be built up in fundamentally new hardware and technology, with the thrust of research and development directed to problems which "are to determine the future of the economy."

The report stresses the point that "the efficiency of social production is not only a scientific-technological or production-economic problem but also a major social problem." A "regime of economies" depends on the working people's day-to-day concern for thrift in the use of resources and productivity. This in turn is essential for the success of the technical policy, which targets increasing output per ruble of assets, and a rise in the product-to-assets ratio. Reducing idle time in the use of equipment, reducing the material-intensiveness of production, introducing material-saving designs and technologies—all this and more will be necessary to achieve the target increase in labor productivity of 27 per cent (as compared with 23 per cent for 1971-75), raising assets per worker in industry by 37 per cent (in agriculture by 59 per cent), and bringing labor productivity growth to the point where it accounts for 85-90 per cent of the growth in national income.

Turning to the improvement of planning and management, Mr. Kosygin defined the "task of economic science" in the new period: "substantially to enhance the role of the plan's quality indicators by raising the efficiency of social production." The plan must become a forceful instrument in improving product quality and assuring the economical use of fixed assets, as well as linking up the plan with advanced science and speeding up the introduction of scientific achievements in production. "For the new five-year plan we have elaborated for the first time concrete programs to resolve the key scientific and technical problems which determine the whole complex of necessary work, including measures for preparing the introduction of new hardware in industry." The plan now includes "comprehensive programs" in which all material and human resources necessary to achieve a given objective are concentrated, to eliminate communication problems and "resolve intersectoral questions." Examples: a program for developing the production basis of atomic energetics; a program for mechanizing manual and arduous physical labor; programs for shaping large-scale territorial-production complexes.

Planning operations are being speeded up, and in this connection it is announced that the plan for 1976 has already been approved. Planning over a lengthy period in the past has enabled management bodies and production collectives to "relax their control of plan fulfillment." This should be corrected.

The State Planning Committee (Gosplan) is charged in the new five-year plan with tasks of new complexity: balanced plan formation, comprehensive programs, economic districting. "If it is to tackle this work creatively and in depth, the State Planning Committee must be released from many of its current concerns. . ." As part of the improvement of the organizational structure of management, many of the detailed planning tasks will devolve onto the middle-level industrial associations, which are to become the main form of economic organization by the end of the Tenth Five-Year Plan. "These associations are a qualitatively new phenomenon in the management of industrial production. They are not a mechanical agglomeration of enterprises, but a coherent production-economic complex organically blending science and production and extensively developing specialization and cooperation." The two- and three-tier system of management in construction, and the development of agro-industrial and inter-farm integration in agriculture, are the forms taken in those sectors by the effort to streamline and raise the democracy and quality of management.

To make plans a better instrument for control and for raising efficiency, there will be greater emphasis on end results, on delivery plans in accordance with contracts between enterprises. It is also planned to complete, within the period, the switch of associations and enterprises with mass and large-batch production to direct, long-term ties, so that the rules of the game remain stable for a reasonable period and enterprises have an incentive to make fullest use of reserves.

Both the profits of enterprises and the wages and bonus system will play greater parts in economic stimulation. Profits should depend closely on the results of an enterprise collective's work, and their use for technical re-equipment, social benefits, etc., be carefully controlled. As for wages, there is to be increasing application of progressive forms of material incentives—remuneration of labor for completed projects and deliveries, and for maintaining planned production with a smaller number of workers. The role of the financial and credit mechanism is to be enhanced, especially through the extension of long-term credits so that enterprises can plan their reequipment and extension over a longer time horizon.

Great importance attaches to initiative and socialist enterprise among economic cadres. "What the modern Soviet economic executive should be concerned with is active use of new scientific and technical approaches, advanced methods in the organization of labor and management, creative quest for reserves in production and thorough consideration of the changing requirements of demand. He must have a sense of novelty, be aware of the lines of perspective and take his decisions with a Party approach and full knowledge of his business and, of course, act as educator in the collective and organizer of production. . . . There is need more broadly to develop criticism and self-criticism, improve control and verification of fulfillment, and steadily to cultivate the Leninist style of work in every echelon of economic management."

Mr. Kosygin spoke of the socialist emulation movement, in which workers, brigades and whole enterprises enter into competitions of plan and counter-plan fulfillment, introduction and mastery of new techniques, etc. This "movement for a communist attitude towards work" must be built in the coming five-year period, especially between enterprises supplying primary materials and those manufacturing the finished products. In the emulation movement, enterprises will adopt counterplans, upwardly adjusted; "this devolves considerable responsibility on planning and supply organs, ministries and government departments, which must quickly and competently respond to the initiatives of work collectives undertaking high commitments."

The Tenth Five-Year Plan envisages deeper involvement of the USSR in the international division of labor, in particular among the countries of the socialist community, and the further transfer of external economic cooperation to a long-term basis. A number of export-oriented industries, to meet the specific requirement of foreign markets, will be set up. Cooperation with the socialist countries "is of a special nature and reflects the durable economic links established in the course of socialist construction and mutual cooperation." The 20-year Comprehensive Program for Socialist Economic Integration poses special tasks in this area. Trade and cooperation with the developing countries will be expanded "on democratic and equitable principles," to "help them strengthen their economic independence." Relations with the industrialized capitalist countries have "new qualitative aspects" in the era of detente, embodied in the practice of large-scale agreements for building of industrial projects in the USSR. These will be continued, as well as participation of Soviet organizations in similar projects in Western countries. "Needless to say, our trade and economic relations will develop faster with countries that show a sincere desire for cooperation and concern to ensure normal and equitable conditions for its development."

The Watchwords: Efficiency and Quality

Alexey Kosygin's report here begins to outline detailed targets, by industry and by sector. This summary will cover only some highlights.

The priority growth of the atomic, metallugical, chemical, and parts of the electrical engineering, radio electronics, machine-tool and instrument making industries has already been mentioned. About 57 per cent of the machine tools in the USSR are less than ten years old, "more than in many Western industrialized countries." Special attention is to be given to development of automated production lines that can be quickly retooled for a variety of output types. In the textile industry, mass production of new spindleless weaving machines and shuttleless looms that cut labor consumption 33-50 per cent, while greatly reducing the noise level, are targeted. Comprehensive mechanization and automation of the country's mines, to greatly improve working conditions in this sector, are in the plan.

The plan includes special measures to protect the environment. For example, in the timber and woodworking industry, timber-felling is to increase only two per cent, with reforestation greatly exceeding that amount. With two per cent more timber, output of chip and wood-fiber boards will increase 60-85 per cent, of pulp 35 per cent and of wooden furniture 40-50 per cent. In other areas of environmental protection, new methods of controlling the ejection of noxious waste into air and water are to be implemented. *All* industries will be switched over to the use of recycled water during the plan period. Discharge of industrial sewage into rivers and lakes by the chemical industry will actually be reduced, despite considerable growth of production. Major water conservation projects will be launched, including study of possible redirection of Northern and Siberian rivers to the Volga basin, Kazakhstan and Central Asia.

The priority growth of group A (heavy) industries—38-42 per cent as against 35-39 per cent for industry as a whole—far from being at the expense of consumer goods production, "is directly linked with the tasks set by the Party for a fundamental restructuring of agriculture, switching it to an industrial foundation and continuing to increase the output of consumer goods." Agriculture, as mentioned above, is a special priority, and the targets of raising power per worker from 17 to 28 horsepower, increasing fertilizer production by 50 per cent, major irrigation works, etc., are expected to raise average output 14-17 per cent, and grain output 18-21 per cent. "Not only will the transfer of agricultural production to an industrial basis create the best possible conditions for introducing advanced machinery and techniques; it will also greatly benefit the further socialist reconstruction of the countryside."

In the light and food industries, progress is balanced against still-existing shortcomings. "The insistent demands concerning the quality, convenience and novelty of goods come not from some restricted group of consumers, but from practically the entire urban and rural population." Increased use of synthetics, tightening links of retailing with industry and agriculture, authorizing production associations to open their own retail outlets where they can study conditions of demand directly, and increasing the responsibility of the local Soviets for control in this area—all these are aspects of the planned attack on these problems.

In capital construction, special emphasis is to be placed on raising the efficiency of investments. In the coming five years, the commissioning of production assets is to outstrip outlays in their construction, and the share of uncompleted construction in total state investments is to fall from the present 76 per cent to 65 per cent by1980. Comprehensive mechanized assembly and prefabrication are to be promoted, and the share of pre-assembled construction raised to 45 per cent of total construction by the end of the period.

The territorial division of labor will be extended, and the eastern regions of the country which are less developed than the European parts of the USSR, will grow at priority rates. (Their industrial production, for example, will increase by 50 per cent.) Territorial-production complexes will be further developed, and new organizational forms worked out "in the immediate future" to cope with these projects. All of the associated social and cultural aspects must be developed.

In summary, Mr. Kosygin returned to the twin themes of the Tenth Five-Year Plan: efficiency and quality. "The higher quality of all our work will assure sensible and thrifty use of the wealth of our society. Communists are no advocates of asceticism, of any artificial restrictions on people's requirements. On the contrary, the full and free development of all of man's faculties, man's creative forces, implicit in communist society, presupposes the creation of favorable material conditions of life. But our socialist life style rules out the extravagance, the senseless waste of material values, labor and energy seen in capitalist society." The problem of raising efficiency and quality is not merely a technical one; "it is also a social, ideological problem," whose solution "will contribute to the consolidation and improvement of socialist social relations and the roles of communist community life."

Kosygin hailed the "mounting creative initiative" of Soviet working people as the "decisive factor" for success in the new five-year period. The USSR's five-year plans have long been a symbol of that country's progress and aspirations to peace. "With the emergence of the socialist community the concept 'five-year plan' also acquired a new, international meaning: it absorbed the fraternal countries' community of aims in building the new life, in shaping and consolidating the socialist world economic system."

"Before us lies a new five-year stretch of the road to a communist society in our country. During these years the creative, constructive activity of the Party, of the entire Soviet people, will be concentrated on the imposing tasks set by the 25th Congress. The work that is being accomplished by our Congress gives deep confidence that the Tenth Five-Year Plan period will see new historic achievements by the heroic working class, the splendid collective-farm peasantry, the people's intelligentsia, in the name of the triumph of the ideas of our great Leninist Communist Party!" □

6

Speeches of Congress Delegates

Following is a small but representative sampling of excerpts from the contributions of delegates to the Congress, from diverse geographic, occupational and ethnic sectors of the population. Some of the speeches were part of the discussion of the Brezhnev report; others of the report by A. N. Kosygin.

K. B. Donenbayeva

Tractorist from the "Kharkov" State Farm,
Borovsky District, Kustanaisky Region, Kazakhstan

Dear Comrades! Permit me first of all to express my heartfelt thanks to the Communist Party, its Leninist Central Committee and Politburo and personally to you, Leonid Ilyich, that I, a rank-and-file working woman, have the privilege of being a delegate to this Congress and of speaking from this high rostrum.

My life is the life of many others. There is nothing exceptional about it. But I must say frankly that I am immeasurably happy at what the Soviet Government has given to me, a simple Kazakh woman. My father and grandfather pastured cattle belonging to others on land belonging to others. They worked all their lives for others and so never knew what the happiness of free labor is like. I do not even speak of the women whose sphere never reached beyond the family hearth.

And indeed, how would it have been possible to believe in those days that I, granddaughter of an enslaved shepherd, should now be driving a powerful tractor over the rejuvenated steppes—that I have even been elected to the highest organ of Soviet power—the Supreme Soviet of the USSR. And that for my modest labor I should receive the Order of Hero of Socialist Labor! All this was possible thanks to the unceasing concern of our Party for each human being, of whatever nationality, from whatever far corner of our country. One sky bends over our whole country, one sun shines upon it!

All the same, it seems to me, that the sun shines over our Kazakh virgin lands more brightly than anywhere else! These lands are indeed the scene of a great exploit by the whole Soviet people. At the call of the Party, by the wish of their own hearts, representatives of all the fraternal Republics came to us and transformed these great virgin spaces with their labor.

In the years of opening up the virgin lands our sovkhoz "Kharkov" alone poured into government warehouses almost a quarter of a million tons of virgin land grain, and our country received from us thousands of tons of meat, milk and not a few other products.

The virgin lands today—Tselina—has become a beautiful, well managed town, with gas, electricity and running water. Every state farm has its own middle school, House of Culture, shopping center with household repair shops, restaurant, kindergarten and the necessary farm buildings and equipment.

Each year the material-technical bases of the sovkhozes are strengthened and enlarged. We are receiving new machines in place of our old ones and the process of mechanization is more and more eliminating heavy physical labor.

Life does not stand still and in order not to fall behind everyone, without exception, must study. I too, have become a correspondence student of the agricultural technicum, even though I have four children!

How we rejoiced when we received as a gift from the workers of the Kirov factory in Leningrad, from our brother workers, that beauty of a tractor, K-701, made with their own hands. With all our hearts we Kazakh people thank the Kirov workers for this magnificent present.

Our state farms are all well equipped technically. But now, in order for the virgin lands to yield still more grain, all our state farms need *more* K-701s and other powerful new machines.

We have a very important request to put to the Ministry of Tractor and Agricultural Machine Building of the USSR. The basic models of the tractors change every five to eight years. But where is the basic renewal of all the various attachments to tractors that are essential for our work? Wide ranging mechanization is so necessary, and there isn't enough of it, therefore such first class machines as the K-701 cannot be used to their full capacity, which lessens their effectiveness. We are waiting for an answer from the designers and builders—an answer in concrete deeds!

I am glad to tell the Congress that I reached the targets of the Ninth Five-Year Plan in three and a half years and I have still bigger plans for the Tenth, along with a whole group of other woman tractorists.

There are more and more "woman mechanizers" in Kazakhstan each year. The life and labor of our working women of the countryside today can in many ways be compared with that of women workers of the city, in their level of education and culture and in their social conditions. Now the problem is to enlarge and improve the scope of services for village working women. We need more modern housing, schools and pre-school institutions; we need to improve the work of the food shops and restaurants and the household services. Of no little importance to women is this question: we women and not only "mechanizers" need comfortable, attractive seasonal working clothes, but too often we see them only in fashion sections of magazines or sometimes on TV shows!

Comrades! In these days, in our region, as throughout the whole country, socialist emulation is growing. In every kolkhoz and sovkhoz the struggle for more Kazakhstan bread is in full swing. In our sovkhoz the representatives of many nationalities work like a single family. But we have always had and always will have a common tongue—the tongue of brotherhood and friendship. We are 250 million sons and daughters of one mother—our socialist homeland. All of us, the united Soviet people, are solidly ranked around our Communist Party and there is no power in the world which can shake our great free brotherhood. It is unbreakable, unconquerable. And however hostile our foreign enemies become, the torch of friendship and brotherhood of all our people will burn brightly forever, because it is unceasingly defended by the great Communist Party of the Soviet Union.

In 1975 an international seminar of women of Asia, Africa and Latin America was held in Alma Ata. Its participants spoke sadly of the lack of rights for women, the unhappy lot of childhood under conditions of capitalism. They noted with great satisfaction the great government concern that surrounds mothers and children in our country. We, Soviet women, respond to this solicitude of our Party with maternal love, warmly supporting with all our hearts its policy of peace, internationalism and fraternity of peoples. We thank the Party for the happiness of our children, for their bright future and for our peaceful labor.   □

Vladimir Shcherbitsky

First Secretary of the Central Committee
of the Communist Party of the Ukraine

In our opinion it is important to emphasize that since the 24th CPSU Congress, the Central Committee and Political Bureau of the Party have done a lot to implement the peace program, to uphold our country's interests in the world arena and to consolidate the positions of the socialist system. A big step has been taken in developing the community of socialist states, in strengthening the Warsaw Treaty, and the Council for Mutual Economic Assistance. We have established the excellent practice of exchanges of party, state and economic experience with friends, as well as mutual visits of cultural groups.

We fully share the appraisal of the position our country holds in the world, and the program of further struggle for peace and international cooperation, and for the freedom and independence of the peoples advanced by Comrade Brezhnev.

Everyone knows, but not everyone wants to acknowledge the truth that the reason mankind has not experienced the horrors of a world war for more than three decades now and detente has become the leading tendency in international life, is above all due to the socialist community, to our great mother-country and our great Leninist Party!

Comrades, here at our Congress which is attended by delegations of many fraternal Communist and workers' parties and national-liberation movements, you feel particularly strongly the community of aims and ideals for which Communists are struggling. It is natural that all of us fully appreciate the potentialities of unity and coordination of our efforts.

The militant call "workers of all lands, unite!" which Marx and Engels advanced, has been resounding in the world for almost 130 years and history shows that the decisive source of the strength of the world communist movement lies in its loyalty to Marxism-Leninism, in its unity of goals, unity of will, and unity of action.

The penetration of Communist Parties by right-wing or left-wing revisionist influences, by nationalistic or other views which are alien to the ideology of the working class, in the final analysis, leads to compromise with the bourgeoisie or to adventurist actions. Fresh evidence of this is the splitting policy of Maoism, which is hostile to Marxism-Leninism, and has become the ally of the most reactionary circles of imperialism in its frantic anti-Sovietism and attempts to wreck detente.

The Central Committee's report furnishes an all-round picture of our achievements in the consistent implementation of the Party's course to increase the effectiveness of all branches of the economy and further improve the well-being of the Soviet people. Of course, these achievements inspire and gladden us all. They are particularly visible against the background of the deep crisis that has gripped the capitalist world and show convincingly that our Party's course is correct. Comrades, our country has indeed become more powerful, and our people live better and have become spiritually richer.

During the past five-year period the economy of the Ukraine developed dynamically and at good and stable rates as part of the national economic complex of the whole country. Its scientific and production potential has considerably increased, and the people's well-being and culture have risen.

The directives of the 24th CPSU Congress for the production of industrial goods and basic farm products, and also the pre-Congress socialist commitments, have been fulfilled ahead of schedule. Some 6.2 billion rubles worth of industrial goods have been marketed over and above annual plans. Thanks to the consistent implementation of the course outlined by the March 1965 plenary meeting of the CPSU Central Committee, our agriculture has risen to a new stage both quantitatively and qualitatively. This is confirmed by the fact that state purchases of grain, potatoes, vegetables, meat and milk have increased 1.3 to 1.4 times.

A total of 80 billion rubles of capital investments were made, and about 300 large industrial enterprises have been built; the people received 1,900,000 apartments. Now these are not bad indices, but at the same time, we soberly appraise everything we have achieved and are deeply aware of our responsibility to the country. The drawbacks mentioned in the Central Committee's report to a considerable extent apply also to our Republic, and we shall do our best to eliminate them.

The plans of the Tenth Five-Year Plan period are truly majestic. They are not easy to fulfill, but if we analyze them we see that they are quite realistic, and the achievement of the planned targets and indices will be another major step in the direction of the implementation of our party's economic and social policy in conditions of developed socialism.

With regard to perspectives for the development of agriculture we shall continue, as before, to take measures for increasing specialization and intensification of production on the basis of inter-enterprise collective and state farm cooperation and agro-industrial integration.

Comrades! The necessity of still further improving the work of our government organs refers first of all, in our opinion to Gosplan, Gossnab [government supplies] and the State Committee on Science and Technique. It is important that the planning process be further perfected, and that decisions be made more concretely in the light of actual conditions.

We consider that it is important to raise still further the role of the primary Party organizations, the district, city and regional Party committees, as organs of political direction, to improve the selection and distribution of cadres, to instill in them a spirit of the highest devotion and responsibility for the work entrusted to them, to strengthen state and Party discipline and develop criticism and self-criticism.   □

Alexey Chuyev

Turner at Ordzhonikidze Baltic Shipyards in Leningrad

Taking part in the work of the Congress one feels with particular force the many-sided dynamic activity of the Central Committee in developing the economy, raising the people's living standards and strengthening peace on our planet. Because of the efforts of our Leninist Party and its peaceful foreign policy, our country lives and works under peaceful skies. This is a great happiness, dear comrades!

Not only we, the Soviet people, need peace. I have visited quite a number of foreign countries, including capitalist states, as a member of delegations. I found that everywhere progressive workers highly appreciate the contribution of our state and Party to easing tensions. But we also know that peaceful coexistence cannot repeal the laws of the class struggle, cannot blunt or weaken the working people's efforts to put an end to capitalist exploitation and monopoly rule. From this high rostrum we voice our inviolable solidarity with our class brothers in the capitalist countries, with their courageous and just struggle for their rights.

I especially value the attention given by the Party's Central Committee to enhancing the role of the working class in production and society, to the practical fulfillment of Lenin's behest that each worker should feel himself not only the master of his factory but also the representative of his country.

Life shows that only socialism ensures the working people wide participation in managing state affairs. Tens of thousands of Leningrad workers have been elected to the Soviets of working peoples' deputies and to Party committees. They play an important role in the trade unions, in organs of people's control and other public organizations.

The general educational level, vocational training and cultural level of the workers has grown immeasurably. Thanks to the steps taken by our Party in improving the training of young workers, the generation of today enters production really well trained and educated. We of the older generation have something to pass on to our successors, and we are putting it into reliable hands.

The working class of our country knows very well that the tasks set before us and the entire practical activity of our Party meet the most vital interests of the Soviet people. The nationwide discussion of the draft guidelines for the development of the national economy for 1976-1980 shows socialist democracy in action.

A constant search for innovation is a characteristic of the Soviet worker. Having been for many years the President of the Leningrad Council of Innovators I see especially clearly what an enormous contribution our rationalizers and inventors make. In the Ninth Five-Year Plan alone, the proposals and inventions of the Leningrad innovators actually saved the country over 700 million rubles.

But, unfortunately, some economic leaders do not always show the necessary concern that the proposals of the innovators are used in production. Too often useful proposals for greater economy and efficiency are unknown outside of the factory where they originated. Much could be done in this connection by the Ministry of Machine Building and Instrument Making of the USSR. In our opinion, it is necessary to increase the responsibility of the Committee on Inventions and Discoveries, and of the Committee on Science and Technology as well as the Ministry and government departments, for making sure that proposals of innovators are utilized.

We fully support the proposals in the Central Committee report on the necessity of speeding up the technical reconstruction of industry. Today in

Leningrad the proportion of obsolete metal-working equipment is higher than the average for the country. Highly skilled workers are working with this equipment, workers quite capable of operating the most sophisticated types of machinery. Speedier introduction of new modern machinery would immensely increase the productivity of the workers. We have had good experience in solving this question in our shipyards. Thus, on the proposal of the Party's regional committee and the USSR Ministry of Shipbuilding, the CPSU Central Committee and the USSR Council of Ministers passed a decree on the complex development and technical reequipment of the shipbuilding enterprises in the city and region of Leningrad. This approach fully answers the demands of the times and we believe it should be spread to all branches of industry.

Leningraders are working with great enthusiasm these days. In this year of the 25th Congress we have taken on special socialist obligations. On the eve of the Congress the Baltic Shipyard Collective has won a new victory. We have finished ahead of schedule the largest atomic icebreaker in the world—the "Siberia." All workers are striving to carry out their own personal five-year plans ahead of time. Our brigade has taken on the obligation of completing this year's plan three months ahead of schedule, and to fulfill the Tenth Five-Year Plan in three and a half years. □

Anatoly Alexandrov

President of the USSR Academy of Sciences

Our country has lived through a most cruel war, through the years of the "cold war" thrust upon us by imperialism and the policy of balancing on the edge of the abyss, but it has never ceased to strive for peace, which is so necessary for all the ordinary people of the world.

Never before has the role of science been appreciated so highly anywhere in the world as in our country during the recent celebrations devoted to the 250th anniversary of the Academy of Sciences. The great role of science was also emphasized here in the report of Leonid Ilyich Brezhnev. We are thankful for the high appraisal of the part played by science in the progress of our country. In no other society does science enjoy such recognition. At the same time we believe that criticisms concerning the need for improving the efficiency of research in certain fields and for the radical acceleration of the introduction of scientific achievements into practice are quite justified.

Much in this respect depends on our own efforts, and we shall achieve tangible headway along this line.

In the sphere of natural sciences and recently to some extent in the social sciences too, the productivity of labor and its quality depend to a decisive degree on supplying scientific workers with modern, highly productive laboratory equipment and computer technology. Today it is impossible to achieve important results with old-fashioned research apparatus. Therefore the restructuring of our scientific establishments is a matter of extraordinary importance for the Academy.

Much is being done in our country to ensure scientific progress. Our social system and system of education make it possible to discover talented people and involve them in science. As a rule an excellent atmosphere of creative work is established in our research institutions. Mutually beneficial cooperation between the scientific establishments in socialist countries and certain Western states plays an increasing role. This will doubtless lead to tangible improvement in the efficiency of scientific work and to the acceleration of scientific and technological progress.

The other side of our work is speeding up industrial use of scientific findings. This requires great organizational efforts, better scientific planning and the most direct mutual ties and activities of institutes and industry. Academic institutions should be directly connected with factories with which they are working, and carry on joint projects with them from the earliest stages.

The emphasis of the Congress on the development of fundamental knowledge in science is extremely noteworthy. It shows that the Party and the government profoundly understand the logic of the development of science and the mechanism of scientific and technological progress. It is very easy to take up small-scale tasks of today and quickly achieve an effective result. But, as Leonid Ilyich Brezhnev has aptly put it, it is not these results that determine the technological progress of the country, and there is nothing more practical than good theory. It is the progress of fundamental knowledge that alters the seemingly established and inviolable scientific concepts, taps new fields in science and technology, brings about new materials, and opens opportunities for the utilization of new and often unexpected phenomena in spheres which have absolutely no relation to the initial field of research.

Atomic technique is now being used in thousands of factories to test in various ways the quality of products, in medicine atomic technology is being widely used for diagnosis and treatment of a number of diseases . . .

[L. I. BREZHNEV: *Is there some sort of an atom bomb against the flu?*]

Against flu? Leonid Ilyich, I can answer you at once. The Institute of Atomic Physics in Gatchin together with the Institute of Mindzdrav, has just developed a vaccine against the flu, which has been tested. Also they are now talking in Leningrad about industrial production of this vaccine. We only need to make the cost of production a little less.

[Alexandrov proceeded to cite a series of instances of the useful application of scientific research in solving the problems of agriculture, livestock, new uses for thermonuclear energy besides the bomb, and predicted that before long the colossal thermonuclear resources of the country would be used for the benefit of the people, as well as many other new sources of energy.]

It seems to me that there are still some problems which should be raised to the level of the government programs, on the basis of long-term scientific prognoses. The most important of these is the further intensification of agriculture. I believe the program of all-around computerization of our economy needs to be raised to the same high level. A single technological policy and organization in this field would radically improve our planning and checking on fulfillment, reaching optimum production, etc.

Outstanding work in the study of cosmic space, carried on under the scientific direction of M. V. Keldysh, has today immeasurably extended the possibilities of television and communications, has made it possible through the "Orbit" system to bring millions of people into the Central Television network, to make sound navigation and meteorological predictions. It is beginning to be used in geological surveying, forestry and probably will be used in agriculture. Lasers are already finding innumerable uses.

Our social science has also had great successes. It should be mentioned that first place here goes to the efforts of our economists to build up the national economy and to carry out research into more optimal ways of developing various areas of the country. Our specialists in social sciences are occupied with the problems of the development of the theory of scientific communism and the world working class movement. A fundamental history of the Second World War is being published.

Our Congress is defining a new stage in the movement for the creation of Communism. Soviet scientists will be reliable helpers of the Party in the achievement of this goal.   □

A. I. Beliakova

First Secretary, Grodnensky District Committee of the
Communist Party of Byelorussia

In the last five years the state and collective farm workers and all the working people of the villages in our district have made great progress in social and working conditions and in productivity of labor. Industrial production has grown by almost 62 per cent and agricultural production by 42 per cent. Average yields of grain and field crops rose from 13.9 centners per hectare in the eighth five-year plan to 24 centners per hectare in the ninth. It went up to 30 centners in the favorable weather conditions of 1974.

Our increased productivity is entirely due to improved quality of work, a result of the better training of our workers. In the collective and state farms of our district there are 850 specialists with higher and middle education, or an average of 30 to one enterprise.

We all recognize that the successes in agriculture are due to the new agrarian policy developed in the March 1965 plenary session of the Central Committee of the Party, and the careful attention given to carrying it out. Just consider that in our district alone government funds expended for strengthening the material-technical base of our agriculture tripled those of the ten preceding years! In that period the number of tractors, harvester combines and other machines in our district has doubled. Use of electric power in our work has grown almost five times, and the use of mineral fertilizers is constantly growing. All this has not only improved the organization of farm production but has radically transformed the character and conditions of agricultural labor.

I would like to give enthusiastic support to the system of specialization and concentration in agricultural production in Leonid Brezhnev's report. The high effectiveness of specialization and concentration on the basis of agro-industrial integration has been demonstrated by life itself.

In response to the concern of the Communist Party and the Soviet Government about improving the material and intellectual life of the Soviet people, in gratitude for the peaceful skies over our country, all our Communists, Soviet people, will give all their strength, knowledge, energy and experience to the great cause of building communism in our country.   □

A. Y. Modogoyev

First Secretary, Buryat Regional Committee, CPSU

Thanks to the concern of the Party and Government and the aid of all the peoples of our fraternal family of nations, the productive forces of the Buryat Autonomous Republic developed at a high tempo in earlier plans. But in absolute growth of social production, the Ninth Five-Year Plan exceeded all the others. In Buryatia industrial production grew by 49 per cent and the productivity of labor by 37 per cent. Our output reached a billion and a half rubles. And, most importantly, quality was much higher because of improved technology. Truly our workers have golden hands!

Such products of our industry as airplanes, electric motors, instruments of automation, river and sea-going vessels, automobile cranes, bridge building parts, woolen goods, window glass, cellulose, cement and numerous other products from our Autonomous Republic are supplied to every part of our country and exported to dozens of foreign lands. Increased geological prospecting has turned up nearly every existing mineral. And all this is happening, dear comrades, in a region where before the October Revolution there was hardly any industry at all and only two per cent of the people were literate.

Weather conditions in recent years were hard on our agriculture. A ferocious drought, floods and other natural disasters did great damage. Nevertheless, our overall agricultural production through those years, especially livestock products, not only did not diminish but actually exceeded that of preceding five-year plans. Now we are building extensive irrigation systems.

I could go on and on about the achievements and rich potentials of our region. But we feel a special obligation to tell the delegates about how Baikal has been saved—that priceless jewel dear to the heart of every Soviet person. As is known, the Party and Government issued a number of decrees on measures necessary to save Lake Baikal from further pollution. These measures have been successfully carried out. In our republic alone 70 purification systems guard the rivers that flow into Baikal from pollution. Sunken logs rotting on the bottom have been cleared away. Timber drifting has been prohibited, both on the rivers and the lake itself. Cutting of trees in the lake basin has been limited and reforestation is going on where large areas have been cleared. New preserves have been established where hunting is forbidden and the safety of the animal and vegetable world assured. Special fish culture plants and hatcheries are being established to restore the supplies of valuable fish like omul (a type of salmon) and sturgeon.

All these and other measures firmly guarantee not only the complete preservation but the augmentation of the riches of the Baikal basin and the lake itself. You need not be alarmed, comrades, about the fate of Baikal. It is in reliable hands. It is being looked after carefully by the Central Committee of the Party and the Soviet Government and the workers of the Baikal region.   □

E. I. Drozdetsky

Brigade Leader at Nagornaya Mine, Kemerovsky Region, Kuznetsk Basin, West Siberia

We know that our Party has always seen its supreme duty in service to the people and concern for their well-being. That is why it enjoys the boundless love and confidence of the workers.

Although I have been living in Kuznetsk coal basin for a long time, I never cease being amazed at the tremendous changes constantly taking place in our industrial region. Coal is being mined in ever-growing quantities; one after another the shops of the West Siberian metallurgical plant and modern enterprises of light industry are being put into operation; town planning is being improved; miners, metallurgical, chemical and building workers have ever higher living standards and their incomes and educational and cultural standards are rising. Working conditions get better and better each year and more and more children's institutions and hospitals are being built.

Such care and attention gives us wings, heightens our enthusiasm and responsibility for our common cause. It makes us want to work still better and more productively and to make the fullest use of our reserves to fulfill the party's plans ahead of time. I say this not for the sake of beautiful words. Those are the opinions and convictions of my comrades in the mines who are always ready to give all their strength to the great work of strengthening the economic might of our homeland.

Some of our enemies abroad try to accuse us of preparations for war. This monstrous lie is hardly worth spending time to answer. From this high tribune I, a mine worker, declare in the name of my comrades in the mine that the most sacred, the most beautiful word for us, the word expressing our deepest desire has always been and always will be the great word "PEACE!"

During the last five years there has been immense progress in the technical reequipment of our mine and practically the whole process of coal mining is now mechanized. The bone-breaking labor of the past is long gone. Machines carry out the heaviest operations. Conditions of work have changed immeasurably. The miner of today is an entirely different person than he used to be. Certainly he is not lacking in physical strength, but the main thing in our work now is knowledge of technique and how to use it.

The miners face big tasks in the Tenth Five-Year Plan. By 1980 coal extraction for the country as a whole is to reach 790 million to 810 million tons, and 161 million tons in the Kuznetsk Basin alone.

We shall continue to do everything in our power to increase the productivity of mining machinery and mechanisms and to lengthen the period of their use. In some cases we find that the modern machinery cannot stand up under the workloads and speeds required of it now. We think that the learned designers should visit us at the coal face more often so that we could work together to create more reliable machinery and raise productivity still further. We are also somewhat troubled because mine reconstruction sometimes goes too slowly. We are told that is because of inadequate capacities of construction organizations. But we are sure that this problem can also be solved, if everything is thought out and planned wisely, thoroughly and efficiently.

As for the miners of the Kuznetsk Basin we shall do everything to carry out successfully all the great decisions made here and work with all our hearts to fulfill the tasks set by the Party ahead of time in order as quickly as possible to complete the material-technical base of communism.   □

L. D. Kazakov

Leader of the Cement Workers Brigade,
Construction Train No. 266, on the site of the
Baikal-Amur Railroad, Irkutsk, Siberia.

It is difficult to express the deep excitement and heartfelt gratitude I felt when I heard the report of Comrade Leonid Ilyich Brezhnev. He spoke with such warmth and concern of the primary importance of conquering the boundless spaces of Siberia, the North and the Far East!

We are proud of the fact that the Party has assigned to us, the youth, the transformation of this rigorous Siberian region, to raise up new cities there, new factories and hydroelectric stations, and to lay the steel rails of a mainline railroad through the dense, impassable forest. On the frontiers of communist construction the young people are continuing the glorious traditions of the Stakhanov movement, the shock brigades, multiplying the exploits of our heroes — the builders of Komsomolsk city, Dnieproges (Dnieper hydro-electric station), the Turksib railroad and Magnitogorsk.

During the years of the Ninth Five-Year Plan hundreds of thousands of young patriots have received travel passes to new addresses: the Kamaz auto works, the Tiumen oilfields in Siberia, the Ust Ilim hydroelectric station and the Sayan-Shushenskaya industrial complex. These special Komsomol construction projects are unique not only in the youth of the builders, but in the special thundering rhythm of their labor, their enthusiasm, selflessness and high sense of responsibility. All this makes communist construction work a real school for the communist training of youth. We not only do our work and fulfill the plans and turn out a high percentage of products. In the process of the work our characters are molded, our dedication to the Party's aims is strengthened.

Today the baton of shock-troop construction has been taken up by the Baikal-Amur railroad. Its significance for the development of the productive forces of Siberia and the Far East is very great indeed.

BAM—the word means thousands of kilometers of steel rails and auto roads, hundreds of bridges, a whole series of large and small tunnels. It means new cities and towns, industrial complexes, opening up the rich resources of the earth beneath for the use of the people. And all this of course must be done in the most severe natural and climatic conditions.

BAM—stands for the main construction work of the youth, a living, shining embodiment in life of the magnificent plans of our Party.

The fate of thousands and thousands of youth is inextricably bound up today with the building of the Baikal Amur railroad. BAM—is a construction project of all the people. We feel the constant attention of all the Soviet people. Hundreds of Soviet enterprises are sending us all sorts of equipment, machinery, tools, warm clothing, prefabricated houses. Dozens of scientific research and designing institutes are working on the necessary plans for us. Priceless aid to our project is being shown by Moscow, Leningrad, the union and autonomous republics. Many regions and areas of the Russian Federation have become patrons of the planning and construction of cities and towns along the main line.

We, BAM builders, understand very well how necessary this railroad is for our homeland, for our people. We understand that it can be built in a short time only with the help of the most advanced methods of work, the most progressive technology. A special role is assigned to socialist emulation. This achieved especially wide application during the preparations for the 25th Congress. The young builders competed for the right of laying the first link, for the right of taking part in clearing the first "taiga landing field," for the right of raising the banner of labor glory.

BAM is a most unique construction project, and demands of each worker special tenacity, courage, selflessness. It is not accidental that we have worked out a code of honor for the young builders of BAM, which contains the following words: "To be a builder of BAM means to fight for the highest quality of work, for economy and carefulness. To constantly learn mastery from our teachers, to serve as an example of the communist attitude toward labor."

Our own brigade consists of 19 people of five nationalities. The average age is 21. I myself, after finishing middle school started to do railroad work. And when the Party called on us, young people, to come and help build the Baikal-Amur railroad, I could not stand aside.

We have a close and strong collective, young people eager to work who put fire into their labor, their whole souls. Each is aware that to be a good builder requires knowledge. Therefore I myself, for example, am studying by correspondence in the sophomore class of the Institute of Engineers of Railroad Transport. The other workers are also studying at institutes and evening schools.

In Siberia we are not guests, but masters! We want to work in the most efficient way possible, thinking not only of today but tomorrow. Looking at the economic side of our work my comrades and I see problems demanding solution. We want to see that towns and cities rising alongside of BAM are built according to a general plan, and are built solidly and well, to last for centuries!

BAM has mastered fine modern technique. In order to preserve it, it is necessary to organize careful and uninterrupted repair and preventive work. There are still not enough travelling mechanical repair shops at BAM. We believe that the USSR Ministry of Transport Building needs to improve the output of mechanical-repair shops on wheels, equipped with everything necessary, and fully guarantee our needs.

Comrade delegates! The vocation of building is one of the most honorable and most peaceful occupations. Our work brings happiness to people. And we unanimously support with all our hearts the Lenin policy of peace carried out by our Party.   □

Yevgeny M. Tiazhelnikov

First Secretary of the Central Committee of the Komsomol (Young Communist League)

Foremost among Komsomol traditions is to take part in all the main fronts of struggle at the call of the Party. An outstanding example of this is seen in the heroic exploits of the workers in West Siberia. This economic miracle of the century is the result of the wise policy of the Party, the decisions of innovators in industry, the labor prowess of Communists and Komsomols and of all our workers. During the Ninth Five-Year Plan the Komsomol sent 30,000 young men and women to this area.

Two years ago the Party commissioned the Komsomol to take an active part in building the Baikal-Amur Railroad. Today 35,000 Komsomols are at work on BAM. Delegate Leonid Kazakov travelled to this Congress on the first few completed kilometers of the railroad.

A work of extraordinary importance, a second virgin lands, is the opening up of the non-black earth areas of the country. Thousands of young men and women have joined in this effort.

During the five-year plan about three million students from colleges and other institutions of higher learning worked in our national economy. The students took part enthusiastically in the building of Gagarin City—a splendid memorial to that outstanding son of our homeland, that fine Communist bred by the Leninist Komsomols.

Every year more than eight million high school students and hundreds of thousands of students of technicums and vocational schools become steeled by work experience during their summer vacations, come to know the beauty of the earth and the true value of bread.

Life itself makes ever higher demands on the Komsomol, dictates the necessity of further strengthening the revolutionary, Leninist training of the youth, the still more active struggle against bourgeois ideology and morality.

Since the 24th Congress, the international ties of the Komsomol have greatly increased and strengthened. There is no greater happiness for the Komsomol, for Soviet youth, than to fight, along with Communists and young revolutionaries of the world, against imperialism and colonialism, for peace, democracy, national liberation and social progress.

Under the good influence of the Peace Program, we can see the rise of an international youth movement. This was convincingly demonstrated at the World Youth Festival in Berlin, an international meeting of the working youth of the world.

At the present time we have started active preparations for the 11th World Festival of youth and students, which will be held in the land of revolutionary Cuba in 1978. □

Pyotr Masherov

First Secretary of the Communist Party
of Byelorussia

The political course of the CPSU is embodied in our massive achievements, which do honor to our Party and to the heroic Soviet people. The giant automobile plant in Togliatti, the mastery of the natural riches of Western Siberia, the complex program for reclaiming the vast reaches of the Russian Non-Black Soil Region, Kamaz (Kama River auto project) and BAM (Baikal-Amur railroad), these and many other examples of the tireless energies of the people are a bright and living confirmation of the creative powers of the land of Soviets, of the mass labor heroism, the cooperation and international brotherhood of the peoples of the USSR.

The working people of Byelorussia have successfully coped with the basic economic and social tasks set in the directives of the 24th Congress of the CPSU. National income increased by 47 per cent in the five-year period. The Five-Year Plan for industry was fulfilled ahead of schedule, in four years and seven months. Industrial output grew by 64 per cent compared with the Eighth Five-Year Plan. The targets of the Five-Year Plan for sales to the state of basic farm produce have been substantially exceeded. All the major projects envisaged by the state plans in accordance with the directives of the 24th Congress have been put into operation. The living conditions of every family, of practically all of our people, have considerably improved.

Comrade Brezhnev has repeatedly pointed to the vital necessity of raising the efficiency of production and the quality of work as the key and determining problem. That our Republic managed to exceed the planned targets for the Ninth Five-Year Plan is due first and foremost to the fact that, guiding ourselves by these directions, we have been working to use as far as possible these intensive factors of production growth. For example, labor productivity in industry grew by 43 per cent, against the planned 40 per cent. Our industry has turned out three billion rubles' worth of output over and above the plan. Grain production by collective and state farms increased by 57 per cent, compared with the Eighth Five-Year Plan period, while annual grain and leguminous crops went up by 63 per cent.

But this is just the beginning of great work. A high level of scientific development, a powerful production and technical potential and the constantly improving professional skills of the workers, collective farmers and specialists, all this makes it possible to secure a steady rise in efficiency and quality in each link of the national economy.

In order to solve successfully the problem of efficiency and quality, it is essential to reduce the time it takes to introduce the achievements of science and advanced practice into production. This, in our opinion, requires an all-round strengthening of interconnections between academic, branch and departmental research institutions, and between fundamental and applied research, as well as an overall improvement of the system of integration between science and production.

Life is also ever more urgently bringing to the fore the problem of regulating inter-branch ties which are growing increasingly complex in conditions of deepening specialization. Many of the questions emerging due to the combining of different branches of industry are, to my mind, far beyond the competency of Gosplan and Gossnab. I think that a more rational solution should be sought in this context and perhaps corresponding organizations should be set up at the USSR Council of Ministers which will be in charge of managing the diversified inter-branch processes.

The main objective of the Tenth Five-Year Plan and its aims oblige us to develop bolder qualitative parameters in planning and management, and enhance the impact of the corresponding indices on the qualitative characteristics of economic activity.

And finally, quality of work is at the same time a major moral category. The implementation of the steps mapped out by the Party depends on the understanding, will, knowledge and experience of the people. That is why we see as our task an all-round improvement of political work among the people, notably in the field of ideological and moral education.

In the broad spectrum of questions of moral training, there are, in my opinion, such problems as forming into one harmoniously developed structure the material and spiritual needs of the individual and steadily developing them. An advanced world view, a socialist way of thinking and acting cannot be handed a person along with the key to a new apartment, a bonus, a free ticket to a sanatorium and other advantages which our people enjoy.

The basic traits of a highly educated person, intellectually rich, politically and morally mature, are established during school years, which in itself gives special meaning to the whole system of public education.

In order to raise the quality of pedagogical work it is our duty to consider seriously the whole complex of the school and teaching problem in connection with the growing demands of life and the perspectives for the development of our society. In our opinion, the schools must more actively accustom the students to methods and habits of independent work.

At the same time, under the conditions of universal middle education, there has been an increase in the number of boys and girls who, after finishing secondary school are attracted at once to the sphere of production. This absolutely requires the further development of polytechnization in the schools, strengthening the labor basis in the teaching and bringing up of youth. This is possible, as Vladimir Ilyich Lenin emphasized, only through the "closest ties between teaching and children's socially productive labor," with the access of the young generation to "the basic processes of industry in general."

In other words, it is a question of organizing the teaching process and educational work so that the whole upbringing of the young people is organically tied in with arming the school children with serious working habits, the fundamentals of labor and professional training.

The political tempering, moral cleanliness and maturity of the youth, of the whole Soviet people—that is our strength, our trusted weapon in the struggle for Communist ideals.   □

Eduard Shevardnadze

First Secretary of the Central Committee of the Communist Party of Georgia

The complex dialectical laws governing our forward advance show us that from the Party and its leaders on the one hand there flow to society and its various social groups political values which illumine the road to a Communist future. And on the other hand, the people themselves, the creators of history, enrich the Party by their priceless historic experience in social creation.

In the center of this unbreakable cycle, ascending in the dialectic spiral, stands the human being, the individual—the basic creative strength of society.

From the report of Leonid Ilyich Brezhnev it is clear that the Party regards the problems and parameters of the all-round perfection of the human being, freedom of speech and action, personal freedom and so on, against the background of the complex socioeconomic development of society and the flowering and drawing closer of the peoples of our Republics. Here, indeed, is the essence of real socialist democracy. It is necessary to speak again of this since in many circles abroad and lately among some of our friends it has become the fashion to speak of the shortcomings of socialist democracy in the USSR.

When we speak of strengthening and deepening the democratic foundations of our society, of individual freedoms and the freedoms of peoples, of the higher manifestation of democracy in Soviet society, we clearly see another side of the problem. Nowhere is there such need for the highest discipline and the highest organization as in a society of free peoples, free nations and free Republics.

From the example of the activities of the Communists of Georgia during the period under report, it is quite evident that it is precisely in the dialectical unity of freedom and discipline, solicitude and exactingness, rights and duties, government and local interests, that the highest manifestation of the creative strength of Soviet democracy has been found.

The Communists of Georgia have come to the 25th Congress of the Leninist Communist Party of the Soviet Union with a feeling of special gratitude to the Central Committee of our Party. After a deep analysis of the socio-political and socioeconomic situation in our Republic, the Central Committee adopted a historic resolution "on the organizational and political work of the Tbilisi City Committee of the Communist Party of Georgia for the implementation of the decisions of the 24th Congress of the CPSU." In addition, the CPSU Central Committee and the Council of Ministers of the USSR issued a resolution "on measures for the further development of the national economy of the Georgian SSR."

In accordance with this, the period under review is naturally divided into two stages for the Party organization of our Republic. In the first stage, prior to these resolutions, there was a drastic decrease in the Republic's economic potential resulting from developments in our Republic over several years. There was an even more tangible slowdown in the tempo of the social and political life and the revival of some negative phenomena. The fulfillment of the directives of the Ninth Five-Year Plan was put in jeopardy.

After the Party and the government made their decisions, the working people of the Republic began to work with unprecedented enthusiasm to achieve the targets of the Five-Year Plan.

We managed to overcome the lag completely. In 1973-75 the average annual rate of industrial growth was 9.6 per cent, labor productivity went up by 7.8 per cent and average annual gross agricultural produce increased by more than 18 per cent, compared with the figure for 1970-72. New industries have emerged in the Republic's economy in the Ninth Five-Year Plan period, including copper and china production and others. The discovery of large oil deposits in Georgia was an event of enormous joy for us.

This is a victory not just for our Republic or our people alone. The working people of Georgia asked me to thank heartily the working people from all the Republics and regions for their great fraternal help which we felt daily in our struggle.

The Tenth Five-Year Plan will be strenuous for us. Our Republic is still lagging behind the average country-wide indices in the key branches.

After the Republic-wide discussion of the draft of the central committee for the 25th Congress we asked the Central Bodies to raise our planned targets for industrial output from 35 to 39 per cent in the draft to 37 to 41 per cent.

This too is not the limit. We are seeking fresh reserves. The all-Union bodies promised us substantial aid in irrigating some of the Republic's regions. If all this goes smoothly, we shall be able, for instance, to produce and sell about a million tons of grapes a year, increase several times the production of fine Georgian wines, achieve a radical rise in the production of tea, citrus fruit and vegetables and overcome the lag in animal husbandry.

Our multi-faceted long-range plans are aimed at improving the individual human being, helping people reach their fullest professional, educational and cultural level, educating every person in the spirit of our ideological and moral principles and making work indispensable for each segment of society and each family.

Our Republic's recent past experience shows that compromise in the sphere of the superstructure damages the economic potential. It must be recognized that many of our contemporaries have not yet rid themselves of all the survivals of the past, of conservative habits and traditions, private property tendencies and egoism, careerism and toadyism, of favoritism and conceit. All this greatly limits the public and political activity of the individual and slows down the process of intellectual development in the spheres in which man is creating material and spiritual values.

The liberation of the members of society from such defects, as well as deep changes in the field of economy, are a most complicated revolutionary democratic process which has its theory and practice. One of the main tasks is to determine optimal ways for the further socialization of each person. Herein lies one of the most crucial aspects of Soviet democracy.

And finally, I should like to mention another reserve for our growth: the personality of a leader. Taking into account the opinions of the people, the Communists had to replace some leaders at the district, regional and republican levels in recent years. There were well-grounded reasons for this. As a result tangible positive changes have been made in all the spheres of life.

The people have taken fresh heart, literally speaking. A simple philosophy can explain this. Advanced socialism creates a historically unprecedented field of activity for the leader—for the highest manifestation of his political, intellectual and organizational abilities in the name of serving the people. When these abilities are in harmonious accord with the objective laws of socialist development, and this potential for progress turns into a real force, then the problem of further headway is solved. This is true of our entire country and of every segment of our society. □

Georgi Markov

First Secretary, Board of the Soviet Writers' Union

Substantial changes have taken place in the Soviet people's intellectual life and culture since the Soviet Communist Party's Twenty-Fourth Congress. New forms of writers' links with reality have emerged and become established over these years. We have witnessed a remarkable merger of labor and poetry, something possible only under socialism. The vital and genuine unity between writers and readers has grown stronger.

The Soviet people have supplied the writers with a vast knowledge of the new phenomena emerging in great variety in the course of the construction of Soviet society and the molding of the human being of today.

The life-giving currents of our existence could not but stimulate intensive creative activity by writers in general. All this has brought fresh forces into literature, mainly from among the young people who are working on the front lines of communist construction.

Progress has been made in all genres of literature in the past few years. There have been significant achievements in poetry, drama and literary translation. Essay writing, journalism and commentary have become more effective and discerning. Considerable improvements have taken place in the realm of criticism and theory.

Remarkable progress has been made in prose writing, particularly its major forms such as the novel and the short story. Books have appeared in which our times and our people are described with philosophical depth and great artistic mastery and which open up new forms of exploring the reality of contemporary life.

In the best works of the recent period, Soviet working people are portrayed in the fullness of their intellectual development, as the creators of material values and of a healthy social atmosphere, as fighters for establishing socialism and the moral principles of communism.

Unfortunately our literature has not yet become all that we would like it to be. And this is not only due to a lack on the part of some writers of a sense of responsibility, self-discipline, exactingness, and certain traits from the old days that somehow have not been outlived, but because literature has its own complexities of development. Indeed our people are creating something altogether new in the world, are striking out along a road no one in history has ever trod before.

The experiences of our Party in the sphere of directing the artistic process and relations with the cultural intelligentsia is developing and solidifying on Leninist principles. In our history there has never been a period such as we are now going through. The Party has established good mutual relations and full harmony with our creative unions, with all the intelligentsia working in the sphere of intellectual labor.

Multinational Soviet literature coexists with and is developing inevitably in close relations with the literature of other nations on our planet. The Soviet Writers' Union maintains literary ties with writers' organizations and writers in more than a hundred countries. Ties between writers in the fraternal socialist countries are particularly close. Literary contacts have become much livelier since the European conference on security and cooperation in Helsinki. The conference's decisions have opened up considerable opportunities for cultural contacts and exchange, and we shall try to use these opportunities to the fullest extent.

Unfortunately, the West often alleges that the socialist world is seeking to hold back the exchange of cultural values. Is this really so? Since the war we have published some 7,000 titles by American authors and 4,500 titles by English and French authors, in total editions of more than 600 million copies. These are impressive figures. And what have those countries published and in what numbers of our literature? Very little, many times less than we have published. So who is hampering the exchange and who is in debt to whom? The answer is clear.

Our society's advance towards communism requires that the role of literature and culture in the life of the people should be further enhanced. The theoreticians of communism in the past could only foresee such a situation. Our experience clearly shows that now this is becoming a law of our society's development at the stage of advanced socialism.   □

V. S. Lebedeva

Senior Operator, Omsk Oil-Refining Combinat, Siberia

A great qualitative stride forward in technology and organization of labor has been taken by our combinat. The power of each single machine has increased. Electronic computer technology daily becomes a more reliable aid in our productive work.

The whole character of labor has changed and the technical-cultural level of the working class has grown. The worker of our combinat today is a person of all-round development, a creative thinker, a specialist in his or her work, a collectivist, a socially active citizen.

In our department there is not a single person who has not finished high school. About 85 per cent of our senior operatives have a high school or college education; the remainder are studying. Without stopping work, I myself completed the Moscow Institute of Oil and Gas. Three thousand of our workers are skilled at two or three different trades, and have saved millions of rubles in economies during the five year plan.

The concern of the Party for the well-being of the Soviet people shines out in the Guidelines for 1976-80. It is very evident in the district where I live. Just a few years ago it was only barren space. Now it is an attractive, well-organized oil workers' town, with apartment houses, pleasant parks, stores, cinemas, a Palace of Culture. During the Ninth Five-Year Plan alone 2,000 oil workers and their families moved into new apartments there. Already there are large facilities for growing and preparing food, guaranteeing fresh vegetables for the Siberians the whole year round!

The development of our huge oil and gas reserves will do much to enrich both Siberia and the whole country. To make the best use of it requires the building of much more housing, schools, and preschool institutions.   □

P. P. Griskevicius

First Secretary of the Communist Party Central Committee of the Lithuanian SSR

The working class of the Lithuanian SSR has fulfilled with honor its duty to its homeland. During the past five years our production increased by 49 per cent. It exceeded planned goals by half a billion rubles—including 200 million in consumers' goods. Four-fifths of this growth was due to increased productivity of labor. Total industrial production during the years of Soviet power in Lithuania has increased more than 46 times.

The correctness of the Party's agricultural policy has been convincingly demonstrated in Lithuania. Climatic conditions were much rougher during the last five-year plan than in the preceding one, yet even under those conditions average agricultural production in the public sector (state and collective farms) was 23.5 per cent more than in the previous five-year plan. Lithuania has become a republic of intensive livestock breeding and dairy farming.

The working people of our republic know well that all our achievements have been possible due to the Leninist national policy of our Party, the unwavering friendship of the Soviet peoples and the constantly strengthening relations of fraternal cooperation. Truly inestimable help has been shown us by all the fraternal peoples, and first of all the great Russian people, whose generosity has won the love and respect of all the peoples of our multinational country.

We understand that the attainment of the goals of the new five-year plan requires still more intensive labor, the elimination of all those mistakes noted in the main report and which equally apply to our republic. We must work much more purposefully and determinedly to carry out measures to heighten the effectiveness of industrial production, to improve its quality, making use of all our internal reserves, speeding up scientific and technical progress and increasing the production of consumer goods. And in agriculture the Party organization will give special attention to intensification and specialization and inter-enterprise cooperation.

In overcoming some of the shortcomings of our vast and complex economic set-up, we must insure that our railroad transport, which has been giving us a lot of trouble, works better.

Thanks to the purposeful work of the Party in the formation of high moral-political and working qualities in the Soviet people, their whole spiritual image has changed. Their educational and cultural level has grown. Today every third person in the national economy of Lithuania has higher, incomplete higher or ten-year education. In our industrial activity physical and mental labor are becoming more and more closely linked.   □

Karen Demirchian

First Secretary of the Communist Party of Armenia

For the Communists of Armenia, as for the whole Party, these past five years have been a period of intense and fruitful labor. The national income of the republic grew by 46 per cent, and its economic potential expanded considerably. The branches producing consumer goods outstripped the others. Our basic industrial production plant grew one and a half times, and many large new industrial enterprises were put into operation. Armenia's first gold was extracted on the very day this Congress opened.

Total agricultural production grew by 21.9 per cent. The material and cultural life of the working people of our republic have greatly improved, their real incomes have risen substantially. Housing of about 700,000 citizens of our republic (total population, 2.2 million) has been improved.

The Party organization of Armenia clearly realizes that the achievements of our republic might have been very much higher if there had not been serious shortcomings in the Party's direction of economic and cultural construction. For a variety of reasons the rate of growth in certain branches of industrial and agricultural production was too slow, and we did not achieve the planned scale of capital construction. The Central Committee of the Party brought this matter sharply to our attention, pointing out how to overcome our difficulties. An outstanding characteristic of the Leninist style of work of our Party's Central Committee is this day-by-day attention to the work and needs of each republic, region and district. The Armenian workers were deeply touched by the special government and Party decree last April, "On Measures for the Further Development of the National Economy of the Armenian SSR.'' We are deeply grateful for this concern that Soviet Armenia become a flourishing republic and for providing the necessary means and possibilities to hasten our economic development and improve the social and political life of our republic in every sphere. Now it is up to us to use our own abilities to the full in realizing these plans.

Our Armenian Party has made a deep analysis of the causes of the shortcomings that have hampered our forward advance. We are taking every possible measure to overcome them, to strengthen Party and government discipline and the individual responsibility of all our cadres. We are working seriously on further development of criticism and self-criticism, on the training of workers in the spirit of a Communist attitude toward labor and the Soviet way of life. This means irreconcilability with any backsliding into philistine, petty bourgeois psychology, money grubbing, bureaucratism and other traits contrary to Communist morality. All of this is warmly and unanimously approved by the workers of Armenia and has had positive results in all spheres of our national economy.

The working people of our republic well know that their achievements are due to the ideas of Lenin, to the October Revolution, to the wise national policy of our Party. They know that they are the result of their own work and the common labor of all the peoples of the Soviet Union. It is in the political, economic and social triumph of our country that their great friendship, the powerful force of socialist internationalism, grows and flourishes. The hearts of all the working people of our republic are filled with gratitude to all the fraternal peoples of our Soviet homeland for their friendship and mutual aid. □

Vassily Prokhorov

Secretary, All-Union Central Council of
Trade Unions

The Soviet trade unions, embracing more than 107 million people, are unanimous in approving the wise policy and many-sided practical activities pursued by the Central Committee of our Party.

Over the past years the Soviet trade unions have been actively contributing to the implementation of the five-year plan. All their experiences and efforts have been used to carry out the resolutions adopted after the Party's Twenty-Fourth Congress to improve the organization of the socialist emulation movement, which has grown on an unprecedented scale and become highly effective. This has made it possible to overfulfill the plans for the marketing of industrial goods to the value of 32 billion rubles, to save 14 billion rubles' worth of materials and more than 19 billion rubles as a result of the adoption of discoveries and improvements. The people have become more active in managing socialist production.

The trade unions have aided the steady increase in the earnings of industrial and other workers and other efforts to raise the people's material and cultural standards.

In the last five years the trade unions' budget for state social insurance has increased by 50 per cent and for labor protection by over 40 per cent; 230 million industrial and office workers and their families, or 80 per cent more than in the previous five-year period, have had treatment or spent their holidays in trade union-run sanatoria, holiday homes and tourist centers.

Taking a critical view of our work, we realize full well that the trade unions have failed to give enough attention to a number of important production problems and to promoting democracy in production in every possible way.

In the last few years, the socialist emulation movement throughout the country has been raised to a qualitatively new level. Our task now is to encourage and further promote it and to urge the trade unions to put into practice the movement to improve quality, to undertake counter-plans, to raise the productivity of labor on the basis of personal creative plans, to hasten the adoption of the achievements of science and technology, to increase the output of high-quality products, and other initiatives. We attach special importance to instilling in people a Communist attitude to work and to enhancing the people's knowledge of economics.

In the light of the Congress' guidelines the trade unions are to be much more active in stepping up the rate of scientific and technological progress. We have somewhat improved our work to meet these ends: the membership of the scientific and technical societies and of the inventors' and rationalizers' societies has increased. The quality of recommendations and proposals submitted and adopted in production has improved. Nevertheless, the trade unions today must do even more in this sphere. Innovations by all workers should be further encouraged and effective forms of close cooperation between scientists and production personnel should be promoted.

More extensive opportunities are opening up for the trade unions to exert their influence on agriculture. Over the last five years the number of agricultural workers in trade unions has increased from 15 to 18 millions. This is of great importance for boosting agricultural production and improving the working conditions and the standard of living of the collective farm workers. The All-Union Central Council of Trade Unions will devote more attention to enhancing the activity of the rural trade unions.

In the Tenth Five-Year Plan period the trade unions are to take an active part in carrying out the program of social development and improvement in the people's standard of living, and show more concern for the conditions of work, life and recreation of the Soviet people.

Even today the trade unions are accorded extensive rights to participate in the running of production and have experience in this field unparalleled in the world's trade union movement. The Party believes that the time has come for the workers to participate still more widely and effectively in management.

In the United States, which is to celebrate its Bicentennial this year, the trade unions unite a mere 21 per cent of the working people. The Soviet trade unions, which were founded by the Bolshevik Party, embrace almost 99 per cent of the working people, that is, virtually the entire working class, all working intellectuals and most farm workers.   □

O.K. Gutseva

Head of Instructional Sector, Sotnikovskoye
Secondary School, Blagodarnensky District,
Stavropol Region, RSFSR

Education in our country is considered the business of the whole Party, the whole people. The transition to universal secondary education has, in the main, now been completed. Its successes are brightly etched in the example of Stravropol. In our region almost one of every three people is studying. Half as many new school buildings have been added to what we had—that means 375 new schools, accommodating 176,000 more pupils.

The decrees of the CPSU Central Committee and the Government on improving village schools were very timely and necessary. The attention of everyone is now centered on the village schools. An intensive process is now taking place of reducing the differences in educational level between the urban and village population.

In 30 graduating classes, our school has trained 125 teachers, 64 doctors, 35 Soviet and Party workers. Among our graduates are engineers, builders, doctors of science and others. We take special pride in the 500 of our graduates who have made up the golden fund of our own state farm "Gigant" and other state and collective farms—mechanizers and livestock breeders, the top specialists and leaders in our agricultural economy.

We have always considered it our duty to develop in our boys and girls a love for their own native region, to train worthy replacements for the working class and collective farm peasantry, those whose hands grow our bread. These are workers of a new type, who combine in themselves the best qualities of the grain farmer and the industrial worker, loving the land and finding their life's calling in work on the land.

Youth is curious and inquisitive and extraordinarily impressionable. Hence, it is doubly, triply important that we older people, teachers and parents, try to direct this urge toward novelty into proper channels, help young people find their place in life and teach them to distinguish what is really new and valuable from that which only appears so at first glance.

I speak of this because today, under conditions of detente and ever broader cultural ties, our ideological opponents, under the guise of exchanging cultural values, information and ideas, are stepping up their attacks against young people first of all. Irresponsibility, cynicism, sloppy clothing, flippancy in personal relations, and in attitudes toward the past and the future — our opponents depict these as "harmless" fashions, and present them as values of the "free world." But behind all this is propaganda for empty-headedness, consumerism and egoism. All these are long-familiar methods with which the apologists of capitalism attempt to influence our youth. "Perhaps," they say, "we can loosen up their patriotism somewhat, make them waver in their devotion to their homeland, and disrupt the revolutionary heritage of the new generation."

It goes without saying that our people are interested in genuine exchanges of cultural riches, they absorb all that is best and most advanced in world culture, and eagerly open the treasure chest of their own culture to all the people of the world. The Soviet people understand very well that such exchanges are one of the main conditions for the strengthening of peace and trust among the peoples.   □

Vassily Starodubtsev

Chairman of the Lenin Collective Farm, Novomoskovsk
District, Tula Region

I t is a great honor for me, a representative of the Soviet peasantry, to address you. I was a grain grower—a rank-and-file collective farmer, worked as plough operator, tractor-driver, and field-crop team leader. For many years now I have been working as collective farm chairman. I have qualified as a candidate of science (agriculture). Great confidence has been placed in me—I have been elected as a member of the Council for Collective Farm Affairs of the Russian Federation.

The resolution of the CPSU Central Committee and the Council of Ministers of the USSR "on measures to further develop agriculture in the Non-Black-Soil Zone of the RSFSR" was for us, workers of regions in the central belt of Russia, a concrete manifestation of the wise agrarian policy of the Party. This resolution opens up vast perspectives for boosting agricultural production in 29 regions and autonomous republics of the Russian Federation. In the Tenth

Five-Year Plan period, large capital investments will be channelled into agriculture in the Non-Black-Soil Zone, the supplies of machines and mineral fertilizers will considerably increase, and large-scale land improvement work will be carried out.

We, Tula agricultural workers, are very satisfied with the fundamental propositions advanced in the report of the Party's Central Committee on the need for further intensifying work on the specialization and concentration of farming on the basis of inter-farm cooperation and agro-industrial integration. The transfer of agricultural branches, livestock breeding in particular, to an industrial basis will make it possible to considerably increase the output of products, while at the same time raising labor productivity and lowering production costs.

The vital importance and the economic advisability of the transfer of livestock breeding to an industrial basis is shown by the experience of the operation on our collective farm of a complex for the production of milk, which has been built after a design prepared by specialists of the collective farm jointly with organizations of the region. We were grateful that our opinions were sought in working out these measures.

There are a number of similar complexes in operation in Tula region today. They have acquitted themselves well: Such complexes are spreading to other regions, too. In this important matter, however, many things are still done in a haphazard manner. We believe that it is high time for the State Building Committee of the USSR to work out a single building and technical policy in setting up livestock-breeding complexes. It is necessary to establish firmly what kind of complexes these should be and to organize the industrial production of structural elements and appropriate technological equipment for them.

However, we still lack enough machinery for comprehensive mechanization of stock breeding. Moreover, some of the machinery and equipment is unproductive and its dependability is below the required level. Experience demands that the Ministry of Agriculture of the USSR, the Ministry of Machine Engineering for Animal Husbandry and Fodder Production and the All-Union Board for the Supply of Farm Machinery, Fuel and Fertilizers should solve more actively questions connected with the transfer of livestock breeding to an industrial footing.

In the current five-year period, large capital investments and considerable material and technical resources are earmarked for collective and state farms. These funds and resources must be put to use wisely and effectively. It is very important to build new projects quickly, using perfected designs and at a high qualitative level. For a number of reasons, however, we do not always succeed in doing so. Plans for rural construction are not infrequently frustrated. This happens, specifically, because the main contractor of our region—the USSR Ministry of Industrial Construction—does not build much in rural areas. It must be said that organizations of this ministry, unfortunately, are very reluctant to go in for rural construction. Yet, the tasks of further developing agriculture in the Non-Black-Soil Zone demand that the contracting organizations of the building ministries should regard the fulfilment of plans for building in the countryside as their most important job. □

A. N. Nikolayev

Building Team Leader

Today we are building a great deal and with different methods than say, 10-12 years ago when industrial house-building was making its first steps. The architecture, finishing and layout of flats has improved. Builders have at their disposal powerful machines and equipment.

Though we are building more and better we should not forget that greater demands are also made of our work and its quality. There are considerable untapped reserves in the building industry and they have to be used in the Tenth Five-Year Plan period.

Serious shortcomings of the organization of building work impede the introduction of cost accounting everywhere. The main shortcomings are lack of clear-cut coordination between all links of industry and frequent stoppage in the supply of parts and materials.

Everybody knows that any construction project begins with its design, the preparation of the site from the engineering point of view, that underground communications have first to be laid and roads built before the building starts. In practice, however, we often come across something quite different. A building team arrives at a site where development should have been completed but finds that the construction of roads and underground communications is still going on. Very often this work is done only after mounting or even completing the building. Thus, sound technological procedures are violated, inevitably resulting in lower quality. Because of incomplete engineering structures, finished buildings take quite a long time to be put into operation. A turn towards better building obviously depends on improvement in the quality of planning.

Work should be organized so that moral and material incentives for workers and leading specialists are connected with the results of work done by the various production units and the central administration as a whole. The point is to create economic conditions which would purposefully stimulate highly productive, coordinated and high-quality work and would enhance the personal responsibility of all workers, at all stages of construction.

Moral and material incentives should promote responsibility and a conscientious attitude towards work and, consequently better quality in building. The system must be improved so that quality is regarded as one of the main indicators in determining the results of work.

Further industrialization is essential for the development of building construction. We are mounting buildings at high rates of speed, just like a factory conveyor line. But painters and decorators who come after us do nearly everything manually; the effective power tools put into use by the Ministry of Building, Road and Communal Machinery are very few. It is high time that engineering workers take up this problem seriously.

We live in an atmosphere of confidence in the future. All our thoughts and aspirations are aimed at working today better than yesterday, and tomorrow— better than today, at devoting all our efforts, knowledge and energy to the work for the implementation of the Party's great plans.   □

G. I. Chiryaev

First Secretary of the Yakutsk Regional Committee of the CPSU

The Yakutsk Autonomous Soviet Socialist Republic is situated in the northermost section of our country. Its colossal natural riches are pouring out in ever greater quantities to help our homeland and its people. There has been a tremendous growth in the mining of diamonds; gold and other precious metals, in hard coal and in procurement of natural gas. The workers of Yakutsk fulfilled the five-year plan ahead of time.

The economic potential of our republic is growing rapidly. In the last ten years our basic industrial fund has increased five-fold, and our agricultural production has grown two and a half times. The well-being of our population and their cultural level is rising swiftly. Two-thirds of our working people have completed high school or college education.

Bourgeois ideologists, in their attempt to distort Soviet reality, often invent tales about the backwardness of our remote areas. But it would be difficult to deceive anyone who has seen our reality with such slander. Throughout the farthest reaches of our vast land, including the Far North, life is boiling with energy, gigantic construction work is going forward. In all this we see the creative power of the Leninist national policy of the CPSU. The Communists and all the working people of the Yakutsk Autonomous Republic are making their own great contribution to Communist construction. At the same time they deeply appreciate all that has been accomplished in all the other fraternal republics, the close cooperation and ever-growing mutual aid of the peoples of our multinational country.

As Leonid Brezhnev said, the unity of our multinational people is as solid as diamonds. We cherish with our whole being the friendship of the peoples, one of the greatest triumphs of socialism.

The Central Committee of the Party and its Political Bureau, and the Government of the USSR devote a tremendous amount of attention to the development of the productive powers of Yakutia. Léonid Ilyich [Brezhnev] has shown special concern for our needs and in 1974, Alexey Nikolayevich Kosygin visited many enterprises of our republic.

The growing scale of our mastery of the North demands improvement of our methods of work in view of the special characteristics of the zone. The study of science and technology adapted to the conditions of the extreme cold must be deepened. We must learn to grow more vegetables and agricultural produce on the spot instead of transporting them from afar. Special training for workers under northern conditions must be provided, new measures to protect them from the cold, frost resistant clothing, better housing, higher standards of living to offset the rough weather conditions. With industry pushing further and further into the North, and vast new mining and industrial complexes planned, transport is a priority problem. The need of special territorial economic planning taken up in Alexey Kosygin's report is of vital importance for the North. □

Sharaf Rashidov

First Secretary of the Central Committee of the Communist Party of Uzbekistan

Gross industrial production in our Republic went up by more than 51 per cent over the last five years, instead of the 46-49 per cent envisaged in the 24th Party Congress Directives. Airplanes, tractors, excavators, cotton harvesters, instruments, machine tools, compressors and other sophisticated equipment—some of it newly developed here—are being produced in the Republic.

Tashkent, risen anew on the ruins of an earthquake, is growing and getting better every year. The ancient cities—Samarkand, Bokhara, Khiva—are also getting younger. New cities and settlements have sprung up and industrial giants have been built in the vastness of the Kyzylkum Desert and Hungry Steppe.

As before, the Communist Party of Uzbekistan concentrates its main attention on cotton growing. At the 24th Party Congress we promised, from this rostrum, to produce 5,000,000 tons of cotton by the end of the Ninth Five-Year Plan. The cotton growers have been as good as their word, even in the face of drought conditions. In the last two years the Republic has exceeded the 5,000,000-ton mark. During the entire Five-Year Plan the country received 24,500,000 tons, 2,300,000 tons more than set in the Congress Directives.

Without any exaggeration, the work of our glorious cotton growers can be called a heroic exploit. And this heroic exploit was possible as a result of the fraternal help that is always forthcoming from all the many peoples living in our homeland. In our Party and in our land there is a wonderful atmosphere of mutual faith, mutual respect and friendship among all the peoples, all the nationalities. The stronger our friendship and mutual fraternal ties become, the greater will be our successes in economic, social and cultural growth and in creating a new highly developed human being.   □

A. F. Yerofeyeva

Spinner at the Ivanovo Textile Combine

Millions of Soviet people, in whose families the bitter pains of war still linger even after more than three decades, know firsthand the price of peace. My father fell in a grim battle near the city of Orel but we, his five children, like the children of our homeland's millions of other defenders, were given a mother's care by our country. We have all achieved a good life. To us, daughters and sons of a soldier, the sensitive attention given us by the Party and the government are endlessly dear.

Hearing the report of the CPSU Central Committee, dealing with the wonderful achievements between two Congresses, we, the delegates, couldn't keep our minds from wandering to our own native area, our own factories and fields, our own labor collectives, our own personal lives.

The closely knit collective at the Ivanovo textile mill and its Party organization have become my mentors and teachers. Although it was built in the first five-year plan our mill has not aged with time, but rather has become unbelievably younger. About 36 million rubles went into technological re-equipment during the Ninth Five-Year Plan. And the production and labor productivity levels set for the end of the plan were already reached in September 1974. The workers themselves drew up a counter-plan and took on additional socialist obligations. We spun about a thousand tons of thread and wove 2.5 million meters of cloth over and above the plan! Our productivity rose more than one-third during the plan and we managed this with fewer workers.

Mine is an ancient and ordinary trade—that of a spinner. My favorite work, my studies at the textile institute and my public duties give my work fullness and meaning. One feels one's growth and one's intellectual maturing.

The demands of the Party, reemphasizing the quality of work, are very important to us. We know that raising the living standards, the growth of the wellbeing of our people, depend above all on the quality of work. For this, we expect the various ministries to provide us with better machines, better equipment, brighter and better dyes for clothing—and then indeed the quality of all our work will be better.

In our collective we have 65 per cent women, and it is on them largely that fulfillment of the plan depends. We are deeply grateful to the Party and government for the constant improvements, year by year, in working conditions and care for women's health. Household services are also being brought closer to the place of production, which is very important for us.

But there is one question that is still being solved a bit too slowly. I am speaking of preschool institutions. We Ivanovo women are making serious requests to some of the republic and union ministries that more money must be invested in day nurseries and kindergartens.

International Women's Year demonstrated once again to the world to what heights Soviet women have been lifted by the Communist Party and government, and what wonderful conditions have been created for our professional and intellectual growth. I am deeply proud that many of my friends have been advanced to high Party and economic posts, women I know as wonderful workers and social activists, loving mothers and passionate fighters for peace.   □

E. V. Shpakova

Director of the Kuibyshev Factory "Rossiya"

Everything our Party does is in the interests of the people, for the improvement of the material and cultural conditions of their lives, to guarantee the peace and security of our country. We are grateful that the question of further struggle to avert the threat of war has such an important place in our Congress. This is natural. Indeed peace is the greatest of all blessings for simple working people.

The food industry is one of the main branches of our economy in our region. Among the many new enterprises of this last five-year period is the Kuibyshev chocolate factory, a modern enterprise with a high level of mechanization and automation, with an output of 25,000 tons of candy a year. Our fine workers' collective developed socialist emulation intensively, and fulfilled the five-year plan in four and a half years. High quality is our main problem. In the past the food industry has not always met the standards desired by the people. We are working on this and will make candy of still better quality in the future.

Our Party gives constant attention to the improvement of the social and living conditions of the working people. The greatest social program in our country's history was carried out during the five-year plan. In our Kuibyshev region alone over 150,000 people received new apartments. Many schools, hospitals and cultural institutions were built.

At the same time I would like to support Comrade Yerofeyeva's plea for building more pre-school institutions. Our factory is young. Six years ago most of the workers who came to our factory were 18-19-year-old girls. Today they are already young mothers. But unfortunately we still have not enough day nurseries and kindergartens. It is well known that the workers in the food industry are mainly women, and the results of their work depend in a great degree on how well their children are cared for. This is not a problem in our branch alone. I believe that Gosplan and the various ministries and government agencies concerned need to allot more funds for the purpose so that the problem will be solved during the Tenth Five-Year Plan.   □

Dinmukhamed Kunaev

First Secretary of the Central Committee of the Communist Party of Kazakhstan

The gigantic scale of work confronting the republic, in the course of which new industrial-agrarian complexes will come into being, brings to the fore the question of accelerated development of industrial and rural construction. All this obliges us to use capital investments with maximum efficiency. This we shall do. But our republic is entitled to count on more effective help from the Union construction ministries and departments and the USSR State Committee for Material and Technical Supply, in solving all problems connected with the successful conduct of construction.

It is quite correct to raise the question of further growth of grain production. Kazakhstan's virgin lands can and will yield more grain and other products of field cultivation and animal husbandry. It is necessary only to accelerate the equipment of virgin land farms with highly efficient machinery and technology, including anti-erosion facilities. We shall concentrate on manufacturing such equipment in the shortest possible time during the Tenth Five-Year Plan.

Land reclamation plays a special role in Kazakhstan. Although it occupies only four per cent of the republic's sown area at present, irrigated land produces more than 20 per cent of the gross agricultural output. This confirms again and again the wisdom of the decisions of the May 1966 plenary session of the CPSU Central Committee. Only land reclamation can guarantee the stability of high harvests of grain and other crops and fundamentally resolve the question of creating a solid fodder base for animal husbandry, which has special importance for Kazakhstan with its many million head of cattle. Any other course would leave agriculture completely at the mercy of the weather.

The possibilities of our lands are very great. Life insistently demands accelerated construction of the Volga-Urals Canal, of a new group of water-lines on the virgin land, plus the utilization of underground water reserves. The time has come, comrades, to examine the problem of the Aral Sea and the replenishment of the rivers flowing into it. All this will completely pay for itself and will ensure the rapid industrial-agrarian development of new and exceptionally promising zones in the interests of the whole Soviet country.

It is deeply regretted that the process of detente has so far not extended to the Chinese People's Republic. We remember very well the time when the Chinese-Soviet border was a border of friendship, of mutual confidence and aid. Now atomic fever and a militaristic psychosis never abate in China, and anti-Sovietism, mixed with the most slanderous fabrications, is cultivated there. By their actions, the Maoists have in fact joined forces with the most extreme international reactionaries. The chauvinist policy with respect to national minorities—Kazakh, Uigur, Kirghiz and Dungan—in Sinkiang, which is contiguous to Kazakhstan, has deprived these people of all rights. It would seem that these national minorities, as well as all the working people of China, could not help but be interested in the improvement of Soviet-Chinese relations; their restoration, on the principles stated in the report of Leonid Ilyich Brezhnev, would be timely and useful and reason and realism should prevail. □

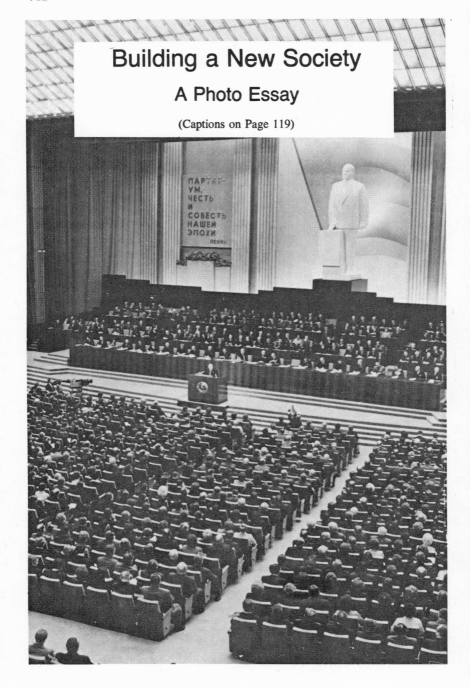

Building a New Society

A Photo Essay

(Captions on Page 119)

A Guide to the Photos

Page 112: The Congress in session — Kremlin Palace of Congresses.

Page 113: A happy moment — welcoming Honor Guard from the Young Pioneers, Soviet children's organization; delegates voting for A. N. Kosygin's report.

Page 114: Top, clockwise from top left: Delegates A. P. Alexandrov, President, USSR Academy of Sciences; tractor operator K. B. Donenbayeva; V. A. Starodubtsev, collective farm chairman from Tula Region; A. F. Yerofeyeva, spinner at Ivanovo textile combine. Bottom: Komsomol leader Yevgeny Tiazhelnikov with fellow delegates.

Page 115: Top: Foreign guests Gustav Husak of Czechoslovakia; Alvaro Cunhal of Portugal, Fidel Castro of Cuba; Willi Stoph and Erich Honecker of GDR. Bottom: Clockwise from top left: Le Duan, Socialist Republic of Vietnam; Dolores Ibarruri, Chairman Spanish Communist Party, the legendary "La Pasionaria" of the Spanish Civil War; Alves Batista, Minister of Internal Information, People's Republic of Angola; Americo Zorrilla, Communist Party of Chile.

Page 116: CPUSA leaders Henry Winston and Gus Hall with Congress delegates; delegation from the international journal Problems of Peace and Socialism — center, John Pittman, editor English-language edition, World Marxist Review.

Page 117: Young Muscovite volunteers leaving for Baikal-Amur railway construction sites; the damming of the Yenisei River in Krasnoyarsk.

Page 118: Romesh Chandra, Secretary-General, World Peace Council, among delegates. A group of delegates posing for someone's camera (obviously not ours!)

Page 119: CPSU General Secretary Leonid I. Brezhnev and Chairman of USSR Council of Ministers Alexey N. Kosygin, reporting to the Congress.

7

Delegates Write about the Congress

Novosti Press Agency, on our behalf, invited some of the delegates to the 25th Congress to record their impressions and thoughts about the Congress. Following are the impressions and thoughts of workers, writers, artists, men and women, from diverse republics and regions, viewing the events of February 25 to March 5 from their personal standpoints.

Konstantin Simonov

Writer

Perhaps the most important feature of the Soviet Communist Party Congress is that taking part in its sessions and speaking from its rostrum are people who shape life—people whose labor is directly responsible for everything that has been created in our country over the past five years, people whose words and deeds do not conflict.

And that refers not only to everything that has been done inside our country but also to our foreign policy, to our persistent struggle for peace, to our constant disinterested help to all nations fighting for their human rights, freedom and independence.

The true internationalism that marks the entire historical activity of our Party and the life of our society, both in word and in deed, was highly, and worthily, assessed in speeches by guests at the Congress who had come from all the continents of the world.

Listening to Comrade Fidel Castro and Comrade Le Duan who spoke with deep feeling about the contribution of our country to the struggle of their peoples for freedom, I, perhaps like every Soviet citizen present in the hall, was proud for my country and my Party—for the country of internationalists, for the Party of internationalists.

I recalled our seamen by the bomb-demolished, charred quays of Haiphong, men who courageously brought everything that fighting Vietnam needed, such as grain—and not only grain.

As a writer and journalist, during the past five years, as earlier, I travelled a lot throughout our country. One of the greatest joys I experienced during the first days of the Congress was seeing again people whom I had met at the places

120

without a doubt. It was a unanimous expression of pride in our Party, in those who guide its activity. That was the main thing.

But there was something else that inspired us. I mean the spirit of sincerity, bold criticism and self-criticism with which the report was imbued. Every Communist present realized this: our accomplishments are so important, socialism's victories are so significant that we are not afraid—morover, we consider it our Party duty—not to close our eyes but to criticize shortcomings with Leninist vigor. We must do this because those who are strong are not afraid to admit that they have not been able, or have not had the time, to accomplish something; because a people which, in Leonid Brezhnev's words, has deeply appreciated the Party's policy and has given its wholehearted support, is capable of overcoming any difficulties in its path.

All the enormous tasks outlined in the report are to serve one and the same goal—the goal for which our great Revolution was carried out, which all of our five-year-plans helped promote, and for which Soviet people fought and laid down their lives in the Great Patriotic War.   □

Kamil Yashen

Writer, Uzbekistan

The continuous succession of days that seem to resemble one another often prevents us from fully appreciating the significance and scale of what is taking place around us. Even space flights have become customary and commonplace, to say nothing of new building projects. That is probably as it should be. For the feat of millions, the enthusiasm for creative work, has in effect become an ordinary thing. Leonid Brezhnev's report contains an excellent statement on this point. As I listened to the report and to the delegates and guests who spoke at the Congress I took a closer look at the people around me. Most of them were representatives of Party organizations at their plants, construction sites and farms. I could easily recognize delegations of Russians and Georgians, Ukrainians and Armenians, Byelorussians and Uzbeks. But it was practically impossible to distinguish a worker from an executive, scientist or engineer. I could not find any outward distinctions to guide me in this matter. A.V. Chuyev who sat at my side in the Presidium was a shipbuilder from Leningrad. On the other side was A.V. Gitalov, a machine-operator from the Ukraine, and farther on A.I. Khramtsov, a gear-cutter from the Uralmash Works and P.A. Malinina, a collective-farm chairman from the Kostroma Region. One could not distinguish them from the well-known social workers, scientists and Party executives, for these working people have become prominent public figures as well.

And I began to think of my native Uzbekistan. Scores of new cities have mushroomed throughout my Republic. Yet the most striking result of our development is the further consolidation of our Soviet way of life, the atmosphere of creative work, genuine collectivism and peoples' friendship.

As a writer I was naturally interested in the report's appraisal of the literary process in the last five-year period. And I can say it was truly inspiring. In the past years intellectuals engaged in the arts have become more productive, and there has been an upsurge in the literature and arts of all the fraternal republics and of the entire Soviet internationalist culture.

The reports delivered by Leonid Brezhnev and Alexey Kosygin were permeated with deep Party concern for the work of writers, artists, composers and workers of the stage, screen and television and gave special attention to budding talents. "Talented works of literature and art are part of the national heritage," said Brezhnev. This shows a Leninist attitude toward creative intellectuals. This is also a pledge that the cultural wealth of the builders of communism will considerably increase in the current five-year period.   □

Sergei Gerasimov
Film Writer-Director-Producer

The 25th Congress is a brilliant example of the Party's ability to analyze scientifically the most complex processes of our time. The policy of the Soviet Government and the general line of our Communist Party have a positive impact on social development all over the world.

The scale of the Tenth Five-Year Plan period cannot fail to inspire a person in any profession, including the arts. We Soviet workers of the stage and screen, painters, and musicians regard our artistic work as the direct sequel of our social life. The people's labor efforts, their impressive achievements and new plans make up the concrete language of life which gives us an understanding of the real world we live in.

Our Western opponents censure Soviet cultural workers for their desire to promote the cause of the state and Party by their art. They see in this an impoverishment of art and a lack of freedom for self-expression. They spare no efforts to divert us from such work, failing or rather refusing to understand that we serve the Party solely from a sense of civic duty.

Problems put forward by life and methods for their solution are an essential part of our art. We must discover for ourselves the springs of human relations in the sphere of production, the intellectual aspect of these relations, and try to stir the people's minds with our discoveries. For instance, many people are moved emotionally when they watch the film, "The Bonus," which deals with workers' honor. Or another example: everyone was profoundly impressed by the film, "Chairman," with problems of the village economy as its backbone. The success of this film far surpassed that usually achieved by a thrilling detective or romantic love story.

Contemporary man has developed an entirely new attitude to artistic values. Art has begun to have a much greater impact on the molding of the human personality. Art, which is called upon to bring up new generations, can achieve a great deal, and this raises immeasurably the artist's responsibility to the people, to their present and future.

We are building a new world on a new basis and in our country economic science is closely linked with art. Or to be more precise, art is connected with all the aspects of the nation's life and serves its interests. The people of present-day society expect us to carry out a profound and serious study of the surrounding world and we are also called upon to do this by the Party Congress. I am sure everyone remembers the words of Leonid Brezhnev to the creative intellectuals: ". . . the well-turned phrase, the play of color, the expressiveness of stone and the harmony of sound which inspire our contemporaries will leave in the hearts and souls of our descendants a memory of our generation, of our epoch, with its anxieties and accomplishments." These are truly inspiring and moving words about the role of our art in contemporary socialist society. □

N. Pereverzeva

Machine operator at "Lenin's Road" collective farm, Rostov region

We are living through happy, momentous days—all of us, delegates and the entire Soviet people. How much effort, energy and knowledge are required to carry out everything that has been planned! But I'm confident our people are equal to the task. I just picture my fellow villagers—industrious people with a well-developed sense of teamwork, and many, many other Soviet people, purposeful and persistent, and I feel absolutely certain: we'll fulfill all our plans.

Not only shall we cope with our tasks, but we shall do so ahead of schedule, and our output will be of high quality. And, as always, our Soviet moral fiber will do us a good service. Grain harvesting was exceedingly difficult last year, for instance, but we gathered the harvest with no losses. We worked with "Kolos" combine harvesters, a very good machine. Our four women-operated combines each put out 7,000 tons of grain.

As soon as the harvest was over, we, advanced workers of the farm, were invited to a meeting with the workers of the Taganrog combine-harvester plant and asked whether we had any complaints about the machine they manufactured. Our talk was very useful. During the discussion not only engineers, designers and heads of departments were present, but also assembly-shop workers and output-quality checkers. Then we visited the shops, not as sight-seers, but to continue the discussion with the work teams.

At the Taganrog plant, we arrived at a unanimous conclusion: the utmost conscientiousness of each Soviet worker is the surest guarantee of success. We resolved to spare no effort whatever in the production sector and to put up with no shortcomings. Then we'd be equal to any task, even the most difficult. That's what the Party teaches us.   □

V. Cherbayev
Team Leader of Turners at "January Revolt" Works in Odessa

H ere, in the Kremlin Hall of Congresses, one gets a feeling that one is part of the great force that is transforming the world. The present achieve-ments of the Soviet people are the direct sequel of the cause of the Great October Revolution. There can be no greater pride than that of being one of the builders of a new life. And the responsibility is enormous! Our fathers and forefathers have laid the foundations of a great cause, and it is our task to advance it to new and higher levels.

The Congress developed a new program for our country's economic and social development. No one can remain indifferent to these great projects. These plans are permeated with concern for the Soviet people and their welfare, and the Soviet people will spare no efforts to realize them concretely.

Our team of turners has also pledged to perform high-quality work. The hydro-cylinders we manufacture bear a "State Quality Mark." Yet this is not enough. It is important to ensure the high quality of the final product of our plant—the high-capacity self-propelled cranes which are urgently needed at many construction sites of the Tenth Five-Year period. To this effect we have concluded socialist emulation agreements with teams working in allied trades: smiths, lathe operators and assemblers. Such creative cooperation of all teams within a single technological chain makes possible timely action to eliminate hitches, ensure an uninterrupted rhythm of work and improve mutual control in all operations. All of us intend to earn the right to stamp our units with personal trademarks and turn them in, by-passing the checking department.

We will also contribute to reequipping our plant technically. For instance, we will install floating cutters, rolling and other appliances in our lathes and take an active part in rationalization and invention.

At the Congress note was made of the present high level of the general and technological education of the working people. The age of the scientific and technological revolution requires that each worker, regardless of his job, possess sound knowledge and great skill. In the preceding five-year period six of our team's eleven members completed the evening department of secondary school without giving up work. In the Tenth Five-Year Plan period all the other team members will complete their secondary education. We will be able to work still better and achieve the new and higher five-year target in four and a half years.

Similar pledges have been taken by all of my fellow-workers at the plant. Each one is discovering new ways to attain better results than in the previous period. We can always find them! The workers on related jobs are not always as careful as they should be, there are cases of violations of labor and technological discipline, and sometimes of spoilage. To eliminate these shortcomings as quickly as possible and ensure smooth production and high quality output is our prime task in the current period which the Party has called a five-year plan of efficiency and quality.

The Party has mapped out far-reaching plans for the economic and social development of our Soviet society. We are confident that all that has been outlined will be achieved! ☐

Nikolay Tomsky
People's Artist of the USSR

One feels immense joy at being alive in such an amazing age and witnessing such truly epoch-making events, as well as for being not a mere observer but a participant in these great social transformations.

It has long been observed that a man realizes his true happiness only when it is achieved through struggle and work, when it helps him to move constantly forward, without stopping, satisfied with what he has already accomplished, while opening before him ever more interesting and boundless prospects.

This is a distinctive feature of our Soviet society—it makes the life of each person invaluable and gives him every opportunity to bring out all his talents and abilities and embody them in beautiful cities, blossoming orchards, poetic words, invaluable works of art and the many great projects which enable him to live an exciting and unique life.

The 25th Congress once again confirmed the sound character of the Leninist policy toward culture and art and underscored their ever growing role in the ideological and political, moral and esthetic education of the Soviet people. From the lofty place it occupies in man's life one can see the boundless and joyful prospects of our art.

The Soviet artist must have great talent, inspiration and creative abilities to enable him to imprint in unfading images the greatness of our epoch and the people's creative achievements. That is why our happiness is so closely linked with a sense of high responsibility and an exacting attitude to our work.

Never before has there been such a situation in our art: thousands of artists specializing in easel painting, graphic arts and sculpture, take part in the biggest building projects of our age, the bases of our five-year plan, in the remotest parts of our homeland, to reproduce in their works the greatness of the Soviet people and their creative feats.

Soviet artists are faced with yet another, no less stupendous, task—to create an esthetic environment for the life and work of the Soviet people. This means that our cities, villages, and our plants and factories should become more beautiful. Today we artists have no end of work to do, and a broad sphere for applying our creative energy and realizing our aspirations. And we carry a high responsibility. For much of what will be created will be the first of its kind.

The quest for the new is the essence of our happiness!   □

Appendix to Part Two

The Credentials Report at a Glance

The data below are adapted from the report to the Congress by Ivan Kapitonov, Chairman of the Credentials Committee.

	Number	Per cent of total
Delegates (one per 3,000 Party members)	4,998	100.0
Delegates for the first time	3,672	73.5
From the Union Republics:		
RSFSR	3,035	60.7
Ukraine	894	17.9
Kazakhstan	218	4.4
Byelorussia	172	3.4
Uzbekistan	159	3.2
Georgia	107	2.5
Azerbaidzhan	96	1.9
Latvia	51	1.0
Lithuania	49	1.0
Armenia	47	0.9
Moldavia	44	0.9
Kirghizia	37	0.7
Tadzhikistan	32	0.6
Estonia	30	0.6
Turkmenistan	27	0.5
Industrial workers	1,703	34.1

Agricultural workers	887	17.7
Intelligentsia (workers in literature, the arts, research, education, health)	272	5.4
Academicians and Corresponding Members of Academies of Science	103	2.1
Doctors and Candidates of Science	442	8.8
Party workers	1,114	22.3
Secretaries of regional and territorial committees and Union-Republic Central Committees	329	6.6
Secretaries of area, city and district committees	635	12.7
Local government, trade union and Komsomol workers	693	13.9
Deputies to USSR and union and Autonomous Republic Supreme Soviets	1,608	32.2
Managers of production associations and enterprises	346	6.9
State farm directors	86	1.7
Collective farm chairmen	142	2.8
Women	1,255	25.1
Members of the Armed Forces	314	6.3
Under 35 years of age	—	12.5
35-50	—	58.0
51-60	—	19.7
Over 60	—	9.8
Heroes of the Soviet Union	67	1.3
Heroes of Socialist Labor	797	15.9
Lenin and State Prize winners	244	4.9

Also present at the Congress were 103 delegations from Communist, Workers', National-Democratic and Socialist Parties from 96 countries.

The Incoming Political Bureau

Newly elected at the 25th Congress:

General Secretary of the CPSU Central Committee: L. I. Brezhnev

Members of the Political Bureau: L. I. Brezhnev, Yu. V. Andropov, A. A. Grechko, V. V. Grishin, A. A. Gromyko, A. P. Kirilenko, A. N. Kosygin, F. D. Kulakov, D. A. Kunayev, K. T. Mazurov, A. Ya. Pelshe, N. V. Podgorny, G. V. Romanov, M. A. Suslov, D. F. Ustinov, V. V. Shcherbitsky.

Alternate Members of the Political Bureau: G. A. Aliev, P. N. Demichev, P. M. Masherov, B. N. Ponomaryov, Sh. R. Rashidov, M. S. Solomentsev.

Secretaries of the CPSU Central Committee: L. I. Brezhnev, M. A. Suslov, A. P. Kirilenko, F.D. Kulakov, D. F. Ustinov, B. N. Ponomaryov, I. V. Kapitonov, V. I. Dolgikh, K. F. Katushev, M. V. Zimyanin, K. U. Chernenko.

Chairman of the Party Control Committee: A. Ya. Pelshe. Chairman of the Central Auditing Commission: G. F. Sizov.

Part Three: The World Input

8

Foreign Guests
Greet the Congress

Gus Hall

General Secretary of the Communist
Party, USA

This 25th Congress of the Party of Lenin is another landmark, a guidepost on the revolutionary path of transition to socialism and to the fulfillment of human society's highest aspirations — a Communist society.

Like a piercing laser beam of light, the basic theme of Marxism-Leninism runs through the very sober, profound and deeply penetrating assessments and projections of Comrade Brezhnev's report.

Just as the building of socialism demonstrates, by the power of its example, the superiority of socialism, so the Communist Party of the Soviet Union, by the power of its example, by its unwavering adherence to, by its resourceful application of, and by the continuous development of the science of Marxism-Leninism, serves as the working pattern for the revolutionary movements throughout the world.

At a moment when the struggles of the historic revolutionary transitions have become increasingly complex, and the ideological pressures build up, at a moment when new strains of the virus of opportunism are being hatched, this power of the Leninist example is of a special and great historic significance.

It serves as a working model because the Communist Party of the Soviet Union, throughout its 78 years, has always zealously guarded the working-class heart, the revolutionary essence of Marxism-Leninism.

The concepts of proletarian internationalism and the class struggle have always been its guiding points of reference. With great skill and persistence the CPSU fights for peace, for detente and for the application of the policies of peaceful coexistence, but with the same persistence it rejects any and all opportunistic accommodations to imperialism.

The new proposals for peace in Comrade Brezhnev's report are a challenge to world capitalist leaders. Because the Communist Party of the Soviet Union never permits consideration of momentary gains to erode the pillar of class principles, it consistently finds the elements of unity between its national and international responsibilities.

It is a high tribute to the CPSU that your Congress has become the occasion for the assembly of one of the largest gatherings of representatives of the world revolutionary movement.

While socialism continues along its steady course of growth and development, while its five-year plans are translated into economic, cultural and social well-being, while the overall quality of socialist life improves, in the capitalist world the general and the cyclical crises are translated into deeper poverty for greater numbers, into economic insecurity and a declining overall quality of life. Political repression and racism become United States capital's main line of defense.

While socialism reaches for new levels of achievement, monopoly-state capitalism develops new dimensions to its crises.

The new theme song of monopoly capital is "austerity." They are saying the people are living too high off the hog. There is a concentrated drive to cut down and to dismantle the social security programs which the working class and the people have won in earlier periods of capitalist development.

The drive for austerity goes hand in hand with the ever rising corporate profits. The cities in bankruptcy are but a reflection of this new dimension of the crises of state-monopoly capitalism.

The daily comparison studies and the great mass awareness of the divergent paths followed by the two world socioeconomic systems has emerged as a decisive factor in the political and ideological arenas of struggle.

Increasingly, socialism is viewed by the masses as the standard of achievement against which all social progress — or lack of it — is measured. It is this shift in the mass patterns of thought that explains the new hysterical note, the new low of falsehoods in bourgeois anti-socialist propaganda.

It explains the fishing with the baited silver lure, and the dredging for any and all anti-Communist, anti-Soviet "droppings," especially if they have radical, left or Marxist coatings.

In our times, the main ideological pressures of imperialism are in relationship to the socialist world and against the Soviet Union in the first place.

Because capitalism increasingly comes out on the losing end in the comparison of the two systems, they have to resort to more intangibles, to political vapor bubbles that appear and disappear, leaving but an odor.

Opportunism breaks through where the ideological pressures of the enemy are the greatest.

Our Party has a basic principled position on these matters. We are not going to fight imperialism by their rules. We are not going to use or repeat anti-socialist and anti-Soviet slander to win acceptance, to win respectability or to prove our autonomy. We will not pattern our policies by accommodation to the attacks against our class, our Party or socialism.

Maoism is the classic example of where the path of opportunism leads to, if it goes unchecked. At the murky bottom of the swamp of opportunism there is counterrevolution. Maoism has reached to that bottom.

The CIA-US corporate and Maoist alliance in support of the fascist butchers in Chile is counterrevolution.

The Maoist-CIA and the racist South African conspiracy against the people and government of Angola is counterrevolution.

The Maoist vile slander campaign against world socialism is counter-revolutionary.

To be silent about these outrageous acts is to be neutral. To be neutral in such a basic struggle is itself an accommodation to opportunism.

There are problems and there are momentary setbacks, but by any yardstick the central fact, the hard core reality of this epoch, is the continuing victorious flow of the world revolutionary process and the growing power and the unity of forces that propel it.

So, dear comrades and delegates, accept our heartiest congratulations, our warm greetings and our best wishes for new and greater victories in your pioneering work in the building of communist society.

May the staunch heroic working-class heart beat strong and in rhythm the world over.   □

Henry Winston

National Chairman, Communist Party, USA

Following is the address, slightly abridged, delivered by Henry Winston at a public meeting in Kiev on March 5, in celebration of the 25th Congress. Winston was a member of the fraternal delegation of the CPUSA to the CPSU Congress.

The quality of life in the Soviet Union is not equalled anywhere else in the world, and the projections that are made for the Tenth Five-Year Plan will improve still further this quality in all areas of life.

This humanism, this profound concern for people, is the real essence of Marxism-Leninism, and it was this fact which was all-pervasive in the magnificent report of Comrade Brezhnev.

The prevention of a third world war is primarily due to the decisive leadership of the great peoples of the Soviet Union, uniting with the peace and national liberation movements all over the world.

The report of Comrade Brezhnev is that kind of document which can help to save humanity from a thermonuclear war, and establish those kinds of guarantees which can help in furthering the building of communism in the Soviet Union and other socialist countries, the anti-monopoly struggles in all capitalist countries, and the fight against colonialism and neocolonialism.

It is an open secret that imperialism's main weapons against social progress are racism and anti-communism. Actively supporting the criminal aims of imperialism are the Maoists. Maoist support to the military fascist junta of Pinochet in Chile which smashed popular democracy, which has imprisoned Luis Corvalan and thousands of other anti-fascists, its support of the pro-fascist apartheid minority which oppresses the Black majority in South Africa, their active support to UNITA, waging war against Angola, not to speak of the bureaucratic, militarist dictatorship over the Chinese people, is but the logical consequence of Maoist class treason.

Whatever disguise Maoism may wear, there is nothing which can disprove the truth that anti-communism has nothing in common with anti-imperialism; that anti-communism is the twin brother of racism and of colonialism.

I feel confident that the people of China will be able to put an end to this scourge, and return their country to the path of Marxism-Leninism. After all, it was Marxism-Leninism, not Maoism, that brought about the victory in China in 1949.

Positive changes are taking place in the world. They are very evident in Europe. This is not due to any kind of benevolence on the part of imperialism, but is primarily due to the massive growth and strengthening of the Soviet Union, the smashing of the policy of containment, and a strengthening unity with all peace forces on the continent of Europe. The Vladivostok and Helsinki agreements point the way to greater successes in the fight for detente and peaceful coexistence, and create favorable conditions for the dismantling of military alliances and bases.

This is very important for us in the United States. Our country is now experiencing very serious problems of inflation and economic crisis, the solution of which is not in sight. The burden of this crisis is being carried on the backs of the working class. Prices of food and all necessities of life are sky high, as are rent, transportation, education and health care. Taxes are going up.

Government figures for unemployment are given as 7.6 million, but labor figures show more than ten million. Unemployment compensation for many has been exhausted, while there is no prospect of finding a job. Unemployment among Black youth is exceptionally high, reaching as high as 30, 45, even 60 per cent in some communities.

Racism finds similar expression among Puerto Rican, Chicano, Asian, Native American Indian and other oppressed minorities. Unemployment is general, but racism makes it special among oppressed minorities.

State monopoly capitalism argues that we're going through hard times in the US and that people must tighten their belts.

Racist persecution against Black people continues to grow. The recent jailing of the Wilmington 10, ten young Black men and women in Wilmington, North Carolina, for defending the most elementary democratic rights against racist policemen is a case in point. These 10 young Black people face a total of 282 years in prison. The Reverend Ben Chavis, a leader of the National Alliance against Racist and Political Repression, faces 34 years.

In the meantime the situation in the US is pregnant with many possibilities. Never in the history of the US has the majority of people opposed the foreign policy of the government, as was seen in Vietnam and Angola. Poll after poll shows that the bulk of the people express a lack of confidence in any agency of government and in the large institutions in the country. The polls also show that the people support such vital measures as detente, cooperation with the Soviet Union and cuts in the military budget.

An effective defense of the living standards of our people makes mandatory a struggle against the military budget which has now reached the tremendous sum of more than 107 billion dollars. The fight to transform those billions into items fulfilling the needs of the people is integrally related to the struggle for detente and peaceful coexistence. The struggle for peace is key to the defense of the economic, political and social rights of our people.

The achievements of the people of the Soviet Union are a mirror through which we can more clearly see our problems and the road ahead. Our guide is Marxism-Leninism.   □

Le Duan

First Secretary of the Central Committee
of the Vietnam Workers Party

It is a great happiness for our delegation to share the joy and pride, together with the Communists and the entire Soviet people, on the occasion of the 25th Congress of the glorious Communist Party of the Soviet Union. Allow me, on behalf of the Vietnam Workers Party and the whole of the Vietnamese people, to convey the warmest and most ardent greetings to the Congress and, through it, to all Communists and the fraternal Soviet people.

The history of the Soviet Union in the past nearly six decades, the history of the stubborn struggle of the working class and the peoples of the Soviet Union under the leadership of the Party of the great Lenin, is a chronicle of events that have exerted a deep influence on the entire course of the world revolution.

All progressive humanity will be eternally grateful to the October Revolution, which has ushered in the era of the triumph of socialism on a world scale. They will always remember the glorious victories of the Soviet Union in the Second World War. These victories saved mankind from the horrors of fascism and created favorable conditions for the emergence of the world socialist system, for the liberation of many colonial countries from the chains of colonialism, and for their winning of the right to be the masters of their own lives.

The Soviet people, overcoming incalculable difficulties, trials and privations, and enduring tremendous sacrifices, displayed iron will and selfless heroism and were the first to build socialism victoriously, and today they are paving the way to communism. The Soviet Union sent the first messenger to the cosmos, laying the basis for the mastery of interplanetary space in the name of the happiness and progress of humanity.

The report, delivered by Comrade Leonid Brezhnev, which adduces concrete examples from experience, gives a magnificent picture of revolutionary heroism and creative talent of the Soviet people which they displayed in the process of the successful fulfillment of the Ninth Five-Year Plan, drawn up by the 24th Congress of the Communist Party of the Soviet Union.

Today the Soviet Union is the world's most powerful socialist land. It has been playing an exceptionally great role in strengthening the might of the revolutionary forces of our time, it supports the national liberation movements and the struggles for democracy and social progress, disrupts the inflammatory machinations of imperialism and defends peace in Europe and in the whole world.

Filled with sincere feelings of comradeship and fraternity, the Vietnam Workers Party and the Vietnamese people regard the Soviet Union's victories as their own, and from the bottom of their hearts wish the Soviet people to win fresh, ever more remarkable successes in implementing the Tenth Five-Year Plan under the leadership of the Communist Party. We wish the Soviet people to reach new heights on their way to Communism and to make an active contribution to the efforts of the peoples of the world aimed against imperialism, colonialism and neocolonialism, for peace, national independence, democracy and socialism.

The Vietnamese people are now experiencing the happiest moment in their 40-century history.

As a result of the general attack and uprising in the spring of 1975, the culminating movement of which was the historic operation in the name of Ho Chi Minh, our armed forces and the people of our whole country were completely victorious in the struggle against the fierce aggression of the American imperialists and completely liberated the people of South Vietnam. Then began the most beautiful era in the history of our country — the era of building a beautiful, united, independent and socialist Vietnam. Our victory is the triumph of the correct revolutionary line and of the solidarity of the peoples of Vietnam, Laos and Cambodia, who for many years fought shoulder to shoulder against the common enemy, for the independence, freedom and prosperity of their respective countries.

Our victory is a triumph of the socialist countries, the communist and working class movement, the national liberation movement, and the forces of peace and progress throughout the world.

The victory which the Vietnamese people won over US imperialist aggression, the full victory scored by the peoples of the three countries of the Indochinese Peninsula pushed back imperialism, expanding the positions of the forces of national independence and socialism in Southeast Asia. These victories brought about a deep change in the correlation of forces, opened up further opportunities for upholding national independence and peace in this region, as well as throughout the world.

At the present new stage, our party is guiding the Vietnamese people in their struggle for the fulfillment of the difficult but glorious tasks aimed at quickly healing the wounds of war, overcoming the aftermath of neocolonialism, completing the country's reunification as a state and its advance along the road of socialism, and actively contributing to the revolutionary cause of the peoples of the world.

More than half a century ago, Comrade Ho Chi Minh, the first Vietnamese Communist, who saw in the October Revolution the only road for saving the people and the country, went to Lenin's country, thereby laying the foundations for the great friendship between the Soviet and Vietnamese people. This friendship and solidarity, the development of which is the subject of the constant concern of the parties and the peoples of our countries, are constantly growing stronger, flourishing and yielding their fruit.

The Vietnamese people are well aware of the fact that, as before, every step forward and every victory that the Vietnamese Revolution scores are inseparably linked with the most important historical events going on in the Soviet Union. The full victory in the war of resistance against US aggression, for the salvation of our country, should be especially emphasized. This victory is part and parcel of the powerful support, the all-round, tremendous, valuable and effective assistance of the Soviet Union.

At present the CPSU, the government of the USSR and the Soviet people are doing their best to help the Vietnamese people restore and develop their economy, to build socialism in the entire country. The deeper the Vietnamese people's devotion to national liberation and socialism, the higher they value the great Vietnamese-Soviet friendship. The Vietnamese people will forever remember this support and assistance, which are permeated with the lofty spirit of proletarian internationalism.

On behalf of the Party, the government and people of Vietnam we express our sincere and profound gratitude to the Communist Party, the Government of the USSR and the Soviet people, our dear Soviet brothers, for considering the support and assistance to the Vietnamese people to be the call of their heart and the cause of their conscience.

Availing ourselves of this opportunity, we wish to express our sincere and heartfelt gratitude to the other fraternal socialist countries, to the Communist and Workers' Parties, the national-liberation movements and the newly free countries, and the international democratic organizations who have rendered and continue to render their deeply felt support and assistance to the revolutionary cause of the Vietnamese people.   □

Oliver Tambo

Acting President,
African National Congress of South Africa

As a result of the international actions of the Central Committee of the CPSU and General Secretary Leonid Brezhnev personally, the peace program of the 24th CPSU Congress is being successfully carried out and has had a tremendous influence in strengthening the peaceloving forces of the world.

The Soviet peace program has also had a profound impact on the national liberation movement which is developing successfully in many parts of our planet. Of special historic significance was the victory of the peoples of Indochina over American imperialist aggression. Simultaneously the heroic struggles of the Arab peoples against imperialism and Zionism were gaining strength and the revolutionary struggles of the peoples of the African continent were spreading. Portuguese colonialism in Africa met its final defeat, and from its ruins arose the progressive governments of Mozambique, Guinea-Bissau, Angola, San-Tomé and Principé, the Cape Verde Islands, all under the leadership of revolutionary democratic parties. The struggle of the peoples of South Africa, Zimbabwe and Namibia grew more active. Attempting to adapt themselves to the changing situation, the reactionary regimes in that part of the world have been forced into desperate maneuvers.

Thus on the one hand, the reactionary terrorist regime of the South African Republic tries to demonstrate an ostentatious love of peace, calling for negotiations with the independent African governments, and on the other exposes its real aggressive essence so clearly demonstrated against the young independent republic of Angola.

This fascist aggression carried on under the usual smoke screen of anti-communism and anti-Sovietism, aroused the indignation of all African society. Many of the African governments expressed their solidarity with Angola. The new republic is now the 47th member of the Organization of African Unity. Its acceptance in the OAU was a decisive blow to those forces which wanted to isolate Angola from its democratic allies and international society.

We want to take advantage of this opportunity to express our deepest gratitude for the timely help of the Soviet Union, Cuba and other socialist powers who, along with support from the progressive forces on the African continent, permitted the MPLA to defeat imperialist aggression.

Through all the years of carrying out its peace program, the Soviet Government has constantly accorded increasing, all-sided support to the peoples fighting for real independence and human dignity, against colonial and neo-colonial aggression on the African continent. We representatives of the African National Congress fully understand that it is due to that help and the help of the democratic forces on the African continent and other countries, that our organization is able to inspire resistance and growing opposition among those sections of our country oppressed by the tyranny of apartheid. We do not doubt that in the future too, the Soviet people will fulfill their international duty with honor.   □

Fidel Castro Ruz

First Secretary of the Central Committee
of the Communist Party and Prime
Minister of Cuba

The Communists of this country were the first victorious detachment of the international working class and the builders of the first socialist state in the history of humankind. For this reason, from Lenin's time on, the congresses of the Communist Party of the Soviet Union have constituted an extraordinary source of experience and learning for revolutionaries the world over.

Revolutionaries have always been encouraged and inspired by the Soviet Communists. Since the October Revolution, it can be said that the new generations of revolutionaries have been raised on its ideas, spirit and principles. No other event had such an impact on the minds of men, the destiny of the peoples and on world progress. Since then, humankind has gone through the most fruitful period of revolutionary change in its whole history.

Today there is a socialist community, and, as a result of the changes in the world situation brought about by the October Revolution and the defeat of fascism, more than 100 colonial and semicolonial nations of all continents were able to take on the hard struggle against the still powerful forces of colonialism and imperialism and attain independence.

Soviet workers paved the way and heroically defended it with their effort and their blood. The 20 million noble, dedicated sons and daughters of the Soviet people who died in the patriotic war was the terrible price paid as a result of the sinister effort on the part of world reaction to turn back the inexorable march of humankind toward the goals of justice, well-being and peace. And that isn't all: with its extraordinary scientific, technological and industrial development, the USSR became a very strong nation in all fields in a matter of decades.

The degree of independence now enjoyed by small countries, the success of the peoples in their struggle to regain control over their natural resources and make their voices heard in the concert of nations, would have been inconceivable had it not been for the existence of the Soviet Union. The peace which exists in today's world, the great privilege which the younger generations have of growing up in a world free of disastrous conflict and the hope for a future of cooperation among nations are due, first and foremost, to the victory of Leninist ideas in this country and their fitting, correct interpretation in setting forth Soviet foreign policy. Objective facts demonstrate, more and more clearly, that world peace, the progress of humankind and socialism are firmly linked.

Changes in the world cannot be held back. Nobody can export revolution or impose it by means of war, but nobody can prevent the peoples from making it, either, and the future belongs entirely to socialism and communism.

We speak on behalf of a people on the other side of the Atlantic, in a continent which was formerly characterized by the absolute domination of the most powerful imperialist nation, on behalf of a people now successfully building socialism 90 miles from the shores of that country.

In doing so, our people contributed with their resolute call for justice and freedom, their sweat and blood and their loyalty to revolutionary ideas. But this would have been inconceivable without the October Revolution and your fraternal support and solidarity, without the existence of the state founded by Lenin.

I can't speak for others, but I know that since the Soviet state was founded, as in the case of our country, wherever a people struggled for its liberation, be it in Europe, Asia, Africa or Latin America, it never lacked the solidarity and support of Soviet Communists. The light of the sun can't be shut out with a finger. True history will not be written by reactionaries, calumniators, intriguers or traitors, whether they go by the name of fascists, bourgeois or Maoists, because history itself will sweep them all away. They seek to destroy the great prestige which has been won by the Soviet people with such heroism, sacrifice and loyalty to the revolutionary cause. The Hitlerites also thought that on the ruins of the Soviet Union they would build an empire lasting a thousand years. But the Soviet Union is indestructible both materially and morally. Nobody can diminish its prestige, because its wise international conduct, its deep sense of responsibility as regards the world revolutionary movement and its loyalty to a principled policy throughout the whole of its existence has inspired limitless confidence on the part of sincere revolutionaries and progressives.

Our people are proud of their relations with this great country. They constitute a model of internationalist practice, understanding, respect and mutual confidence. Never has the Soviet Union, which gave our country such decisive help, come to us demanding that we do anything, laying down conditions or telling us what to do. Never before in the history of international relations, long governed by self-interest and force, have such fraternal links been known to exist between a mighty and weak nation. Only socialism can make possible this kind of ties between peoples.   □

Michael O'Riordan

General Secretary of the Communist Party of Ireland

Our country was the first colony of the British Empire, and to maintain its domination the imperialists applied the technique of "divide and rule." Today, in Northern Ireland we have daily evidence of the results of such a policy, in the form of British military harassment; in assassinations; bombs in public places, in prisons that are full.

Due to British imperialist policies we neither have peace, employment or social advance in our island. There has also been a subjective contradictory factor in that bourgeois political figures have dominated the internal political scene in the two states carved out in Ireland by the British ruling class. The record of such political leaders has been their constant betrayal of the people in the national, political and economic spheres. But now there is a change in the form of emerging working-class leadership.

Our working class despite intense pressure recreated the 100 per cent unity of our trade union movement in a united national trade union center covering the Protestant and Catholic sections of our working class in both the Northern and Southern states in our island. This powerful Irish Congress of Trade Unions last year for the first time elected as its President a Communist in the person of Andrew Barr, National Chairman of our Party, and also elected him to be the first Communist on the Executive Committee of the European Confederation of Trade Unions.

Comrades! Our people are faced with the grave problems not only of unemployment, but of life and death, and the whole future of our people.

At this magnificent Congress we have heard the answers to problems that confront our people, such as—

Can a people overcome the divisions created by imperialism? The answer is here in the powerful multinational state of the USSR!

Is a small country helpless and weak in the face of imperialism? The answer is here in Vietnam!

Can an island people lying beside the powerful imperialist exploiter defeat this imperialist power and go on to building socialism, though it is separated from the socialist camp? The answer is here in Cuba!

All these answers are here thanks to the heroic people who provided them, and thanks to the consistent internationalism in practice of the CPSU, and thanks to the change in the balance of forces in the world brought about in the first place by the Party of Lenin; and which we are confident will be further altered in favor of humanity by this 25th Congress.   □

Erich Honecker

First Secretary of the Central Committee of the Socialist Unity Party (GDR)

The implementation of the CPSU peace program has brought about a radical change from the "cold war" to detente and the affirmation of the principle of peaceful coexistence between socialist and capitalist countries. The power of the Soviet Union and its peace policy have to a decisive degree been responsible for a new situation in the world.

The Helsinki Conference gave international legal status to the results of World War II and postwar developments, creating the decisive prerequisites for transforming Europe into a stable continent of peace.

The period since the 24th Congress has coincided with the general *de jure* recognition of the German Democratic Republic under the rules of international law. This, dear comrades, was no accident. It was due to the Leninist foreign policy of the Soviet Union, the concordant action of all the socialist countries and the international solidarity of the progressive forces of the world.

It is now, first of all, essential to make detente irreversible, to supplement political detente with military, to realize detente in action, to end the arms race which imperialism continues to drive ahead, and step by step to achieve disarmament.

Influential imperialist circles continue to oppose the process of detente. Their attempts to falsify the meaning of peaceful coexistence, inflame the arms race, and provoke new tensions must be decisively rebuffed as also must the "superpower," chauvinistic policy of the Peking leadership, which has demonstrated its hostility to socialism and peace. This 25th Congress of the CPSU summons the Communist and working class movement to new heights of struggle and to closer unity on the basis of Marxism-Leninism and proletarian internationalism.

Your Congress has evidenced anew that the CPSU is the most steeled and experienced section of the international Communist movement. Therefore our Party has always considered the constant deepening of a close fighting alliance with the Party of Lenin as the main criterion of proletarian internationalism. This has been, is and will be the basic guide to our thoughts and actions!

The Treaty of Friendship, Cooperation and Mutual Aid signed by our countries, October 7, 1975, is the basis of the still closer relations between our countries.

Our Party, our government and our people have united their efforts to achieve our common Communist aims and for the further solidarity of our socialist nations.   □

Carlos Altamirano

General Secretary of the Socialist Party of Chile

On behalf of the Chilean people and the Socialist Party of Chile, we express our gratitude to the Soviet people for the deep-going solidarity they have shown in both words and deeds under the conditions of temporary defeat suffered by the Chilean people. The Soviet Union and other socialist governments and people condemned the fascist dictatorship, broke diplomatic relations with the Pinochet regime and have headed the struggle for the diplomatic and economic isolation of the fascist junta, consistently following the policy of proletarian internationalism.

Some governments, however, contrary to their internationalist duty, have directly or indirectly helped the fascist tyranny. China has given $100 million to aid the Pinochet regime and recently decided to supply the Junta with arms to be used against the Chilean people.

The position of the CPSU inspires our Party and our people with a still greater feeling of responsibility. International solidarity makes it possible for the Chilean working people to broaden the struggle within the country. Even thirty months of terror have not resulted in strengthening the fascist dictatorship, and tens of thousands of our comrades are continuing the underground struggle.

We have learned important lessons from our temporary defeat. The powerful people's movement that has developed in Chile was possible because of the unity of the working-class parties—the Socialist and Communist. Both parties guaranteed a leading position to the workers within the broad coalition of

Popular Unity forces. Back in 1956 the Chilean working class created its political front. Under the leadership of the two Marxist-Leninist parties, a revolutionary program was developed envisioning the establishment of a new government and the transfer of power from the hands of one class into the hands of another. The Popular Unity Party won 50 per cent of the votes in the 1971 elections, and had still greater influence in society. This was an unprecedented success under conditions of bourgeois democracy. Having won this victory, the people's movement committed its biggest mistake in overestimating the stability of the political regime in Chile and the solidity of the democratic system of the country. Using the millions of dollars obtained from the CIA, the ITT, the Anaconda and Kennecott companies, imperialism and the bourgeoisie provoked economic chaos, and social anarchy, resorted to political terror and began to search for any means to strangle democracy as they have done in analogous historical situations.

At all stages of the development of the Soviet state down to our day, you, Soviet Comrades, have waged a heroic struggle and have achieved outstanding economic successes by making gigantic advances in science, technology and culture. The road you have traversed is full of sacrifices in the name of building a new life and generous help and solidarity with the struggles of other peoples. This is well known in heroic Vietnam, in glorious socialist Cuba, in the People's Republic of Angola and by all of the peoples waging a struggle for freedom and socialism.

We will always seek to be worthy of the solidarity of the peoples of the world. We will follow Salvador Allende who has shown us a wonderful example of revolutionary honesty and revolutionary consistency, which the people of Chile will never forget.   □

Moses Garoeb

Member of the National Executive, Administrative
Secretary of the South West African People's
Organization of Namibia

From its foundation up till now, the Soviet Union has consistently supported all people who have struggled and are still struggling today to free themselves from all forms of oppression.

Namibia is one of these countries which still remain under foreign domination. The Namibian people have taken up arms to liberate themselves. And, in our struggle to liberate our country, we are proud to say that the Soviet Union and the socialist countries have consistently supported us: morally, politically and diplomatically. That is why we know that victory will be ours in the end.

Today, there is a general panic in the imperialist camp because of the advances made and the victories being scored by the national liberation movements, particularly in Southern Africa. There is a general outcry by the racists and imperialists because of the so-called "intervention by the Soviet Union and Cuba" in Southern Africa. But for the liberation movements the situation is clear: the Soviet Union and Cuba and other socialist countries are merely carrying out their internationalist duty which is to provide assistance to all peoples who are fighting for their liberation.

Today in Southern Africa, the forces of national liberation—in Namibia, Zimbabwe and South Africa—are poised to deliver the last decisive blow against white minority regimes. These regimes know that with the determination of the African people to free themselves and the consistent aid from the Soviet Union and other socialist countries it is merely a matter of time before they are finally defeated.

We want to assure this Congress that SWAPO will leave no stone unturned, will spare no life, however precious, to ensure the total defeat of South African racists in Namibia. We have never doubted, and never will, the support the Soviet Union is rendering our people and our movement. We want to be worthy of the support given us.   □

Farouk Kaddoumi

Member of the Executive Committee of the
Palestine Liberation Organization

While sharing with you our happiness at your great achievements both in the heroic work of your own people in all spheres in building socialism, and in your great contribution to guaranteeing peace on earth and to the struggles of the peoples for liberty and independence, at the same time we want to stress the great debt we owe you for the principled line and comradely position in support of the fighting Palestinian people. We highly value your support of our just struggle for the restoration of our inalienable national rights to self-determination and the establishment of our own independent government. One of the brightest examples of that position was at the meeting of the UN Security Council in January during the discussion on the Palestine and Middle East question, when the voice of the Soviet Union was one of the loudest, friendliest and most sincere in defense of the cause of our people!

The decision of the Rabat Conference designating the Palestine Liberation Organization as the only legitimate representative of the Palestinian people symbolized the victories won by our people and added real strength to our.

movement in many spheres. This meant growing solidarity of many sections of the people around the PLO. This solidarity was confirmed by the mass demonstrations for several months running in the occupied territories of our homeland.

Our people highly value the constant efforts of our friend the Soviet Union for the establishment of a just peace in the Middle East. We highly value the Soviet initiatives toward a durable solution of the problems of establishing the national rights of the Palestinian people, toward guaranteeing the PLO the possibility of participating in all international efforts having the aim of establishing a just and equal peace within the framework of the UN and in accord with its decisions on the Palestinian question.

Not long ago the Palestinian revolution was confronted with evil plots and attacks in Lebanon. In spite of the dangerous scale of these plots, our Palestine revolution, its power doubled with the help of the patriotic and progressive forces of Lebanon, emerged from this crisis stronger, more steeled, firm and unified. This provoked the hostile imperialist powers to step up their attacks and hatch new plots. For this reason we must be even more attentive and vigilant.

We are living through this historic moment in your great struggle along with you. We believe in the inevitable victory over the forces of world imperialism, racism and reaction.   □

Ezekias Papaioannu

General Secretary, Progressive Party of the Working People of Cyprus

The imperialists have not relinquished their plans to dismember Cyprus and turn it into a NATO springboard with a view to establishing control over the Suez Canal and the oil-bearing areas of the Middle East. These adventurous schemes have not materialized so far because of the Cypriot people's staunch resistance, international solidarity and, mainly, because of the Soviet Union's powerful support.

Imperialists have always tried and are still trying to present the Cyprus question as a feud between the Greeks and Turks whereas in reality it hinges upon the contradictions between the people of Cyprus, both Greeks and Turks, on the one hand, and imperialism, on the other.

The Cyprus question can and must be resolved in a peaceful way by means of the withdrawal of the Turkish and other foreign troops from Cyprus territory, a return of the refugees to their homes, a search for the missing persons and their release, a settlement of the constitutional problem and holding of negotiations between the Greeks and the Turks under the aegis of the Secretary General of the United Nations and on the strength of the relevant resolution adopted by this international organization. Besides, the international aspect of the Cyprus question should be considered at an international conference, the convening of which has been repeatedly urged by the Soviet Union, and effective and dependable international safeguards should be instituted.   □

Cheddi Jagan

General Secretary of the People's Progressive Party of Guyana

Because the Soviet people have built an advanced socialist society and are confidently advancing to communism, the prestige of Marxism-Leninism has grown. Consequently, more and more people the world over are looking to it as a solution to their own problems and for the fulfillment of their aspirations.

In the English-speaking Caribbean area with predominantly colonial and neo-colonial rule and bourgeois ideology, Marxist-Leninist ideas are gaining ground despite the fact that in many territories scientific-socialist and progressive books, pamphlets and periodicals are banned. Capital and goods are permitted to move freely in the territories comprising the Caribbean Common Market, but Communists find obstacles placed against their free movement.

But Marxist-Leninist ideas cannot be barred. It is easier to stop tomorrow than to stop communism.

However, we must combine revolutionary confidence and optimism with vigilance. Our enemies have become more cunning. Comrade Brezhnev has rightly warned about revisionism of Marxism-Leninism. Maoism, Trotskyism, Marcusism, New Leftism and other currents, though posing in revolutionary garb, are distortions which sow ideological confusion and thus objectively aid imperialism and capitalism.

We must also guard against the denial of the general laws of scientific socialism, attempted on the basis of particularism and exceptionalism. Exponents of "African socialism" failed to support the MPLA and lined up on the same side with imperialism.

Experience has demonstrated that under revisionism short-term opportunist gains can lead to long-term losses to the working class movement and degeneration into petty-bourgeois nationalism.

The CPSU has also relentlessly pursued the Leninist foreign policy of peaceful coexistence, working for detente and disarmament. This determination has resulted in advances on many fronts in keeping with the Peace Program adopted by the CPSU 24th Congress. If the Soviet proposal of a ten per cent cutback in defense spending by all the states in the United Nations Security Council is accepted the beneficiaries would be particularly the developing countries.

Ever since the Soviet Union's birth, history has recorded its consistent and · incomparable practice of lending moral solidarity and material assistance to peoples the world over struggling for freedom, justice, peace and social progress. By the CPSU's resolute commitment to the lofty principles of proletarian internationalism, the Soviet Union is rightly regarded as a true friend and ally of "third world" countries, living proof of which is expressed, within more recent times, in the victory of Vietnam, the emergence of Bangladesh and the successes presently scored by the MPLA of Angola. □

Mamadi Keita

Member of the Political Bureau of the Central Committee of the Democratic Party of Guinea, Government Minister

The 25th Congress is taking place at a time when Africa is living through a stormy phase of its history. In Angola, international reaction, acting wilfully and stupidly, flying in the face of reality and defying the will of the Angolan people, vainly tries to maintain the position of an omnipotent master. The dark forces of reaction, international imperialism, fascism, racism, apartheid, have joined together to block the irresistible process of the complete liberation of Africa, which has been oppressed, exploited and tortured by these bloodthirsty vampires for too long. These forces would like to deal a mortal blow to the progressive countries of Africa, to crush the will of the African people for independence and weaken their fighting spirit. They are trying to arouse sympathy on all sides, slandering the real friends of the African people. But Africa has fully awakened and matured. Today it knows better than anyone else who are its real enemies and who its real friends.

The imperialist, fascist forces, racists and supporters of Apartheid—all these liars with their poisoned tongues are spreading fables that the USSR and revolutionary Cuba are trying to procure bases and get a foothold in Africa for strategic reasons. The USSR and Cuba need no apologists for their actions. Revolutionary Africa will answer for them. Let the imperialists and racists explain their actions.

The help of the socialist countries and in particular the help of the USSR and Cuba are wholly selfless and completely in accord with the methods and principles of socialist internationalism. More than that, it must be said that the people of Angola, their lawful government, asked them for this help. In the name of the people of Guinea, its Party and its government and its respected leader Akhmed Sekou Touré, our delegation would like to express our gratitude to all the socialist countries and other progressive forces, and first of all to the Soviet Union and Cuba, for their great help to Africa.

The situation today is completely clear. On the one side, international imperialism, its allies and lackeys who know very well that the establishment of a progressive and independent Angola is a powerful factor in the development and victory of the liberation struggle in Namibia, Zimbabwe and South Africa; and on the other side the revolutionary and progressive countries of Africa and all the progressive forces in the world which are trying to make an end to colonialism and foreign aggression.

The people of Guinea are firmly in the same ranks with their brothers from Angola on all fronts of the struggle—political, diplomatic, economic and military.   □

Harilaos Florakis

First Secretary of the Central Committee of the Communist
Party of Greece

In our country, after the collapse of the dictatorship of the colonels, under-lings of the USA, there is an upsurge of the popular, democratic movement which is led by the Communists, and which sees its goals in struggle for national independence, liberation from US domination, democratization of the country and for decent living conditions.

As a result of transition from the cold war to detente, more favorable conditions are being created for consolidating peace and cooperation among peoples, as well as for the struggle waged by our people.

At the same time, the imperialists, NATO and internal reaction, using the allegation of a "communist menace" as a cover, intensify their onslaught against democracy and steer the Greek government to the right, to a more reactionary course. They go to all lengths to drag our country back into the NATO military organization, and to convert Cyprus into a springboard for attack against socialist and Arab countries.

These intrigues, which form an integral part of the policy of imperialism as a whole against the forces of progress and socialism, are openly supported by the CPC Maoist leaders. Characteristically, in our country anti-Sovietism—this major ideological weapon of the imperialists—manifests itself mainly in the form of well-known accusations and lies inspired by the Chinese leaders. Two or three Maoist groupings in our country, which are at loggerheads with one another, see the main danger in our Party and in the Soviet Union, and not in US imperialism or NATO.

The CPG could withstand all persecutions, successfully oppose hostile ideologies and constantly be in the vanguard of the people's and national struggle only because it kept its loyalty to the Marxist-Leninist teaching on the leading role of the working class, and Lenin's teaching on the party of a new type.

Our people successfully withstood all trials thanks to the invaluable support of socialist countries, first and foremost, the Soviet Union, and the international communist and working class movement. The unity of the Communist and Workers' parties is a great material and moral force. The coordinated efforts of the enemy can and must be counteracted by the Communist and Workers' parties which are guided by a single theory—the invincible theory of Marxism-Leninism, and which oppose world imperialism with a jointly worked out strategy.   □

Representative, Communist Party of the Philippines

L earning from its long experience of excessive dependence on foreign imperialism, which only aggravates its problems, particularly under conditions of deepening crisis of world capitalism, the Philippines is beginning to take measured steps towards greater identification with the non-aligned group of countries—ASEAN nations in particular—and their struggle for a new international economic order. It has established diplomatic relations with eleven socialist countries, and is taking steps to formalize diplomatic relations with the Soviet Union. While its economy continues to be heavily linked with foreign monopolists, its new policy of national and collective self-reliance tends towards greater political and economic independence.

Responding to the call of President Marcos for national unity in pursuit of his new policy of self-reliance, the PKP, in line with its policy, decided to cease its armed struggle and achieved an agreement with the government resulting in its legalization as an organization, as well as legalization of its associated mass movements and the release of its political prisoners. They are supporting the agrarian reforms and the shift in foreign policy of the government, as well as other progressive reforms, but oppose all measures against the interests of the working people and those tending to strengthen foreign monopoly domination of the country. Simultaneously, the PKP is popularizing its program for a democratic, independent national development of the Philippines.

Despite the limitations of martial rule on its mobility, enemy harassments and other difficulties, the PKP is pursuing its policy of working and struggling with the masses of working people, and extending its contacts with other patriotic and democratic forces, within and outside the government. It seeks to forge militant working-class unity, cement the worker-peasant alliance, and create the broadest front of progressive, democratic and patriotic forces. It is determined to arrest the advance of reaction, supported by foreign monopoly and abetted by ultra-Left adventurism, and pursue a national-democratic program, involving profound structural transformations, which could lead to a non-capitalist path of development and eventually to socialism.   □

Gaston Plissonier

Member of the Political Bureau
and Secretary of the Central Committee
of the French Communist Party

Dear comrades, a deep crisis has hit our country. It is not a classical economic crisis; it is a global crisis that has spread to all the spheres of national life. It is the crisis of the capitalist system. That is why our Party tells the working people that society must be reshaped and that the way to socialism should be taken resolutely.

It is this aim that was the focus of attention at the recent 22nd FCP Congress. Our Party at the Congress offered the people a democratic road to socialism which is in accord with the conditions in our country and of our time. This is a path of deep-going economic and political reforms which are aimed at eliminating the domination of capitalist monopolies.

Naturally, this socialism—relying on the principles of scientific socialism—will have the specific features of our country. It will be socialism of France's colors. In this way, for example, the various parties, attracted by socialism, will take part in building socialism on the basis of equal rights and duties.

In order to win the difficult battles that we shall have to fight against the big bourgeoisie at every stage, we regard as necessary the existence of a powerful movement of the majority of our people, with the alliance of left parties being its pivot. Even today the working class plays the part of vanguard, the part of a motive force in the struggle for democratic changes and socialism. Tomorrow it will represent the decisive force of the working people's representative power, which will guide the building of new society.

Imperialism, which is forced to retreat, nevertheless continues its dangerous intrigues. A proof of this is the policy of the French Government. In point of fact, it has reinstated our country in NATO, favors the hegemonistic designs of West German imperialism, takes no part in any negotiations on disarmament and declares that it is ready to abolish our national independence within the framework of a military-political bloc of a "little Europe" of the trusts.

Our Party vigorously fights against this policy, which is prompted by fear of the rising working class and democratic movement and by a desire to preserve the social and political status quo at any price. In these conditions, we raise still higher the banner of independence and national sovereignty and the right of our people to freely decide their own destiny.

Dear comrades, the firmness with which we defend the cause of our working class and our people, our independence of judgment and action, will never lead us astray from our internationalist duty. At the same time we believe, as was pointed out at the 1969 international meeting, that the existence of some differences between communist parties must not in any way interfere with the joint struggle for common aims.

Close ties of fraternity and solidarity bind the French Communist Party with the Communist Party of the Soviet Union. Steeled in hard tests, they are based on two inseparable principles—the principle of proletarian internationalism and the principle of independence. We strive to strengthen them consistently, because we are aware that by doing so we serve the interests of peace and socialism.

Friendship between our peoples is deeply rooted. The working class and the people of France do not forget the great sacrifices and the decisive contribution made by the Soviet people to routing Hitler's Nazism. They highly appreciate the gigantic achievements of socialism made since the October Revolution. □

Jesus Faria

General Secretary of the Communist Party of Venezuela

Positive changes are taking place in the world. In Venezuela, too, there are certain changes, although they do not proceed as rapidly as we would like them to. In Venezuela the extraction of iron ore and oil, of which we have plenty, today is in the hands of the state. The government firmly supports the people of Panama in the struggle to retrieve the Canal Zone. In OPEC Venezuela champions just prices for oil. As for Latin-American integration, including economic integration and in particular the Latin-American economic system, our present government also pursues a course which clashes with the policy of the imperialist circles of the United States.

The Communist Party of Venezuela opposes such measures of the government as run counter to the people's aspirations, and criticizes them, but we always support the government unhesitatingly when it comes to defending the national interests of the country from the encroachments of imperialism and countering its policy of pressure and intimidation.

Dear Soviet Comrades, the statement by your Congress on solidarity with political prisoners and victims of persecution by the fascist and reactionary regimes is an important manifestation of true internationalism. I myself have spent many years in prison, and the solidarity of the peoples throughout the world, and particularly of the Soviet people, was always of great help to me. ☐

Franklin Irizarry

Deputy General Secretary, Puerto Rican Communist Party*

Someone has said that detente means class collaboration. Nothing could be falser. Those who speak of war as a means of speeding up the revolutionary process are, in the last analysis, the allies of imperialism.

For the Communists of Puerto Rico, the peace policy of the Soviet Union has very great significance, and we do everything possible to make it widely known. The Maoists have attempted to carry on activities on our island, poisoning the minds of the youth. But the Maoists now find themselves in a difficult position. They could in no way justify the position of Peking in relation to Angola—a position coinciding with that of the imperialists and the South African racists.

We should like to declare here our firm support of the Marxist-Leninist policy of proletarian internationalism followed by the CPSU. We cannot understand how it is possible now, at the end of the 20th century, to reject internationalism, which Marx and Engels considered a powerful weapon of international working class unity.

In Puerto Rico we have been fighting for national independence since 1868, when our first republic was proclaimed. The Spanish armies crushed the patriots at that time, but the struggle has not ceased. In 1898 US marines invaded Puerto Rico and to this day Puerto Rico remains a colony of US imperialism. Our island is a US military fortress, a base for aggression against the Dominican Republic, Cuba, Venezuela, Panama and other Latin American countries.

Our Party carries on the struggle under difficult conditions: actually it is in a semi-legal position. Today our country is undergoing an economic crisis which

---

* Felix Ojeda, General Secretary of the Puerto Rican Communist Party at the time of the 25th Congress, died on April 21 following an illness. In May, the Party's Central Committee elected Franklin Irizarry General Secretary.

is the consequence of our dependence on the US economy. Some of the largest multinational imperialist monopolies, including big oil, chemical and pharmaceutical plants which poison the air and water of our island, have branches on our soil. Moreover, our workers are paid only a third as much as US workers, although the cost of living in Puerto Rico is 25 per cent higher than in the United States. Forty per cent of our working force is unemployed.

In these days while we are in the land of Lenin, we see how much has been done by your people to respond worthily to the 25th CPSU Congress. We want to express our deepest admiration for all that you have shown us in so short a time, for all that you have taught us. And we shall take back to our native land this knowledge, and the love of your great people who have received us like their own sons. □

Nicolas Chaoui

General Secretary, Central Committee of the Lebanese Communist Party

In assessing the nature of the conflict in Lebanon, we have proceeded from the existence of two main opposing forces in our part of the world: the Arab national-liberation movement, on the one hand, and local reaction, Israel and imperialism, on the other. In stoking the fire of war, Lebanese reactionary forces served as an instrument for carrying out the US-Israeli plan which is aimed, in the final count, at defeating Palestinian resistance and destroying the other detachments of the Arab liberation movement; these forces therefore wanted to enforce the US version of a settlement, ignoring the problem of the Palestinian people, and to prepare conditions for continuing Israeli aggression.

Lebanese reactionary forces, which for five years had resisted in vain the rising wave of the popular movement, began to increase the scale of armed clashes. In these conditions, with armed action being taken against the Palestinian resistance and the progressive patriotic movement, we had no choice but to take up arms as well.

We have always insisted, and still do, that a political balance be established in the government and in the armed forces, and that reforms necessary for improving the situation and normalizing life in the country be introduced. We are for banning force as a means of settling disputes, and for rectifying the consequences of the civil war.

That is the only correct path towards ensuring peace in our country and healing its deep wounds.

At the same time we are convinced that there can be no peace in Lebanon and in our part of the world in general until Israel has withdrawn its troops from all the occupied Arab lands, and until the Palestinian people have been given the opportunity to return home and set up their own national state.

We regard the Soviet Union as the chief ally of the Lebanese people and all the Arab peoples, and as the mainstay of a just settlement in our part of the world based on the complete withdrawal of the aggressor's armies from all the occupied Arab territories and ensuring the Palestinian people its national rights. □

Yusuf Dadoo

Chairman of the South African Communist Party

This jubilee Congress marks yet another milestone in the life of a Party with a record, unequalled in history, of advancing mankind's struggle against the tyranny of exploitation and for a life of peace and plenty.

The policy of detente is inseparable from the struggles of the oppressed for freedom and national liberation. A lasting peace and the elimination of all possibilities of world or regional armed struggles can only be finally achieved when all peoples are rid of the burden of imperialist domination. That is why the glorious victories in the recent period by the peoples of Vietnam, Mozambique, Cambodia, Laos, Guinea-Bissau and Angola are historic blows for world peace as well as for national liberation. The role which your Party played in each of these victories is in the best tradition of proletarian internationalism. It underlines once again the now historic reality that imperialism no longer has a monopoly of power and that those struggling for liberation are now doing so with fraternal support of a strong and powerful socialist world.

The Maoist clique no longer even pretends to hide its collaboration with imperialism and the world's most extreme reaction. The people of Africa will never forget its criminal intervention in Angola on the side of Vorster racist forces, the CIA and the local representatives of imperialism—Holden Roberto and Jonas Savimbi.

In Southern Africa the defeat of Portuguese colonialism, and the events which followed, have opened up new and exciting possibilities for all the liberation forces. The political and physical conditions which have emerged for the pursuit of the struggle to destroy racism and foreign rule, are more favorable now than ever before in history. The perspective of a Zimbabwe under majority rule and a Namibia which is free and independent is immediately attainable.

In imperialism's most important citadel—South Africa itself—the situation has become progressively less favorable for the survival of racist supremacy. Vorster is no longer cushioned by states hostile to the liberation forces. The victories of our brother fighters in former Portuguese colonies have demonstrated to the mass of our people the urgency and feasibility of striking successfully at the racist regime. There can be no compromise with racism and imperialist domination. Our Party in alliance with the African National Congress which is heading the liberation struggle in South Africa will pursue with relentless and grim determination the struggle to rid our country of white supremacy and win people's power.   □

Luis Carlos Prestes

General Secretary of the Central Committee of the Brazilian Communist Party

In trying to justify their crimes, the US imperialists and Brazilian reactionaries continue their slanderous accusations against the international communist movement and the Communist Party of the Soviet Union. This, however, evokes growing admiration and affection for the Soviet people on the part of the working people of Brazil, all the patriotic and democratic forces of our country. We never forget that it was the Soviet Union that suffered the greatest losses in the struggle against fascist aggression; we remember that humanity was rid of the horrors of fascism first and foremost owing to the heroism of Soviet soldiers and the entire Soviet people.

Figures showing the achievements of the Soviet people in economy, plans for further raising the standards of living and social development are the plainest and the most convincing proof of the indisputable superiority and historic inevitability of the socialist system to the peoples in capitalist countries, who suffer from the deepening crisis, when poverty and famine enter the homes of tens of millions of unemployed.

Your successes give us, Brazilian revolutionaries and Communists, a new powerful weapon which helps us in our everyday explanatory work, in the hard struggle to develop political awareness and cohesion of the working people. It is much easier to conduct this work already today, owing to the successes of the policy of detente which deprives the Brazilian reactionaries of their last arguments, making outdated and useless their anti-communist outcries concerning a "Soviet menace" and world communism.

But we are aware that the US imperialists have not given up their evil schemes. The reactionaries are aware that is is impossible to do away with our Party and therefore they try to terrorize the Party's leaders. During the last twenty months, ten members of the Central Committee of our Party were arrested, subjected to torture and killed in the dungeons of the Brazilian military. Thousands of patriots, Communists and non-Party people are languishing in the reactionaries' prisons.

But the Brazilian people led by its courageous working class and its communist vanguard will crush the forces of reaction.

We struggle for socialism because we know that only in conditions of socialistsociety is it possible to fully resolve the problems facing our people, to establish a genuinely democratic system which, in Lenin's words, will be millions of times more democratic than any bourgeois democracy.   □

Yumzhagiin Tsedenbal

First Secretary, Central Committee, Mongolian People's
Revolutionary Party. President, Presidium of the Great
People's Khural of the Mongolian People's Republic

There still exist forces trying to prevent by every means the relaxation of international tension, to return the world to the "cold war" times. These forces are partnered by the Maoist leadership of China, which has elevated anti-Sovietism and anti-socialism to the rank of its official policy. The current Peking leaders regard the country of the October Revolution, the great Soviet Union, as their chief enemy and act openly as advocates of a new world war. Ganging up more and more with anti-Communists of different stripes and developing ties with the reactionary regimes and racist-fascist cliques, they are waging a fierce struggle against detente, pursuing a great-power hegemonistic, expansionist line in foreign policy, carrying out intensified preparation for war and militarization of all the areas of the life of Chinese society, and creating an atmosphere of distrust and emnity between states.

Allow me to assure you, comrades, that together with the Soviet Union and the other fraternal socialist countries, together with all peaceloving forces the Mongolian People's Republic will go on fighting persistently to deepen detente, to turn the Asian continent into a zone of lasting peace and security of the peoples.

The past five years have been a period of deepening and perfection of all-round cooperation among the fraternal countries of socialism, of a further rallying of the ranks of the world communist movement on the principles of Marxism-Leninism. It should be specially stressed that the CPSU, which possesses the richest experience of building a new society and performs the role of trail-blazer in the struggle for communism, contributes decisively to the growth of the might of the world socialist system, to the consolidation of its international positions and the enhancement of the influence of socialism on the course of world development.

Allow me to express deep-felt cordial gratitude to the great Leninist Communist Party of the Soviet Union, the Soviet Government and all Soviet people for consistent internationalism and many-sided assistance in our building of a new life, for big-heartedness and the fraternal feeling of fellowship, for the bold building of the highroad to a radiant future.   □

Shripad Amrit Dange

Chairman of the National Council, Communist Party of India

Our country, which has become a special target of US imperialism, is passing through an extremely critical and complex situation with its contradictory features. The struggle against imperialism and reaction, which want to reverse India's development in a counterrevolutionary direction, has become unprecedentedly sharp. Last year, the rightist and fascist forces made a diabolic bid for the seizure of power. They used the parliamentary forums and democratic freedoms to build up a violent agitation to "destabilize" the situation. Taking advantage of the economic crisis and exploiting the discontent of the people they raised demagogic slogans and incited assassination, sabotage and other acts of violence and anarchy.

The main reason for this ferocious attack is that during the recent period, the government of India undertook significant progressive measures in response to popular demand. After nationalizing banking and general insurance, the government nationalized coal mining and a number of textile mills. By an Act of Parliament, the privileges, purses and pensions of the feudal princes were abolished. Then the government took over the oil industry and strengthened the public sector of the national economy. It also made some moves against the multinationals in the drug and chemical industry. And above all, it carried out several progessive amendments in the constitution of the country aimed at weakening the positions of monopoly and feudal property interests.

Hence Right Reaction acted with such fury. Their aim was to push our country away from the policy of peace and nonalignment, away from friendship with the Soviet Union and other socialist countries and take it into the imperialist camp. They sought to destroy not only democracy but also the unity and independence of the nation.

The Right's bid for power has of course been foiled by the bold, preemptive actions Prime Minister Indira Gandhi took by declaring national emergency. But the sources from which such a threat arises still continue. However, some measures have been taken by the government to fight some of the glaring features of the economic crisis. The Prime Minister has announced the 20-point economic program which will, if it is faithfully implemented, not only improve the living conditions of the down-trodden masses particularly in the rural areas, but will also be a blow to reaction. The struggle against reaction's social and economic base is steadily developing in our country.

Our Party which has been in the forefront of the fight against Right Reaction and fascism is supporting all these measures and is working for uniting the patriotic and democratic forces, particularly the toiling masses, to safeguard our independence and take the nation forward to radical social and economic transformations.

The broad masses including many following the ruling party are more and more realizing that the capitalist path cannot solve their basic problems. I am therefore happy to inform you that the membership of our Party this year has risen to six hundred thousand.   □

Gisele Rabesahala

General Secretary, Independence Congress Party of Madagascar

We know that the recent successes won by the national liberation movement are the outcome of the heroic struggle of the peoples of the developing states. However, we would like to emphasize the fact that these successes have been scored in a healthier international climate and in the conditions of detente, which have come about as a result of the untiring efforts of the Soviet Union and the CPSU.

After having been subjected to colonial and neocolonial oppression by French imperialism for 80 years, our country is today undergoing positive changes which are an expression of the people's striving for independence and complete liberation. On December 21, 1975, ninety-five per cent of our population expressed their support for the program of Didier Ratsiraka, President of the Democratic Republic of Madagascar and President of the Supreme Revolutionary Council, and have thus chosen the road of development leading to socialism.

The program contains the following declaration: "For the people of Madagascar, a socialist revolution is the only possible way towards accelerated independent socioeconomic and harmonious cultural and humane development."

At present the implementation of the program of a socialist revolution in the Democratic Republic of Madagascar involves a series of economic, social and political measures aimed at overcoming the social and economic domination of French imperialism and laying the foundations of a new society that will be free of all kinds of oppression and exploitation of man by man. As the program points out, "this choice made by the Malagasy people of the socialist path of development is also their contribution to the cause of defending peace throughout the world.''

The importance of the choice of the socialist path of development becomes still greater when one considers that in this part of the Indian Ocean imperialism, faced with the upsurge of the liberation struggle in South Africa, Namibia, and Zimbabwe, is using the racist regime of the South African Republic not only to enslave African peoples, but also to preclude a progressive orientation of independent African countries.   □

Todor Zhivkov

First Secretary of the Central Committee of the Bulgarian Communist Party, Chairman of the State Council of the People's Republic of Bulgaria

The positive shifts in the intricate complex of relations in the present-day world are the result of the joint efforts of the countries of the socialist community and the international working class movement, the efforts of the peaceloving peoples. They are the result of the actions of many diverse forces, including realistically minded politicians in the capitalist countries. However I cannot but express here as well the deep conviction of our people that the greatest, decisive service in strengthening peace in Europe and the world over has been performed by the Soviet people and the Communist Party of the Soviet Union.

Ever since the Soviet Union came into existence the enemies of socialism have been at pains to eclipse the radiance of the great Soviet land. Today, trying to outdo one another in anti-Soviet propaganda, the slanderers have struck up a new song, bemoaning the freedom of the Soviet man, the democracy of Soviet society. Monopolists and latifundists, surviving war criminals and their successors, fascist gangs and Israeli aggressors are shedding tears.

Today it is clearer than ever that the Soviet Union is the first state in history of genuine democracy and humanism. Power in the Soviet Union really belongs to the people. All the material and intellectual values created by the people belong to them. People breathe freely from one end of the vast Soviet country to another.

Today it is clearer than ever that if peace prevails in the world, if newly-free countries reject dependence on imperialism and embark upon the road of social progress, if the possibility of peaceful transition from capitalism to socialism opens up before some peoples, all this is in a vast, decisive measure due to the fact that there exist in the world the Soviet Union, the world socialist community.

We want to recall once again from this rostrum words spoken by an immortal son of our people, Georgi Dmitrov, words which remain valid today: The attitude towards the Soviet Union is the touchstone of revolutionarism and internationalism, the watershed between the forces of progress and the forces of reaction.

It is an elementary truth that the force and influence of the communist movement lie in its unity and cohesion. And in our time as well real unity and real cohesion are only possible on the basis of Marxism-Leninism and proletarian internationalism.

Under the banner of Marxism-Leninism and proletarian internationalism victory was scored in the revolutionary struggle of the workers and peasants of Russia. Under the banner of Marxism-Leninism and proletarian internationalism the world socialist community came into being and is developing and gaining strength. Under this banner the great army of Communists of all the world took shape and has been hardened. Under this banner the army of Communists is rallying broad masses of the people, waging a successful struggle against imperialism and reaction, overcoming difficulties and victoriously marching forward.   □

Nicolay Ceausescu

General Secretary of the Romanian Communist Party, President of the Socialist Republic of Romania

Mankind is living through an epoch of profound revolutionary social and national transformations. An important role is being played in these changes by the socialist countries (and I want to note the considerable contribution of the Soviet Union), by their achievements in socioeconomic development, their foreign policy of peace and cooperation. A positive influence is exerted also by the policy of the young independent states, by the struggle of the peoples who ever more forcefully express their will to decide their own destiny freely, without any outside interference, by the revolutionary movement of the working class, by the actions of other democratic and progressive forces all over the world. A characteristic feature of our epoch is a new stage of the general crisis of capitalism extending to all spheres of socioeconomic life, the growing aggravation of contradictions in the capitalist world.

All these changes have paved the way for a new policy in the world arena, the policy of detente. It should be borne in mind, however, that there exist considerable reactionary forces capable of jeopardizing this policy and world peace.

Proceeding from these realities, Romania has pursued, and pursues now, together with the socialist countries, all other peaceloving peoples, and the progressive forces of the world, an active foreign policy, making its concrete contribution to the realization of mankind's striving for security and progress, to the solution of the complex problems of our epoch.

Esteemed comrades, I would like to note from this rostrum the comradely relations existing between the Romanian Communist Party and the Communist Party of the Soviet Union, to express our determination to work in the future as well for the constant development of the friendship, cooperation and solidarity of our Parties.

The Romanian Communist Party develops close bonds of friendship, co-operation and solidarity with all Communist and Workers' parties and acts to strengthen the cohesion of the international communist and working class movement and to help establish a new unity, based on respect for the right of every party independently to shape its political line, revolutionary strategy and tactics, to contribute creatively to the development of Marxism-Leninism, to the enrichment of the theory and practice of the revolution and socialist construction. We are participating actively in the preparation of the conference of European Communist and Workers' parties, wishing to further fruitful and democratic exchange of experience between parties, the consolidation of their solidarity and co-operation.   □

Stane Dolanc

Secretary of the Executive Bureau, Presidium of the
Central Committee of the League of Communists of
Yugoslavia

We attach great importance to cooperation between the LCY and the CPSU. The existing distinctions and peculiarities reflect differences in the ways of development of modern socialism and its practice, as well as the peculiarities of the international position of our countries. They are to be expected and determined historically and socially, and therefore they can on no account be an obstacle to the further all-round development of our relations. This approach is natural and accords with our mutual interests.

We value highly the Soviet Union's contribution to the preservation of world peace and the easing of international tension, to which socialist Yugoslavia too gives maximum possible support.

To become stable, the process of detente must spread to all spheres of international relations and to all regions, with all states participating on an equal footing in the solution of vitally important problems of the present-day world.

The need for a radical change in the existing system of international economic relations is obvious. It is an obvious duty of all developed countries to make— also in their own interests—a contribution to the solution of these problems.

A constant and growing threat to peace is posed by the continued arms race. Unless there is a turn to practical disarmament, and not only control over armaments, even the already achieved results of detente will be called into question.

The struggle of peoples and countries for complete economic and political independence, sovereign and free development, equality and democratic cooperation, for as successful material and cultural progress as possible, acquire ever greater importance in international relations. The policy of nonalignment, which socialist Yugoslavia also pursues, serves precisely these aims. This policy took shape in the struggle against imperialism, all forms of exploitation and domination, in the fight for liberation, development, the overcoming of the division of the world into blocs, for the democratization of international relations and active peaceful coexistence of all nations, for peace and progress.   □

Janos Kadar

First Secretary of the Central Committee of the Hungarian
) Socialist Workers' Party

The foreign policy of the Hungarian People's Republic is clear-cut and widely known. We stand for the multilateral cooperation and coordinated international actions of the socialist countries. We see the basis and guarantee of the peaceful life, untroubled socialist construction and national independence of our people in that our country is a member of the Warsaw Treaty. Of great help in our socialist construction is economic cooperation within the framework of the Council for Mutual Economic Assistance. We are doing all we can to further the realization of the jointly elaborated Comprehensive Program of socialist economic integration.

The attitude towards the Soviet Union is a question of special importance, a question of principle to us. Hungarian-Soviet relations rest on a firm foundation: we are bound together by the common ideas of Marxism-Leninism, communism, proletarian internationalism, by the identity of our vital interests.

Last year the historic Conference on Security and Cooperation in Europe was held in Helsinki. True, the aggressive circles, the "cold warriors" are waging stubborn rearguard battles, launching counterattacks from time to time. But there is no doubt that if the forces which cherish peace and reckon with realities display staunchness in struggle, the Helsinki recommendations will be implemented and will exert their beneficial influence in Europe and in other parts of the world. The socialist countries and the Communist and Workers' parties of the world are in the vanguard of this struggle.

The Hungarian Socialist Workers' Party considers that the principles of socialist patriotism and those of proletarian internationalism are inseparable, and it educates the Communists, the people, the younger generation in this spirit. We condemn national narrow-mindededness, bourgeois nationalism, anti-Sovietism, divisive activities undermining the unity of our movement, and especially their crudest manifestation—Maoism.

Today, when great problems affecting mankind's destinies are being solved, when the forces of progress are scoring ever new successes, when the international communist movement is in an upsurge, when the Communist parties independently shape their policy, tactics and strategy, the responsibility of every individual party has grown. Our Party is convinced that the importance of proletarian internationalism increases in the present epoch, and therefore it is important to develop contacts between Communist and Workers' parties, to strengthen the Marxist-Leninist unity of the international communist movement.   □

Alves Batista

Member of the Political Bureau, Central Committee of the Popular Movement for the Liberation of Angola

The Central Committee of the Popular Movement for the Liberation of Angola (MPLA) sends its heartfelt, revolutionary and fraternal greetings to the 25th Congress of the CPSU and the Soviet people. Their efforts towards the strengthening of peace throughout the world, and their moral, political, and material assistance to the national liberation movement, express their consistent policy of proletarian internationalism. They will never be forgotten by the MPLA and the Angolan people.

The achievement of independence by the peoples of the former Portuguese colonies is striking evidence of the further intensification of the general crisis of capitalism. Thanks to the unbending will of our great and long-suffering people who are fighting under the leadership of their revolutionary vanguard, the MPLA, the course was resolutely set for the declaration of the country's independence on November 11, 1975, and for the establishment of the People's Republic of Angola.

That road was not an easy one. On the eve of our declaration of independence, US imperialism, using the troops of South Africa's fascist regime and other reactionary forces, recklessly unleashed bloody armed aggression against our country in order to seize Luanda, the capital of Angola. The purpose of that diabolical plan was clear: to do away with the MPLA and, on November 11, to place at the helm a reactionary clique of traitors to our national interests.

It was in the midst of those dramatic days that the MPLA addressed its historic appeal to the nation: to take up arms and direct all effort towards the defense against imperialist aggression. In that situation and in spite of the fact that the regular troops of the South African racists and the mercenaries were 20 kilometers from Luanda, the Central Committee of our movement in the person of its devoted leader, Comrade Agostinho Neto, President of the MPLA and of the People's Republic of Angola, performed the heroic act of declaring national independence.

Thus the entire history of our struggle for freedom and the glorious and unforgettable day of November 11 confirm the revolutionary grandeur and the force of proletarian internationalism. The aid of the socialist countries to the Angolan people was timely, effective, vigorous and resolute. The selfless assistance of the countries of the socialist community and the solidarity and support of the progressive forces of Africa and other continents, played a truly decisive role in our victories over the imperialist aggressors.

We shall not mention all the socialist countries which gave and continue to give moral and material support to us. We should like, however, especially to note the disinterested help of the Soviet Union and the courageous practical actions of our Cuban brothers. And we regret that one socialist country acted in unison with imperialism against our people.

Our victory over Portuguese colonialism became possible thanks to the aid of the Soviet Union. Therefore permit me from this high rostrum, once again, to express our respect and gratitude to the Communist Party of the Soviet Union, the Soviet people, and all socialist countries.

At the present time the struggle is continuing in Angola, for final liberation and consolidation of the country. We have inherited an utterly wrecked, plundered and devastated land. The main economic task now is to free the country completely from the grip of the monopolies and to establish fruitful cooperation with all countries throughout the world on the basis of respect for national sovereignty, territorial integrity, non-interference in internal affairs of each other, and mutual advantage. We consider our cooperation with socialist countries of primary importance. As to the political aspect, our urgent task is the strengthening of the organizational structure of our movement and the creation of conditions for the development of the MPLA into a political party based on scientific and revolutionary theory.

We realize that tremendous difficulties lie ahead. We know that imperialism has not yet laid down arms and that it is ready for more adventures. Whatever forms it takes, our people, under the leadership of the MPLA, will smash all reckless imperialist acts of aggression.

We express the most profound feelings of solidarity with all nations fighting for their liberation.   □

Americo Zorrilla

Member of the Political Commission and
Secretariat of the Central Committee
of the Communist Party of Chile

Because of the exceptional importance of this Congress, our Central Committee decided to send one of our leaders from within the country to bring you the fraternal greetings of the Chilean Communists. Our Party would have liked to be represented by our general secretary, Luis Corvalan. But he is in a fascist torture chamber. However, we can assure you that Comrade Corvalan is with us in spirit.

We have been delegated to transmit the gratitude of the Chilean comrades for your fraternal solidarity. We shall always be thankful to you for immediately breaking relations with the fascist regime, which, together with the imperialists, bears the responsibility for the murder of President Allende and innumerable crimes against the people. The solidarity shown by your parties, by the countries of the socialist community and by all progressive, democratic forces in the world, have inspired the working class and the people of Chile in the struggle against the fascist dictatorship.

Once again the people of Chile have been convinced that both in grief and joy they can count on the friendship of the Soviet Union. Life has confirmed that our Party made no mistake when its founder, Recabarren, gave a high evaluation of the historic role of the Soviet Union and declared that anti-Sovietism was one of the worst forms of anti-Communism.

The report sums up the struggle of the CPSU in the international arena against the aggressive forces of imperialism. We welcome the efforts for the further development of detente. The rage of the fascists when they are confronted with each successful step is evidence that this course answers the needs of the progressive forces.

International solidarity is the most important factor for the victorious fight of the people. Chile has felt deeply the strength of international solidarity. At the same time, by the example of our own country and of Angola we are convinced that the Maoist leaders have retreated from the principle of proletarian internationalism and joined the ranks of the American imperialists, the racists, the fascist junta, on whose hands is the blood of thousands of Communists and other patriots.

Socialist Cuba has shown that sooner or later the people of Latin America will triumph. This conviction was confirmed by the extraordinarily significant meeting of the Communist Parties of our continent in Havana, and the first Congress of the Communist Party of Cuba. The policy of the most reactionary circles of the United States, directed toward setting up the bloody fascist regime of Pinochet in Chile, and similar regimes in Uruguay, Brazil, Bolivia and other countries, cannot stop the liberation movement. The mass of the people, and first of all the working class, is fighting for the overthrow of the fascist junta, for democracy, in order to clear the way for revolution against imperialism and oligarchy.

The organization of the Popular Unity government was a great victory for the working people of Chile and the whole people. Deep social changes took place in the three years this government was in power; the creative activities of the workers reached an unheard-of scale. The fascists will never be able to wipe all that from the memory of the Chilean people.

Our Party does not hide the mistakes it made in that period. We are studying them thoroughly in the spirit of criticism and self-criticism, drawing the necessary conclusions from both achievements and mistakes. At the same time we are listening attentively to the opinions about the Chilean experience in the international communist and working class movement. The union of communists and socialists, the coalition of the parties of Popular Unity, continues to exist. We are taking the course of creating a patriotic anti-fascist front. Therefore we are very glad that the delegation from the Socialist Party of Chile, headed by its general secretary Carlos Altamirano, is present at the Congress.

The main strength of the anti-fascist resistance is in the working class. Coming out against the policy of dictatorship, the working class is defending not only its own interests. The interests of all the social groups suffering from fascism summon them to struggle. It is widely known what cruel repression by the fascists is caused by any manifestation of dissatisfaction, any act of resistance. Nonetheless, in Chile not a single day passes without struggle. It takes different forms. Meetings where the workers voice their demands, strikes that restore their confidence in their own strength, create conditions for a new rise in the resistance movement. The ideological struggle and underground propaganda are expanding.

Two and a half years after the coup, not only is the junta completely isolated in the international arena but it lacks the slightest support from the masses inside the country. The Christian Democrats, the Catholics and other church groups and the petit and middle bourgeoisie, which in their time supported the reactionary junta, are now allied to a certain degree with the Popular Unity parties' opposition. Many of the military are unwilling to play the role of butchers. The masses of the people see that anti-facist unity is the most urgent question.

We believe that we have not yet done enough and are trying to activize further the opposition of the masses. We explain to the people the necessity of fighting still more decisively for unity as the most important condition for victory, and that in the struggle against the dictatorship, the working class should play its own role in solving the serious problems that face Chilean society.

It is now clear that Pinochet will not be able to retain power. All the crimes, torture and concentration camps will not save fascism. The people will overthrow and conquer it!   □

Nguyen Thi Binh

Member of the Central Committee of the National
Liberation Front of South Vietnam, Foreign Minister of the
Provisional Revolutionary Government*

The Vietnamese people have won a complete victory in our national liberation struggle and are in the springtime of a new era—an era of peace, independence, unity and a socialist Vietnam. While we rejoice endlessly at this great victory and the bright prospects opening before our homeland, the people of South Vietnam are even more overcome with gratitude for the October Revolution—the greatest revolution in the history of humanity, prologue to the victorious struggle for the independence, freedom and happiness of the people of the whole world. With a feeling of love, faith and admiration, the people of South Vietnam constantly follow and rejoice at the wonderful achievements of the fraternal Soviet people in building and defending their homeland and in simultaneously making a gigantic contribution to the struggle of the peoples for peace, national independence, democracy and social progress.

In our long and rigorous struggle to save our homeland from US imperialism, as well as in our present stage of building a new life, the people of South Vietnam constantly draw on the victories of the heroic Soviet people to mobilize our own strength and all-conquering faith. And more than that, the Communist Party, the government and people of the Soviet Union, in a true spirit of the highest internationalism, constantly gave enormously effective help to the Vietnam people, and continue to do so now.

The land of Vietnam, on which no shadow of the aggressor remains, is at peace, and the people of Vietnam, under the deathless banner of Ho Chi Minh and the glorious Party of the Vietnamese working class, have entered with enthusiasm into the new stage of their revolution, the stage of uniting their homeland and building socialism. In one half of Vietnam socialism has already

* Following proclamation of the Socialist Republic of Vietnam on July 2, 1976, Madame Binh is now Education Minister of the unified cabinet.

shown its preeminence. Without the socialist North, acting as our great base of support, South Vietnam could not have won its great victory. Therefore the advance of the whole country to socialism is the most reliable road to the strengthening and development of those victories for which the Vietnamese people were forced to endure such suffering and make such sacrifices.

There are still many difficulties to overcome, remnants of aggressive war and colonialism. But the people and the National Liberation Front of South Vietnam are firmly convinced that the Vietnamese people will achieve new victories in the peaceful construction of their homeland and make an active contribution to the cause of revolutionary struggle, the cause of maintaining peace in Asia and throughout the world. In this we are counting on the same help from the Soviet Union and other socialist countries and all our friends around the world.   □

Jean Pierre Chister-Chicaya

Member of the Special Revolutionary Staff, Member of the Politbureau, Congolese Party of Labor

(Mr. Chister-Chicaya presented greetings from Marien Ngoabi, Chairman of the Central Committee of the Congolese Party of Labor and President of the People's Republic of the Congo, who had expected to be present, but was detained by revolutionary duties.)

We Congolese people highly esteem the role of the great land of Lenin and other socialist countries in the recent victories of the progressive forces of the world and want to take this opportunity to thank warmly Comrades Leonid Ilyich Brezhnev and Fidel Castro, the Soviet and Cuban people and their parties, for their support to the courageous people of Angola, who are fighting under the banner of the MPLA against a broad imperialist, racist and fascist coalition knocked together by American imperialism and the racist regimes in South Africa with the support of their local lackeys.

However, the struggle is far from over and we issue a flaming call from this tribune for still greater unity and solidarity of the socialist countries and all progressive forces, since there exist in the world many zones where fascist dictatorship, racism and apartheid still rage. We must expose before the whole world the strangling of the people of Chile by the Pinochet Junta and demand the immediate and unconditional freedom of Comrade Luis Corvalan.

For the same reason we call attention to the heroic struggles of the peoples of Namibia, Zimbabwe and South Africa against the dictatorship and degradation forced upon them by the racist and fascist regimes of Vorster and Ian Smith.

The People's Republic of Congo makes its own modest contribution to the struggle of all these peoples. In order to strengthen the struggle against imperialism within the country, the Congolese Party of Labor laid the basis for radicalizing the Congolese revolution at an emergency plenary meeting of its Central Committee, December 5-12, 1975.

The movement for radicalization has as its basic aim the reorganization, cleansing and strengthening of the Congolese Party of labor and its mass organizations, the strengthening of the economic struggle in order to tear from the hands of the imperialists the vitally important branches of our economy which remain under their control. Finally, the radicalization movement must lead to the intellectual decolonization of the Congolese who are still too often influenced by West European bourgeois models of culture and especially models of former colonial powers.

This movement is thus a deep-going, long time process, a day-to-day struggle which demands a high degree of vigilance on the part of Congolese revolutionists. The Congolese people are determined to carry on this difficult struggle under the banner of the Congolese Party of Labor in order to deliver telling blows against imperialism. Their victory in this struggle would be a real contribution to the weakening of the imperialist camp.

The highest aim of these struggles waged by progressive forces throughout the world is the final elimination of the exploitation of man by man and the building on our planet of a better world—the world of communism. □

Alvaro Cunhal

General Secretary of the Portuguese Communist Party

A delegation of the Portuguese Communist Party attended the 24th Congress of your Party five years ago. At that time our Party was illegal and was subjected to fierce persecution on the part of the fascist dictatorship. Portugal and the Soviet Union had no diplomatic relations, and friendship between our Parties was in effect the only form of relations between the Portuguese and the Soviet peoples.

Today we are conveying to the 25th CPSU Congress and the whole Soviet people, warm militant greetings from the legal, mass Portuguese Communist Party. For two years our Party has been taking part in the government and playing a decisive role in the implementation of profound democratic reforms in our country. Therefore, we convey to you greetings from a Portugal freed from fascism, from a new, democratic and revolutionary Portugal.

You must know, comrades, that you Soviet Communists are much needed by the working masses in all countries. Unfortunately, a great part of mankind is still under the imperialist yoke. Imperialism is preparing new wars, it is exploiting hundreds of millions of people and wants to perpetuate its reactionary domination.

The very existence of the Soviet Union, your entire activity in building the world's first Communist society, your selfless struggle for peace and security is like sunshine for our planet.

The constant and active solidarity of the Soviet people with the Portuguese people—a solidarity which revealed itself even during the period of fascism—was today warmly expressed in the speech of Leonid Ilyich Brezhnev. Your solidarity arouses deep feelings of gratitude in all the revolutionaries of our country.

Despite the rough and uneven course of the revolutionary process, despite vacillations and contradictions in the organs of power themselves, the Portuguese Revolution has achieved remarkable successes. Extensive freedoms have been won and an end has been put to the colonial war. A positive contribution has been made toward the independence of peoples formerly under the yoke of Portuguese colonialism. The living standards of the working people have been improved. The banks, the key industrial branches and transport have been nationalized. Workers' control has been established and the workers are now actually involved in running hundreds of enterprises. Agrarian reform has begun in vast areas of the country, where after a persistent and courageous struggle the rural workers and petty landowners took over control of almost 1 million hectares (1 hectare=2.47 acres) of land that formerly belonged to the big landowners, and have organized cooperatively run industrial enterprises and farms on these lands. Thereby they made the first heroic steps in reorganizing Portugal's agriculture on new principles—without either exploited or exploiters.

All this is a historic victory of the Portuguese people. And all these are deepgoing, irreversible, democratic changes.

It is true that new difficulties and dangers have recently arisen. Imperialism and world reaction, backing and encouraging the country's reactionary forces, are resorting to all kinds of pressure, blackmail and interference against the Portuguese Revolution.

The Chinese leaders, in their turn, having no wish to establish relations with democratic Portugal, since its government includes Communists, at the same time invite the General Secretary of the reactionary People's Democratic Party to visit China and promote the activity of the Maoist groups in Portugal which are a direct instrument of reaction.

Domestic and international reaction are attacking the Portuguese Communist Party with particular force. And this is not accidental. The Portuguese Communist Party firmly believes that although Portugal is a small country situated in capitalist Europe and a member of NATO, the Portuguese people have full right to choose a sociopolitical regime in keeping with their will.

Rumors are being spread that the Portuguese Communist Party allegedly wanted to seize power by way of revolution, depending on a revolutionary minority only. That of course, is not true. We are not adventurists. We proceed from the laws of scientific socialism and try to convince the broad masses that our policies are correct. But we do not wish to retain the foundation of monopoly capitalism which might again lead Portugal to fascism. Our people suffered enough during the years of fascist power and do not want its yoke around their necks again.

Portugal's reactionary forces, counting on the active support of international reaction, are now trying to solve the country's basic problems in their own interests. They are counting on the policy of anti-Communism and unity with the right carried on by the Socialist Party. The right forces themselves helped bring about the split in the Armed Forces Movement which led to the well-known uprising in November of last year and the defeat of the left wing of the army.

The anti-Communist campaign is taking on an increasingly aggressive and violent character. Our Party's headquarters are being set on fire and blown up. There are some areas in which Communists can operate only under conditions of semi-legality or illegality. Reaction has seized positions in the government apparatus, is demanding the liquidation of our democratic gains and attempting to create conditions for the restoration of the dictatorship.

However, the working class is beating back reaction and again taking the initiative into its own hands. Notwithstanding the complex and difficult situation we continue to have faith that the Portuguese people will guarantee the further development of the democratic process. We are doing everything possible to eliminate the split and to strengthen the MFA and achieve the unity of the armed forces in the name of the defense of democracy and national independence.

We are sparing no efforts for the development of the workers' and peoples' movement, strengthening the trade unions, the peasants' league, for the mobilization of the broadest masses for struggle, for the unity of all Portuguese anti-fascist forces.

We consider that mutual understanding and joint actions by Communists and Socialists are of special importance. Recently such actions have developed on different levels, despite the opposition of some of the leadership of the Socialist Party.

At present our main task is the defense and consolidation of the freedoms and other gains of the revolution. A return to big capital of the nationalized branches of the economy and the enterprises at which workers' control has been established, and the abolition of the agrarian reform would mean restoration of the dictatorship.

The existence of a truly democratic regime in Portugal requires liberation of the country's economy from the domination of the monopolies, big landowners, and imperialism. It is possible to defend, strengthen, and develop freedom and democracy in Portugal only by advancing along the road to socialism.

Despite the wave of anti-Communism, the Portuguese Communist Party already has a membership of more than 100,000 and continues to grow. The strengthening of the Party is the necessary condition for the defense and continuation of the revolution. Democratic Portugal can be built only with the active participation of the Communist Party in all spheres of national life, including the government.

We are inspired and fortified in our struggle by the international solidarity of democratic and progressive forces, the national liberation movement, the fraternal solidarity of the Marxist-Leninist Parties with which we are united in our great international family of the Communists and by the support, belief, and solidarity of the glorious Soviet people.   □

Jason Moyo

President of the Foreign Administration of the African National Council of Zimbabwe

The invitation to our delegation to attend the CPSU Congress is further evidence of the broadening and deepening of friendly relations between the people of the Soviet Union, its leader, the great Communist Party founded by the immortal Lenin, and the people of Zimbabwe, who are carrying on their struggle today under the banner of the African National Council headed by Comrade Joshua Nkomo, from whom I also bring greetings.

The Soviet Union, the world's first socialist government, is justifiably called the bulwark of socialism. You are laying the road to the world of the future for all countries still languishing under the yoke of capitalism. You have been delivered from the horrors of capitalist exploitation because in your country the workers are at the head of the government and run production themselves. Due to the policy of the Communist Party, all people are equal. And now you are firmly defending all your gains in the battles for freedom, developing the economy of your country, pursuing a policy of solidarity with the peoples of the whole world fighting for their national liberation and real independence.

The people of Zimbabwe are among those whom your country is aiding in their struggles for national liberation. In our war of liberation we know that your constant support is due to the policy of the CPSU. We know that everything received from you has been created by the devoted work of the

Soviet people. You can understand therefore why your Congress means so much to us. In the name of the Zimbabwe people, I express our deep thanks to the Communist Party of the Soviet Union for its solidarity in our struggle for national liberation. Please understand that this is not just a polite expression on our part, but signifies our high regard for the relations existing between us which we wish to develop and strengthen.

The liberation of Zimbabwe, Namibia and South Africa is an especially complex task, considering the global strategy and economic interests of NATO in this area. NATO spares no efforts to hang on to its last foothold in Africa. But the fighting people of these lands are fully determined to end racism and oppression in their lands forever.

We rejoice at the victory in Angola. At the same time we must not forget that the fight for the final liberation of South Africa demands still greater efforts. □

William Kashtan

General Secretary of the Communist Party of Canada

We believe the 25th Congress, like the 24th, will have outstanding significance due to the new initiatives of the Soviet Union in the struggle for peace and its efforts to make detente irreversible and extend it to the military sphere. Detente, despite the alarums of some people, has not led to the ending or weakening of the struggles of the anti-imperialist and democratic forces against imperialism and reaction, but on the contrary has made new successes possible.

Today, under the deepening economic crisis in the capitalist world, the communist countries have the obligation—more, the duty—of taking up the problem of democracy with new energy, not in order to retreat under the attacks of capitalism but to expose the false claims of those who pretend to be defenders of democracy. There must not be the slightest retreat in the defense of socialist democracy. Any tendency to appease the anti-Soviet and anti-Communist circles in this respect can only result in great damage to our cause.

Our Party condemns the Maoists and their splitting, anti-Soviet and anti-Communist policy. It is well known that the Maoists describe themselves as fighters against imperialism and defenders of the "third world." It is now clear to all that they are rather the allies of imperialism and act as its stooges in their attacks on the real national liberation movements. Whether one speaks of Angola, Chile, Western Europe or West Germany—everywhere the Maoists are found in the same camp with the most reactionary forces of imperialism, including the South African racists. The struggle for peace and against imperialism cannot succeed without a constant struggle against Maoism.

Our Party believes that the present situation requires still greater cooperation and unity among the Communist and Workers' Parties, and the strengthening of proletarian internationalism. We cannot agree with the viewpoint which advocates its weakening. Our Party has always sought to combine patriotism and internationalism in such a way that they complement and strengthen each other. For that reason we support every measure directed toward tightening the unity of the Communist and Workers' Parties, and censure policies and actions undermining the international unity of these parties. That is why, as before, we stand for the convocation of an international meeting of Communist and Workers' Parties.

Our Party welcomes every step toward strengthening the economic, cultural and scientific exchanges and ties between Canada and the Soviet Union. We see in this as well as in the development of trade relations between our countries not only an additional guarantee of jobs for Canadian workers, but also an important factor for strengthening Canadian independence in the light of attacks by US imperialism.   □

Meir Vilner

General Secretary of the
Central Committee of the Communist Party of Israel

Together with all progressive forces throughout the world we are inspired by the growing might of the Soviet Union, by its tremendous successes in economic development and improvement of the Soviet people's living standards and its achievements in the fields of science and culture. This is a decisive factor for changing the relation of forces in the world in favor of socialism and the successful struggle for peace, democracy, national and social liberation and socialism.

We regard one's attitude toward the Soviet Union as a question of principle and paramount importance. Whatever form it takes, anti-Sovietism damages the struggle of the working people and of all forces which are opposing imperialism and advocating peace and socialism.

Dear Comrades, in our country frantic anti-Sovietism has become a banner of the ruling Zionist circles. They are selling their country for dollar handouts and are sacrificing our young people on the altar of war. As Communists and Israeli patriots, we resolutely condemn the anti-Soviet campaign of the Israeli government and Zionist leaders. We are indignant at the shameful anti-Soviet farce which they recently staged in Brussels under the pretext of false "concern for Jews in the Soviet Union." Any unbiased person is fully aware that it is not in the Soviet Union but in Israel itself and in other countries of the so-called free world that national discrimination is taking place.

Together with other peaceloving forces, we Israeli Communists are fighting for a radical change in Israel's official policy and for a policy of peace and friendship between the peoples of our country and the Soviet Union.

We consider our chief task the struggle to eliminate the hotbed of war in the Middle East and to establish a just and stable peace on the basis of respect for the rights of all states and peoples of our region. We are against the occupation of the Arab territories and the barbarous repression and terror resorted to by the Israeli authorities against the population of these territories. We stand for a realistic and just peace on the basis of the fulfillment of the well-known resolutions of the Security Council and the UN General Assembly. We are working for the withdrawal of the Israeli troops from all the Arab territories occupied in 1967, for the recognition of the legitimate national rights of the Arab people of Palestine, including their right to national statehood, and for ensuring the sovereignty and territorial integrity of all the states in the Middle East, including, naturally, Israel. We are for the resumption of the work of the Geneva Peace Conference on the Middle East with the participation of all interested sides, including the Palestine Liberation Organization.

We have achieved fresh successes in our hard and complicated struggle for peace, in defense of the interests of the working people, against discrimination of the Arab population, and for the creation of a united front of all the peaceloving forces of Israel. In the recent elections to the municipal council of the city of Nazareth the list of candidates submitted by the Democratic Front received more than two-thirds of the vote, while a member of our Party's Central Committee was elected Mayor of the City. The general positive trends in the international arena are beginning to be felt on the Israeli scene. □

Enrico Berlinguer

General Secretary of the Italian Communist Party

Our delegation is glad to be present at this Congress and to bring you fraternal greetings from the Italian Communist Party, with its more than 1,700,000 members. We Italian Communists especially value what has been done in creating a system of international relations based on the principle of peaceful coexistence. All this was made possible by your contribution in implementing the program of peace adopted at the 24th Congress.

Under present conditions, as never before, the idea and possibility of internationalism is viable and realizable. From the experience of our country and our Party, we can say that new broad masses of workers and youth of various political views are more and more actively participating in the struggle under the banner of international solidarity. This has been manifested in the solidarity with the peoples of Vietnam and the rest of Indochina, with the peoples of Mozambique, Guinea-Bissau and Angola, Portugal, Greece, Spain and Chile.

In general the whole developing movement for the liberation of the workers and the peoples has become stronger in its drawing power and in its mutual ties. Humanity is striking out along new and varied roads. Therefore, in our opinion, recognition and respect for the complete independence of every country, of every progressive movement and every Communist and Workers Party is of the greatest significance in both principle and practice. Relations between the Communist and Workers Parties must in our opinion be permeated with the spirit of friendship and solidarity. At the same time we are for open and candid presentation of differing experiences and positions. It is well known that in the Communist movement there exist different viewpoints on a whole series of questions, including the most important ones, and we believe they should be considered in the spirit of complete comradeship, within unbreakable norms of equality and respect for the independence of each Party.

All developed capitalist countries, especially in Europe, are now in the throes of a deep crisis in their economic, cultural and intellectual life. We are not forgetful of the experience of the twenties and thirties when the workers' and democratic parties made opportunistic compromises and sectarian mistakes. The most reactionary forces of big capital in a number of countries were able to change the relation of forces to their own advantage, establishing fascist and fascist-type regimes. A similar danger can arise in our times. However, there are also many positive developments. Criticism of the defects and corruption of the capitalist system is taking on a mass character, even on the part of the non-proletarian sectors of the population. There are growing tendencies toward socialism. There is increasing unity of the workers in their struggles.

The position of our Party in Italy today is stronger than ever. In last June's municipal elections the Communist Party won the support of more than 33 per cent of the voters.

Thus it became still more evident that the deep crisis in our country could be solved only if the Communist Party participated in the political leadership on an equal basis with other peoples' and democratic forces. As a direct result of the last elections we joined with comrades from the Socialist Party and representatives of other democratic forces in the administration of several large regions and such large cities as Milan, Turin, Naples, Bologna, Florence and Venice.

This was possible, first because through long years of intensive work and struggle we have established close ties with millions of workers, with the intelligentsia, with broad masses of women and youth. It is also the result of our concrete proposals for unity, our active participation in all the fights to defend the interests of the people.

Actually confronting, as we are, the real possibility of socialism, we must show what we consider necessary and uniquely possible for Italian society. We are fighting for a socialist society which would be the highest manifestation of the development of all our democratic victories and which would guarantee the observance of all the personal and collective liberties, freedom of religion and culture, art and science, a society reflecting the contribution of different political forces, so that the working class may perform its historic role within the ranks of a manysided, democratic system.

Comrades! Today, as the 60th anniversary of the Great October Revolution approaches we wish you successful work and new achievements in the further development of socialist society, and in our common cause of the struggle for peace and progress throughout the world.   □

Dolores Ibarruri

Chairman of the Communist Party of Spain

Dear Soviet Comrades, we have not forgotten and will never forget your fraternal solidarity and the sacrifices you made in our struggle against fascist aggression. They helped to strengthen the warm friendship between our two parties. This friendship has always been a great inspiration to us during all our continuing struggles.

The policy of peace pursued by the Communist Party of the Soviet Union and the Soviet Government, which stands out so clearly in the report of Comrade Brezhnev, is the decisive factor in safeguarding peace on earth. Wherever people are fighting-for their freedom, for winning or strengthening their national independence, they feel the solidarity and support of the Soviet Union. This is a powerful bulwark against which the aggressive policy of imperialism will be smashed.

By the whim of history we Spaniards are in a paradoxical position. Our people, who were the first to take up arms against fascist aggression; losing three million of our sons and daughters, even now, thirty years after the defeat of Hitlerism, are still compelled to continue the struggle against the last fascist regime in Europe. In that struggle today two generations who have not known war are actively participating, and fighting against the reactionary regime in our country with youthful energy and thirst for freedom.

Now, after the death of the dictator, Spain has entered a phase of fierce battles, not to be compared with any others of the postwar period in their scope, depth and fighting spirit. Participating in this broad movement, headed by the working class, are peasants, people of the free professions, intelligentsia, women, the Catholic church, students and even certain sections of the army and the government workers.

This struggle is necessary because in spite of the death of Franco, institutions and organizations of a fascist nature remain. Today we can declare that real anti-fascist unity, for which the Communist Party and other democratic forces have fought for so many years is becoming an actuality.

In official Spain nothing has changed. Spain itself has changed into a Spain yearning for work and culture. It is entering a decisive struggle to win democracy and liberty. Millions of Spaniards are demanding democracy, a real change in the political regime which will mean that there is no place in our country for fascism and its laws and institutions.

Only a provisional government, in which all the democratic forces would be represented, could establish freedom, represent the voice of the people and begin the establishment of a new order. First of all, we must speak of unity in the struggle for democracy. There has already been established a Committee for Coordination of the actions of two organizations uniting the basic opposition forces—the Democratic Council in which the Communist Party is taking part, and the Platform of Democratic Agreement. We hope in the near future to complete the process of establishing a single organ which will embrace the entire Spanish democratic opposition.

It is our Party which is taking the initiative in carrying out a policy of national agreement, supported today by the widest circles, beginning with the workers up to the higher Catholic priesthood, which considers that the road to national agreement lies through amnesty for all political prisoners and emigres.

The correctness of this policy, consistently followed by our Party, is evidenced by the agreement on unity which has been achieved among the different political forces fighting for democracy. We already may see our country on the horizon as a democratic Spain.

I want to express the firm hope that we, Spanish Communists, inspired by Marxism-Leninism, will succeed together with our whole people in establishing in Spain a democratic structure opening the way to socialism.   □

Mohammed Siad Barre

President, Supreme Revolutionary Council,
Somali Democratic Republic

The national liberation movement today is rushing irresistibly forward. Now that colonialism of the old type is disappearing, imperialist domination takes the form of neocolonialism. This new form of domination is much more stubborn, and the struggle against it is difficult. In order to defeat colonialism in its classical form it was sufficient to have an anticolonial movement for the creation of an independent state without radical changes in its internal social-economic structure. However, we all know that also gave rise to the danger of the transformation of an independent government into an artificial superstructure over a system retaining all the oppression and exploitation of the past. The fight against these developments requires a new movement to tear the means of production from the hands of imperialism, ending the old forms of social relations: in other words, a socialist solution is required. Many liberated countries have recognized this and entered upon a non-capitalist road of development, leading to socialism.

In Africa, imperialist aggression has taken on particularly abominable forms. In the southern part of the continent racist governments have been set up, based on the exploitation and cruel repression of the native population, who are deprived of all civil and human rights. The imperialists make use of these regimes to pile up profits, to exploit their resources, in order to prevent the social and economic development of an independent Africa. However, with the victory of the former Portuguese colonies, the noose has been drawn tighter against the racist regimes in the south. This has goaded the imperialists into stupid and desperate actions from the support of reactionary cliques to direct armed intervention. They attempted to block real independence for Angola, headed by the MPLA.

All these attempts failed. The independence of Angola was assured thanks to the fighting spirit of the Angolan people, the true and tested MPLA leadership and the selfless help of the socialist countries and the progressive peoples of Africa. But it is characteristic of imperialists that they do not master the lessons of history. If they experience a disaster in one place, they try to reverse their losses in another, using the same approaches and methods. Therefore we well know that the imperialists will struggle to the end, whether in Namibia, French Somalia or South Africa.

After the revolution of October 1969, the people of Somalia were filled with determination to continue their national and social liberation to the very end — the victory of socialism.

The revolutionary maturity and moral strength of our people were manifested with special clarity under conditions of the recent economic difficulties experienced by the poorer countries as a result of the crisis gripping monopoly capitalism and the terrible drought which meant serious losses to our people and our natural resources.

The people of Somalia will never forget how the Soviet Union, in the true spirit of Leninist internationalism, speedily came to our assistance, sending us their comrades — young drivers and flyers along with trucks and airplanes. As a result, 120,000 people were transported from the places suffering from drought and relocated in new places.

The Soviet Union has given material and moral support to liberation movements in Africa, Asia and Latin America. Without this solid help many victories over imperialism would have been impossible. We extend the warmest gratitude to the Soviet people, their party and their government and their leaders who are marching confidently along the road of peace, socialism, freedom and friendship.   □

Gustav Husak

General Secretary of the Central Committee, Communist Party of Czechoslovakia, President of the Czechoslovak Socialist Republic

The Communist Party of Czechoslovakia is preparing for its 15th Congress. This Congress will sum up what we have achieved in the five years since we were able to overcome the sharp crisis in our Party and our society, and work out the tasks of further construction of a developed socialist society.

The results achieved, in carrying out the decisions of the 14th Congress, in the development of our national economy, the rise in the material and cultural level of the people and other spheres, have been the most remarkable in the history of socialist Czechoslovakia. The ideological and organizational unity of the Party was strengthened, closer ties with the people established and the leading role of the Party in society was enhanced.

These good results confirm that the policy of our Party, worked out at our 14th Congress, was correct and realistic. Our people accepted this policy as a vital matter. In their day-to-day work they successfully carried it out and their social and labor activities have created favorable conditions for the work of the 15th Congress.

Only through friendship, alliance and many-sided cooperation with the Soviet Union and the other countries of the socialist community can we create the necessary conditions for the socialist development of Czechoslovakia, its freedom and independence, and a peaceful life. The Czechoslovak people do not forget the tremendous sacrifices by the Soviet people for our liberation in World War II. We highly value the fraternal help which the Soviet Union, as a true friend and ally, has given us during the course of 30 years for the building of socialism, and wish to express our deep gratitude to the Soviet Communists and the whole Soviet People.

The history of the Communist and workers' movement confirms that unity, class and international solidarity are the most effective weapons in the revolutionary struggle for the social liberation of humanity. Our movement has often had to struggle with various opportunist, revisionist and nationalist influences. At the present time we consider it necessary to oppose actively the Maoist leadership of China, which is openly linking up with the most reactionary forces in the world. This policy is hostile to socialism, progress and peace and therefore our Party will continue to fight against Maoism and all forms of opportunism.   □

Edward Gierek

First Secretary of the Central Committee, Polish United Workers' Party

For many generations the Polish people have fought for their independence, for progress, for statehood capable of guaranteeing their security and development. In this struggle they have made great sacrifices, and traditions forming their consciousness have been born. Poland, our homeland, which was born by the merging of the struggle for independence with the social revolution, is the realization of the most vital yearnings of our people guaranteeing them a sovereign state, dynamic economic development, the flowering of science and culture. This is the result of the unbreakable alliance of friendship between Poland and the Soviet Union. Our unity is the imperishable confirmation of the value of internationalism.

Fraternal Polish-Soviet relations were forged by the historic processes and events of the 20th Century. The sources of the ideological unity of our parties arose in the joint struggle of the Polish and Russian working class in the 1905-7 revolution. The Great October Socialist Revolution meant the realization of Lenin's proclamation of the right to self-determination, the annulment of unequal treaties, opening for Poland the road to independence. Our people will never forget the liberating mission of the Soviet Army, the Soviet soldiers shedding their blood and giving their lives for the sake of a free Poland. We have strengthened and deepened our friendly ties in the course of the whole postwar period.

Our Party attributes enormous significance to the strengthening of cooperation among socialist states. The economic cooperation which we have intensified in the course of carrying out the program of socialist integration of the CMEA countries, simplifies and hastens the socioeconomic development of each of them. The political and defense alliance of the Warsaw Treaty countries, guaranteeing the security of our peoples, has become at the same time the basis for greater activity for detente and for increasing peaceful relations between countries of differing social systems.

We have done a great deal to create the necessary prerequisites for the strengthening of peace in Europe. We have done everything possible to prevent and to stop any threats that might arise, thereby creating an international atmosphere favorable to peace.

Today we can say with satisfaction that our continent has lived under peaceful conditions for over three decades, that many hotbeds of war have been stamped out, and aggressive forces have been beaten back in many parts of the planet. And due first of all to the improvement in Soviet-American relations, we have made progress along the road of weakening and averting the dangers of a new world war.

We also value highly the realistic approach of the governments and leaders of many Western countries to the question of peaceful coexistence. The strengthening of detente and making it irreversible is of vital importance to all nations, as is defeat of the attacks against detente by the various forces of anti-Communism, militarism and cold war.

The strengthening of our international security and peace is a great and noble aim. Poland will continue to act in accordance with the Final Act signed at Helsinki, and try to carry out all its main principles and conclusions.   □

Francisco Mendes

Principal Commissioner of State, Guinea-Bissau; Member
of the Permanent Secretariat of the Executive Committee
of the African Party for the Independence of Guinea and
the Cape Verde Islands

At the 24th CPSU Congress, the immortal leader of our Party and great friend of the Soviet Union, Amilcar Cabral, spoke with incomparable eloquence of our gratitude to the courageous Soviet people for their selfless fraternal aid and constant support for our just cause.

The great honor has now fallen on me to express the deepest appreciation of our Party and the people of Guinea-Bissau and the Cape Verde Islands, for the Soviet Union's many-sided and unconditional support.

During many years of bitter war against Portuguese colonial domination we have had plenty of opportunity to appreciate the lofty sense of internationalism of the Soviet people. And today, as we begin the struggle for the development of our country, we know that we have true allies at our side in the Soviet people and their Party. Solidarity with them is more important than ever in the building of a new life, and progress and peace on our land.

The results of the European Security Conference at Helsinki once again confirmed the foresight of the Soviet leaders, which made possible a climate of peace and cooperation among governments with different social systems. This means new hopes for a better life to the young nations as well.

Dear Comrades! The true Leninist principles and aims of the Great October Revolution and the Communist Party of the Soviet Union have transformed the

USSR into the most powerful force ever created by man in the interests of the cause of peace, the liberation and progress of the peoples, their wellbeing and full development. Their many-sided help has strengthened our independence and our national reconstruction and the peace and progress of our African homeland. ☐

Jose Cuello

Member of the Secretariat of the Central Committee of the Dominican Communist Party

When in 1965 we Dominican revolutionaries had been surrounded by 42 thousand American marines we repeated Pablo Neruda's immortal verses dedicated to the Soviet people who in the Battle of Stalingrad had forced the Nazis to abandon their plans for a "thousand-year Reich." "Capital de la gloria, resiste," repeated the Dominicans in their small heroic country.

American imperialists dictated to our country compromise terms by force of arms, being well aware that they would not be able to crush the resistance of the people inspired by the great examples of the past, without arousing the hatred and indignation of mankind that had resolutely condemned the intervention.

But that uprising—in the wake of the victory of the Cuban revolution—could have been Latin America's first uprising of the military supported by the people. Subsequently the experience of Peru, Panama and Ecuador showed that the armies of the Latin American countries were beginning to be involved in the struggles of their people.

In the fierce struggle being waged on the continent American imperialism is turning away from the reformist model of development, outlined in Kennedy's Alliance for Progress as an alternative to the national liberation revolution and socialism, to the Brazilian model which has manifested itself in the most criminal, bloodthirsty form in heroic Chile, the country of Salvador Allende and Luis Corvalan.

As for our country, the compromise settlement has resulted in the adoption of the reformist model fraught with the constant, and at times openly expressed, threat of fascism. The fascists' attempts to win undivided domination have, during the last ten years, cost the Dominicans more than a thousand lives. All the constitutional guarantees have been trampled underfoot, including freedom of movement and freedom of speech, let alone other political freedoms. All of this goes hand in hand with embezzlement of government funds.

Between 1972 and September 1975, American mining companies had taken out of our country 372.5 million dollars worth of bauxite, nickel, gold and silver for which the Dominican government received only 105.1 million, or 28.2 per cent of the total.

This kind of "reformist model" for Latin America is being opposed by the Communists of this continent. The struggle against it is being waged by the Dominican Communist Party; it is also waged in Bolivia, Uruguay, Guatemala and Haiti and other countries of Latin America where despotic traditions go far back into the distant past.

Socialism, of which Cuba is Latin America's first and an heroic example, is becoming increasingly attractive to the masses of the continent whose aspirations accord with those of the peoples all over the world. In the Soviet Union socialism has a sound foundation of universal peace which is a factor opening up broad prospects for the peoples' struggle. It is an economically advanced and rapidly developing power which selflessly shares its knowledge and resources with the peoples fighting for independence and winning it. Finally, in the Soviet Union socialism has a powerful military, political and moral force that has hampered imperialist designs aimed at eliminating by force or by blockade the gains of the peoples of three continents.   □

Gordon McLennon

General Secretary of the Communist Party of Great Britain

The unprecedented world attention devoted to your Congress represents a recognition of the initiatives for peace, detente and disarmament by the Soviet Government.

Deep social, economic and political crisis grips Britain. Over a million-and-a-half workers are now unemployed, others are on short time, millions are living on or below the poverty line, and in the second half of 1975, there was the biggest drop in general living standards for 20 years. Cuts of nearly five billion in government spending on public and social services over the next two years will further reduce standards in education, transport, housing, health and social welfare. These cuts will also mean a further increase in unemployment. Meanwhile British military expenditure this year will be almost five billion. Long established democratic rights are under attack. The crisis of British policy in Northern Ireland deepens.

Differences can and do exist in the international communist movement on certain questions, and our views on these questions are well known. Our solidarity and joint action with your Party and other brother parties will continue to be fully expressed in the common struggle for peace, against imperialism and for socialism. In doing this we will be carrying forward the internationalist tradition and record of our Party.   □

Part Four: Before and After

9

IGOR MARTYNENKO

Pre-Congress Discussion: The Guidelines Belong to the People

n December 1975, the Central Committee of the CPSU issued for nation-wide discussion the draft "Guidelines for the Development of the National Economy of the USSR for 1976-1980." The draft was printed in all newspapers, and broadcast over radio and TV. Prepared by thousands of specialists in the center and in the localities, the draft had been thoroughly discussed at different levels before its adoption. Indeed, its preparations began at trade union meetings in each plant and meetings with factory committees, in which initial economic suggestions, criticisms, wage demands and other issues were raised. Opinions of the workers in each industry were then transmitted to the responsible ministries, which prepared draft proposals for the National Planning Commission. Consideration of these proposals continued at various levels until the draft was placed before the entire country.

After publication Soviet citizens, while approving it as a whole, submitted amendments, suggestions and remarks through the press, radio and television, at meetings of Party, trade union and Young Communist League organizations and at meetings at factories, offices and farms.

The results of the discussion were summed up at the 25th Congress, which adopted the final text of the Guidelines. Many millions of people attended those meetings and took an active part in the discussion. This was typical of the Soviet practice of insuring the participation of the people in the preparation of decisions on major problems facing the state and affecting their own lives. In this crucial process even thousands of experts will not substitute for the creative initiative and experience of millions of working people. This latest discussion was on a scale never before attained; as socialism develops more and more people can and must play an active part in the political process both in the Party and in the Government. This is the essence of Soviet democracy.

IGOR MARTYENKO is a commentator with Novosti Press Agency.

185

What follows is only a glimpse of this vast discussion, with examples of the kinds of questions raised from different forums and parts of the country.

In the course of one month after the publication of the Guidelines Soviet periodicals printed tens of thousands of remarks, proposals and amendments to the draft. Of the comments published in *Pravda, Izvestia* and *Trud* (the central organ of the Soviet trade unions), half were from workers and collective farmers. The rest were from Party functionaries, government officials, trade union officers, scientists, technical specialists, students, pensioners and housewives. None of the comments rejected any major proposition of the Guidelines. But there were many further suggestions, and elaborations of criticisms and analyses of faults that were discussed in the draft itself.

"I suggest that the Central Committee's draft introduce a special point on the necessity to tie in the development of production with the construction of houses, cultural and service establishments and schools, and to take to task executives who ignore this rule," V. Chizhov, a school director from Central Russia, wrote in *Trud*.

"We still do not have a single system of control of the quality of work in agriculture," F. Sterlikov, an assistant professor at the Kuibyshev Agricultural Institute, wrote in *Trud*. He suggested setting up a special quality control service similar to that in industry.

V. Sturza, a furniture factory worker from Kishinev, observed that prices on higher quality products did not always cover the growth of costs and this influenced the performance of the producing factory. He suggested increasing the role of wholesale prices in stimulating the output of high quality products.

Many spoke of the need to increase each worker's responsibility for product quality, the importance of economical use of machinery and materials, and the necessity of improving standards of work. A. Chekin, a driver from Saratov, suggested that stricter measures of responsibility be introduced for the wasteful use of materials. V. Vilkov, a building team leader from Dzerzhinsk, and A. Ikaunieks, a milling machine operator at the railway car building plant in Riga, Latvia, thought it necessary to increase the responsibility of managers of sub-contractor enterprises for failures in order fulfillment.

A. Ginzburg, a reader of *Izvestia* from Irkutsk, noted: "In the Tenth Five-Year Plan period the population of the Baikal area will grow sharply following the construction of the Baikal-Amur Railroad. This means that more health-building establishments should be built in this region in order to make better use of environmental factors for restoring people's health and capacity for work. I propose that this be included in the draft." "I think that the draft Guidelines should specially emphasize the role of moral stimuli, which become the main motive force of our successes as we advance towards communism," O.

Serdyuk wrote to *Pravda* from the Kirovograd Region in the Ukraine.

Among the many recommendations in the environmental field came one from Y. Emaletdimov from Kazan, chairman of the standing commission for the protection of nature of the Supreme Soviet of Tataria, who observed that natural features must be taken into account, in addition to administrative subdivisions, in planning environmental protection measures.

Two leading members of the Rostov regional council for nature preservation, writing in *Izvestia*, called for an amendment to make strict observance of environmental protection laws a condition for any award to individuals or enterprises for achievements in production.

Questions of social development occupied a special place in the comments. For example, I. Skrabis, a pensioner from Krasnodar in the south of Russia, wrote in *Izvestia*: "The draft envisages improvement of working and living conditions for women, specifically the extension of partly paid leave to give working women a chance to look after their infants until they are one year old, and providing working mothers with greater opportunities for working a shorter day or a reduced working week, or to work at home. I think if we really want to improve the life of working mothers the leave should be paid in full." (At present women in the USSR receive a 112-day maternity leave with average wages paid.) One can find many other remarks and suggestions on how to improve the working and living conditions of working women.

There is a section in the Guidelines dealing with the further development and improvement of democratic forms of management of production. Many people proposed that special points be added on raising the responsibility of economic executives for the promotion of the initiative of the workers, on making wider use of workers' meetings, the societies of rationalizers and inventors, and on developing new forms of production democracy.

Newspapers carried many letters discussing the program for further improving the system of secondary, vocational and higher education. The letters contain many further recommendations aimed at the further improvement of the Soviet educational system. Foremost among these problems is to raise the educational levels of as many working people as possible to the point where they can participate in running the state. There were also proposals aimed at improving medical services, the social insurance system, the holiday industry, and other services for the people.

While letters to the papers are important, they don't create the dynamism and excitement of the meetings, where workers and leaders meet face to face and hammer out proposals and concepts.

A meeting to discuss the Guidelines took place at the Moscow plant which manufactures Moskvich cars, known in many countries. Fitter N. Sudarikov said: "Our team has discussed the draft, and we fully support it, because it lays good guidelines for the country's social and economic development. We take improvement of our work qualifications very seriously, because the quality of output directly depends on it. Our task is to work the Guidelines into a specific, actually guiding program to achieve our goals. We will need, and we confidently expect, help from the senior comrades here."

V. Kolomnikov, director-general of the plant, addressing the meeting, said: "When speaking of the prospects of the plant in the tenth five-year period we must not lose sight of social development tasks. In the past five years we have built more than 200,000 square meters of new housing, a stadium, a high school and an out-of-town camp. But we must continue, and even increase construction of apartments, holiday homes and health centers for our workers."

In Alma-Ata, capital of the Soviet Central Asian republic of Kazakhstan, the Guidelines were discussed at a meeting of the workers of a house-building plant. (This plant prefabricates parts from which houses are assembled.)

Opening the meeting, Mikhail Chormanov, secretary of the Party committee of the plant, said: "The production line has reached full capacity. The task now is to double the capacity in the same production area, without stopping the plant, to build houses with larger rooms, kitchens and bathrooms. As the draft says, a growing part of capital investments should be spent on retooling and reconstructing operating enterprises. This will make it easier for them to go over to the manufacture of new items."

The plant's director, Nikolay Kondratyev: "The government has allocated 19 million rubles for the reconstruction of our plant. That's a big sum! But it would have taken roughly three times as much money to build another plant."

Then Nikolay Logachov, a team leader, took the floor: "All our workers are interested in reconstruction. Our team has discussed the whole thing, outlined general and individual tasks, and thought out the placing of personnel. We'll cope with the plans."

The Priuralsky state farm lies far from any large city. Its 30,000 hectares* of land almost border on Bashkiria, and the regional center, Chelyabinsk, is more than 300 kilometers away.

The farm machinery operators had a lively discussion of the tasks the Guidelines had set for the workers in agriculture.

Alexander Golovin, the state farm's garage mechanic: "I would like to touch upon a problem very important to us farm machinery operators. The draft notes that in the tenth five-year period agriculture will receive many new tractors, combine harvesters and other agricultural machines. That is a very important and timely measure. The renovation of machinery on our farm is conducted in the form of supply of heavy-duty K-700 and K-701 tractors. I suggest that a

---

* One hectare=2.47 acres.

special provision be introduced in the draft for increasing the output of trailers and spare parts, which will make for the fullest utilization of the technical possibilities of the powerful tractors. It is also necessary to renovate the automobile fleet of the farms. This will help make state farms more efficient."

Many of those present supported repairman Sergey Panov, a Party member, who spoke in favor of determining what personal contribution everyone would make to the implementation of the tasks outlined by the Party for the tenth five-year plan period.

The speakers also discussed the plan for the state farm's social development in the coming five years, including better conditions for work and recreation. Over the past years a block of modern two-story houses and a kindergarten have been built on the state farm. The farm's workers, however, want further improvement in their living conditions.

In 1975, the coal miners of the Ukraine (a republic in the European part of the USSR) produced 216 million tons of high-grade coking and other grades of coal, nearly ten million tons more than was mined in 1970, the whole increase being achieved through higher labor productivity. The Ukraine's Donbas, the country's oldest coal basin, tripled the number of walls equipped with complete sets of machines and nearly completed the going over to coal mining with the latest narrow-cut machines.

The successes, however, could be much greater. Therefore the Communists working in the mining industry see to it that new machinery supplied to the mines in ever increasing amounts is effectively used since it is there that great reserves for increasing efficiency are to be found.

The part of the "Guidelines" dealing with Kirghizia envisages further development of the power industry, specifically, the construction of the Kurpsai hydro-power station since Kirghizia still lacks sufficient electric power. The republic has experience in building such installations. It already operates Central Asia's largest Toktogul hydro-power station with a capacity of 1.2 million kilowatts, one of a series of power stations to be built on the Naryn River. The total capacity of these stations will be seven million kw.

One more problem which is given great attention in the republic is improvement of the fuel and power pattern. This involves joining the local gas pipe line operating in the south of Kirghizia to the system of centralized gas supply in the Fergana Valley.

The MELZ plant in Moscow is one of the Soviet Union's largest enterprises manufacturing electro-vacuum instruments, TV kinescopes and electric lamps. Here is what the chairman of the Party committee, Konstantin Dunyakov, said at the general workers' meeting held to discuss the draft:

"In the recent period 295 consumer articles manufactured by our plant have been certified as being of top quality. That is 80 per cent of the total. But if we lay stress, not on these 80 per cent, but on the remaining 20 per cent, it will become clear that we cannot rest content with this state of things. We must increase the output of articles bearing the Quality Mark."

"Lenin pointed out on many occasions that communism would grow out of the conscious labor of millions of working people," Nina Korovina, a worker, said at the meeting. "A high level of organization is a condition for efficient labor. Poorly organized labor bores, annoys and tires out the worker. Therefore the Party organization must concentrate its efforts on improving the organization of the labor of every worker, team leader, foreman, engineer—all who participate in the production process."

The draft lays the main emphasis on the development of the industrial base of the Soviet economy. But great attention is paid in it also to agriculture.

Tractor team leader I. Prakh, at the general meeting of the members of the Rodina collective farm in the Krasnodar Territory, said: "Having discussed the draft plan, our team has undertaken an obligation to raise the fertility of our fields still higher. We have all conditions for this. But many problems still remain to be solved. The level of technology on our farm by far does not meet present-day demands. The share of manual labor remains large, as a result of which field and other operations take too much time and we lose part of the crop.

"The draft provides for comprehensive mechanization of grain and sugar beet growing. We are sure that the tasks set by the Party will be successfully accomplished."

The oilfields of the Azneft oil administration in Baku—capital of Azerbaidzhan, a Soviet republic in Transcaucasia—have existed for many decades, and it is becoming more and more difficult to extract oil from the beds that have lost much of the pressure in them.

"We are convinced that there is a way out," M. Gambarov, a worker, said at a general meeting. "Not long ago we successfully tested the 'travelling fire' method, by which oil is forced to the surface with the help of fire in the oil well. The Guidelines call for a 25-30 per cent increase in oil production; I think we must build this new method into our working plans."

M. Bairamov, head of the engineering and technological service, said at the meeting: "We have studied the Party's draft closely, and we know our tasks. By the end of the tenth five-year period the extracting of oil and gas in off-shore fields, both existing and newly discovered ones, will have grown considerably. The draft calls for more active measures to protect the natural environment. We call on all our experts to pay more attention to passing on their experience to young workers, and above all to teach them to love labor, to see in it life's main purpose, and to educate the younger generation of oil workers on the traditions of the militant, multinational working class of Baku."

Many more such examples could be cited. Alongside expressions of support concrete problems were raised, and suggestions aimed at speeding the realization of the tasks of the new five-year plan, at making it a five-year plan of efficiency and quality. The organs of the press, the presiding boards of Party and workers' meetings lost no time in submitting the proposals to competent organizations, pressing them to adopt concrete measures on each proposal.

The continuing deepening of inner-Party democracy was seen in the report and election campaign in the Party on the eve of the 25th Congress, which coincided with the discussion of the draft Guidelines. Meetings in the primary Party branches were attended by more than 94 per cent of the Communists, with one in four of those attending taking part in the debate. The campaign was extensively covered in the press, and on radio and TV, thus in effect turning the Party committee reports into reports to all the working people.

Take, for instance, the work of the Tatar regional Party conference. (The Tatar Autonomous Soviet Socialist Republic lies in the upper reaches of the Volga.) Many delegates spoke of shortcomings, including those in agriculture. In 1975, some collective and state farms had failed to fulfill the plans for the sale of grain and meat to the state. Their heads tried to blame this on unfavorable weather conditions, but the delegates came to a different conclusion. It is true that the drought did considerable damage, but it could not be held responsible for everything. Delegates pointed out that in the same hard conditions many farms had grown good crops thanks to the skill and care displayed by the working people.

The conference in Tataria, like other Party forums, showed that the Party has no secrets from the people. On the contrary, it sees to it that all Soviet people are informed about its work and plans, its difficulties and successes.

The discussion of the draft ended on the eve of the opening of the 25th Congress of the Communist Party. Even before the Congress a special commission of the Politbureau of the CPSU Central Committee considered the people's suggestions. Together with the proposals made by delegates at the Congress, these amendments to the draft Guidelines were submitted to a commission of Party and government workers, ministers, scientists, representatives of the public and industrial workers, elected at the Congress. The draft with the amendments adopted by the Commission was distributed to the delegates. The suggestions and additions that were not included in the document will be considered by the appropriate agencies throughout the country.

The Central Committee noted that the draft Guidelines had been discussed constructively and in a businesslike manner everywhere, in all regions, territories and republics. It has shown once again the Soviet people's vital interest in the fulfillment of the tasks set by the Party. □

10

IGOR MARTYNENKO

After the Congress:
Bringing the Plan to Life

The Tenth Five-Year Plan of Economic Development has been characterized as a plan for increased efficiency and high quality. This, however, does not mean that the overall growth of this country's economic potential and living standards have been relegated to the background. More funds than ever before have been allocated for capital construction and agriculture, improvement of working and living conditions, and development of culture during 1976-1980.

The main goal of the current five-year plan is to secure a maximum return for every ruble invested, every ton of raw material used and every hour spent.

In this connection the Congress stressed the need of steadily raising labor productivity. This will account for about 90 per cent of the total growth of industrial output, and for the entire growth of output in agriculture and the building industry.

In order to achieve this growth of labor productivity, the workers themselves decided to apply the time-tested method of socialist competition to the improvement of both labor productivity and quality. Socialist emulation, or friendly competition among individuals and groups of workers to boost production or fulfill targets faster, arose as a great movement in the 1930s, during the initial period of massive industrialization of the Soviet Union. These competitions have always been based on finding better and more efficient ways to work, not on simply working faster. They do not involve "speed-up" or placing extra strain on workers, practices which would violate the extensive Soviet labor protection laws which are strictly enforced by the trade unions. The same extends, of course, to the new emphasis on emulation in improving quality of production.

Considerable excitement is generated among the workers as daily scores of teams are posted on factory bulletin boards. Winning teams receive special banners and emblems, which they take great pride in keeping, if they can. Photos of winning team members appear on factory walls, and wall newspapers carry special writeups of their progress. A recent innovation is that workers getting the highest quality results may stamp their own products and bypass the inspection department.

The entire emulation method, which draws the workers into the inventive and rationalization process, helps realize the goal of bridging the gap between manual and mental work.

An example of how the new style of socialist emulation works can be seen at the Moscow Electrical Engineering Factory. Shortly before the Congress opened, the teams headed by Communists Metelkin, Amosov and Kuznetsov announced that they would compete with each other and that the motto of this competition would be ''workers, guarantee the quality of goods produced in the five-year plan period!'' The three teams signed a joint agreement on a socialist emulation drive based on mutual assistance and cooperation. Their example was followed by workers at many other Soviet factories.

Formerly, when a team finished a component and turned it in, the workers no longer had anything to do with it. Under the new arrangement the team keeps an eye on the part until it has been integrated into the finished product, whether car or machine tool. The essence of the new style emulation between teams is to help one another and to share experience and know-how so all will be better equipped to eliminate shortcomings in the labor process.

Social advancement in the USSR is possible only because the workers exercise their creative abilities in industry, agriculture, scientific research, etc., because they make full use of their civil rights, and participate increasingly in public life. Under socialism something truly marvelous has taken shape in the character of the Soviet people—the sense of being their country's full masters, well aware of the connection between their own work and the creative activities of all their fellow workers. They keep their country's best interests at heart, and the interests of all are the concern of every individual.

Therefore if a skillful worker turns in a good performance at the factory or in the field and is ahead of his coworkers, he usually wants to pass on his experience to others. Probably no group is more respected in our country than these outstanding workers. Many are famous throughout the country. They are written about in the press and are elected members of the organs of government bodies.

Soviet people are vitally interested in seeing their factories do a good job. To fulfill production targets efficiently and on time, a factory must operate at full capacity. How can the targets be exceeded without installing additional facilities?

Of course, the main role in production is played by the conscious activity of people. Working for themselves and for their society, they think not only about what and how much to do but also how to do it better and faster. In other words, the workers themselves analyze the process of production.

Workers make up 65 per cent of the ''production conferences'' in all Soviet factories. Here workers share equally with management in solving problems of production as well as working conditions, and management is obligated to take their proposals and complaints into consideration. If management fails to act on measures decided at these conferences, the factory trade union may arrange a replacement. In 1975 alone, more than a million proposals drawn up by such conferences for raising production efficiency and improving working conditions were put into effect.

For twelve years a team of women insulating tape binders at the Vladimir Ilyich Electric Cable Plant in Moscow have been in competition with their counterparts at the Electrosila Plant in Leningrad. When I visited the plant, here is what the Moscow women workers told me about this socialist emulation:

"We have not been competing with our sister workers in Leningrad just to be ahead of them. This is no cinder track at a stadium where time and speed are decisive. We are competing in a much more important field—we are looking for more ways to raise production efficiency for everyone's benefit.

"We learned that the Leningrad workers had found new ways to raise efficiency and reduce labor expenditure. This started us looking for additional possibilities in our own factory. We figured that if we made better and fuller use of insulating material we would be able to save wiring and tape enough for an extra machine a day. This was our reply to the decisions of the Party Congress."

The decisions of the Congress have aroused new initiatives and new ideas. Today socialist emulation drives to implement the main plans and counterplans have spread to all parts of the country, involving more than 80 million people.

The socialist emulation drives between individuals are supplemented by competitions between teams, between shops and between large production collectives, and even between whole factories and whole industries. One distinguishing feature of this type of socialist emulation today is that all the pledges the workers take on are scientifically worked out.

For example, a worker has noticed that by introducing some sort of innovation in the production process he can turn out more products than planned. After thinking the idea through he consults the foreman and the shop economist, and works out details with them. This is how counterplans are brought about, *i.e.*, pledges which a worker, and then the personnel of a whole workshop and later a whole factory, assume in order to exceed the planned production target figures.

The initiative of working people takes different forms. For example, a team of excavator operators at the Sokolovsko-Sarbaisky ore-dressing mill in Kazakhstan developed its own plan which proposed to raise labor efficiency by 30 per cent through better use of new technology. The initiative was taken up by 220 other teams. As a result, the ore-dressing mill exceeded the targets for raising production efficiency and turned out more than 200 thousand tons of ore concentrate in excess of the plan.

The team of Moscow subway builders headed by Ilya Shepelev which I visited was expected to meet its production targets in 13 months, but succeeded in doing so in ten and a half months.

"The key to how they did it lies in the new organization of socialist emulation," Shepelev told me. "Although socialist emulation was popular among the metro-builders before, too, the new method of doing different jobs as one complex for which the whole team is responsible has opened up new possibilities. Actually, the emulation itself, which brings out the urge to work faster and better, led us to accept this collective cost-accounting method."

Shepelev's team has 45 workers, fifteen of whom are members of the Communist Party. The Communists have their own party group.

During work in a Circle for the Study of the Fundamentals of Economics, Shepelev and his colleagues made a detailed study of the team (collective) cost-accounting method which was originally used in the housing construction industry. Such circles are part of the nationwide system of party education, in which each Communist participates according to the CPSU rules.

A team pledges to do a certain type of work and also assumes full responsibility for the state of affairs on the building site. It has the incentive not only to work faster and save building materials but also to make more effective use of machinery, reduce expenses by raising efficiency and the standards of professional skills. This form of cost accounting enables every worker to exert his influence on the day-to-day progress of construction.

After discussing various aspects of this method at a meeting of their Party group, the Communists proposed to apply it in their work. The management accepted the proposal.

It may be asked: what about the workers who are not Party members? Right after the Party meeting, the Communists explained to each one the essence of the new style of work. The non-party members of the team fully supported the proposal.

Pushcha-Voditsa is a large state farm that supplies nearby Kiev with early spring vegetables and fruit. The first vegetables, such as tomatoes, cucumbers, lettuce, squash and eggplants, arrive at the food stores from the hothouses at a time when the streets of the Ukrainian capital are still covered with snow. Over the past five years the state farm was expected to grow 16,470 tons of vegetables and, instead, it grew 16,814 tons in four years. Nevertheless, there was no overproduction or overstocking. Actually the more vegetables were grown at the state farm, the lower was their price, and therefore they became more readily available at the store. This is one of the characteristics of a socialist economy.

The state farm has 85 hectares of arable land and 300 hectares of orchards and berry fields. Over the past four years, the farm increased the number of hothouses and raised the yield of vegetables by 50 per cent. As a result, gross profits rose from 1,700,000 rubles in 1971 to 3,200,000 rubles in 1975.

The farm's Party committee is headed by Nikifor Ivashchenko, who is well versed not only in farming techniques but also in the best ways to use the latest achievements of science.

Thanks to Ivashchenko's tireless efforts, the hydroponic method of vegetable growing, for example, burgeoned into an industry that yields high profits. The hydroponic hothouse has gravel for soil, and all the necessary nutrients here come from special solutions. Vegetable growing has become much less work, and the expenditure of water and nutrient substances has been cut appreciably.

Recently, on Nikifor Ivashchenko's proposal, work was started on the construction of another hydroponic nursery complete with automated equipment.

Such problems as mechanizing laborious farming operations, perfecting production technology, introducing new sorts of seeds for better crops, maintaining working relations with research institutes, training agronomists specializing in truck gardening—all come into the focus of attention of the Party organizations of the state farm.

Trekhgornaya Manufactura is one of the oldest textile combines in the USSR, built 176 years ago. Now consisting of several textile mills, it is rightly called the citadel of the Moscow workers who fought against the tsarist troops in December 1905, in the days of the first Russian Revolution. Later, in October 1917, Trekhgornaya Manufactura was a revolutionary stronghold of the Russian working class, a place where Lenin met and talked to revolutionary workers on many occasions.

Vera Andronova, secretary of the Party organization of one of the mills, has been working here for about 25 years. When I talked with her, she was looking through the list of women workers, studying their records in order to recommend the worthiest for government awards on the basis of their performance in the last year of the Ninth Five-Year Plan period.

Andronova said she was in a quandary trying to decide. for, in her view, almost all the women workers at the mill deserved the highest honors. "Take Neonila Smirnova, the secretary of the Party bureau of one of the departments," said Miss Andronova. "Neonila is also a member of the district Soviet. This in itself is a great honor. And not only honor, for being a deputy to the Soviet means a lot of work too. A deputy must serve as an example in everything, and particularly in work. And this is exactly what she does. Neonila Smirnova's team produced 830,000 square meters of quality textiles to mark the opening of the 25th Congress."

· The women of the combine take pride in their work, and with good reason, for they turn out almost 900 kilometers of textiles a day. Some of the textiles go to stores in Moscow and elsewhere in the Soviet Union, and some are exported to the foreign market.

"All the textiles produced at our combine are of top quality. Over the past several years output has grown 12 times," explained Vera Andronova.

The party secretary of the Odessa branch of the All-Union Orgenergostroi Institute (construction of power facilities), Oleg Vysotski, said that a great deal of attention is now paid to socialist emulation based on the individual plans of every member of the institute staff.

Quality of work is regarded as the result of the creative initiative of the participants in the socialist emulation drive, achieved by a new system of planning. The staff has been divided up into groups which include specialists who not only develop a project but also see it through to the final production stage. Socialist emulation within each production group fully corresponds to the collective nature of work at the institute and makes it possible to combine better the individual abilities of each specialist.

The effectiveness of socialist emulation based on individual plans can be judged from the following example. A group of engineers (Pyotr Spiridonov, Vladimir Greenstein, Pavel Kuchuk, Nikolay Sternfeld, Grigory Shatalov) undertook to design a new transformer substation. Each was given an individual assignment. But what they were actually doing as a team was to resolve a complicated technical problem to make a compact transformer installation accommodating high-performance equipment and means of automation, instead of the costly transformer substation.

The new technical ideas were reduced to a formula used for making estimates and relevant drawings for the proposed high-power installation. The results obtained by each engineer were discussed at a Party meeting of the scientific and technical board of the institute. After that the installation was recommended for mass production.

Soon afterwards, the Electroshchit factory in Kuibyshev produced more than two thousand transformer installations designed at the institute. The new installation made it possible to reduce the expenditure of metal and labor.

Socialist emulation holds out great promise as a method for raising the efficiency of the individual worker and whole collectives. But it happens sometimes that a pledge does not exactly correspond to the capabilities of those who make it. That is why in Yakutia, for example, pledges are, as a rule, submitted to public discussion at general workers' meetings.

Following is an excerpt from the minutes of one such meeting, at the freight truck depot in Yakutsk, where driver Georgi Oleinikov defended his proposal to work more than required in the plan of that organization.

Yury Mitryashin (worker): Georgi Oleinikov will tell you about his personal plan, item by item, and he will also explain in detail how he is going to exceed this year's production target figures. The speaker must show us that all the calculations and figures in this plan are well founded.

Oleinikov: Before making a plan of my own, I looked up the overall estimates for the whole year ahead. I must admit that I would not have been able to figure all that out, had it not been for specialists who helped me.

Oleinikov went on to explain how he was going to haul 280 tons of freight beyond the official plan. The explanation ranged over many factors such as better use of the trailer, faster refueling, more mileage without overhaul.

Oleinikov's case was argued by 15 of his colleagues who took up every little detail, asked questions, weighed pros and cons.

Voice: Last year you met the target figures that stood at 120-130 per cent, and why do you pledge only 110 per cent this time?

Oleinikov: You know that the high percentage for the last year came mostly from overtime, that over the last quarter of the year I worked an additional thirty hours a month. But this time I am planning to pack every thing into the normal working day. Actually, every minute is accounted for.

Oleinikov later gave an account of how he had carried out his pledge in full.

What is the individual plan? It is a pledge taken by a worker using such untapped reserves of productive energy as proficiency, innovations, rationalization proposals, the ability to save time, etc. Public discussion means that the organization of socialist emulation has reached new heights, which is particularly important today.

The Serp i Molot steel mill in Moscow is being modernized to raise efficiency of production in line with Congress decisions. This mammoth job has absorbed the entire attention of the local Communist Party organization. "We must organize the whole thing in such a way as not to lose a single person," said manager Vassily Isayev when I visited the plant. These words, signifying one of the primary objectives of the management during the reconstruction, served as a fresh reminder that there is no unemployment in the Soviet Union, and in fact has not been since 1930. The question of ensuring stability of personnel has always been uppermost in the minds of the Serp i Molot management. Every worker displaced by modernization of equipment is placed in a new position and provided with all necessary retraining.

"Modernization began early in the Ninth Five-Year Plan period," Nikolay Drach, deputy chief engineer, told me. "Since then we have spent 37 million rubles, and now we are planning to double that. We are remodeling all the departments. The whole plant will be retooled from the bottom up. In other words we are going to have a brand-new plant stuffed with new machinery and equipment, some time in 1983, when Serp i Molot will celebrate its centennial.

The idea is to increase overall production by 80 per cent and efficiency by 100 per cent.''

With the reconstruction work in progress, it has taken the Communists and all the workers at the plant a great deal of effort to ensure the continuous operation of all its departments and divisions. This reconstruction also means the building of apartment houses for workers, a clinic, child-care facilities, canteens, and holiday homes.

Serp i Molot today is a place where many new innovations have been introduced, where discoveries and initiatives of all sorts are given the green light, where, according to the Soviet economist Alexey Gastev, "the indomitable friend of invention brings us millions of rubles saved.''

Yury Kamenski, a Party member, explained to me that it would be impossible to exceed the production target figures by merely reducing the time needed for smelting operations, because the technological process rules out any speed-up. To increase production the entire system of metal smelting had to be altered, in fact replaced by a better one. And this is exactly what the workers and engineers of Serp i Molot did to double metal output.

This creative approach to work, to various problems connected therewith, has produced very good results. Suffice it to say, that six grades of steel developed at this plant were awarded the quality mark and are now listed as quality metal by the most exacting world standards.

The creative atmosphere gave every Communist, and every advanced worker at Serp i Molot an incentive to look for better and more efficient ways of production. Young people are keeping up with the veterans. A socialist emulation drive was recently announced for raising the quality of the metal smelted here. This competition is an essential part of the program for improving the efficiency of production, for accelerating scientific and technological progress. □

Part Five: In Conclusion

11

Freedom for the Prisoners of Imperialism and Reaction!

Statement of the 25th Congress
of the Communist Party of the Soviet Union

Adopted unanimously on March 1, 1976

Expressing the will of the Soviet Communists, of the entire Soviet people, the 25th Congress of the CPSU solemnly proclaims its fraternal and unbreakable solidarity with the Communists, with all fighters against imperialism and reaction, and above all with the victims of fascist repressions, those who are incarcerated in concentration camps and prisons, and who are subjected to brutal torture. The inhuman ordeal that has fallen to their lot is the class revenge for their heroic participation in the noble struggle for the interests of the working people, for the triumph of the ideals of peace and democracy, national independence and socialism.

Despite the angry protests of broad sections of world opinion, the fascist junta in Chile continues to trample on all norms of law and to keep in confinement the General Secretary of the Communist Party of Chile, Luis Corvalan, the outstanding son of the Chilean people and a prominent figure of the world communist movement.

The Congress demands in all firmness: Release Luis Corvalan!

Release our comrades—members of the Communist Party of Chile leadership J. Cademartori and J. Montes, leaders of the Socialist Party E. Ponce and C. Lorca, other Popular Unity leaders, and the thousands of other prisoners of the fascist regime—Communists, Socialists, all patriots and democrats!

In Uruguay, the authorities have started another wave of repressions against the progressive forces. We demand: Release Secretaries of the Central Committee of the Communist Party of Uruguay J. Pérez and J. L. Macera, release all Uruguayan Communists, the President of the Broad Front of Uruguay L. Seregni and other democrats!

Antonio Maidana, Chairman of the Paraguayan Communist Party, has been kept in prison for 18 years. A tyrannical military dictatorship holds sway over the whole country. Release Antonio Maidana! Release M. A. Soler, Secretary

200

of the Central Committee of the Paraguayan Communist Party, and hundreds of other Paraguayan patriots!

In recent years, two General Secretaries of the Guatemalan Party of Labor, B. Alvarado Monzon and U. Alvarado Arellano, were brutally killed in quick succession in Guatemala. In Brazil, leading members of the Communist Party and the democratic opposition are disappearing without a trace in prisons. In Argentina, the reactionary forces are subjecting the Communist Party and other progressive organizations to systematic terror. Terror does not cease in Haiti.

The Congress expresses its resolute protest against all these persecutions, and demands an end to them.

Outstanding leaders of the national liberation movement of Africa—Amilcar Cabral, General Secretary of the Party of African Independence of Guinea-Bissau and the Cape Verde Islands, and Eduardo Mondlane, President of the Front of National Liberation of Mozambique—lost their lives at the hands of imperialist agents.

The racists' rule over the peoples of the South African Republic, Namibia and Zimbabwe is a challenge to the conscience of mankind. Inhuman treatment by jailers caused the death of Bram Fisher, an outstanding humanitarian and an unbending fighter against racism and social injustice. Many leaders of the Communist Party of South Africa, the oldest Communist Party on the African continent, are kept in prison in appalling conditions. Disgrace upon the racists and their henchmen! Release all participants in the national liberation movement in the south of Africa!

Thousands of Communists have been killed in Indonesia. To this day there are tens of thousands of political prisoners in prisons and concentration camps. Release the Communists, all the patriots of Indonesia!

On Palestinian territory occupied by Israel, fighters against aggression and for the sacred right of their people to have their own independent state are arrested and kept in prison.

In Spain the authorities still refuse to restore legitimate freedom to many hundreds of political prisoners—Communists, Socialists and other democrats. The Congress supports all those who champion the just cause of the Spanish people.

The Congress emphatically condemns the persecution of and discrimination against Communists, consistent champions of peace and the security of peoples, the most dedicated fighters for the interests of the working people and for a better future for mankind. The Congress declares its full support for the heroes and persecuted fighters in the revolutionary and liberation movement and sends them its fraternal greetings.

The 25th Congress of the CPSU supports and approves the proposal made in the report delivered by Comrade L. I. Brezhnev, General Secretary of the CPSU Central Committee, for erecting in Moscow, as a symbol of the Soviet

Communists' undying devotion to the great cause of proletarian inter-nationalism, a memorial to the heroes of the international communist, working-class and national liberation movement, to the selfless fighters for people's happiness, who fell at the hands of the class enemy.

From the experience of the heroic Bolshevik Party and of many generations of revolutionaries of other countries we know that any attempt to halt the march of history by terror is doomed to failure.

The 25th Congress of the CPSU calls on all the Communists of the world, on the working people of all countries, on all public and political organizations, to intensify the struggle to end the terror and repressions against the vanguard forces of progress, democracy and socialism, and to fight for the release of all prisoners of reaction.

The CPSU, the peoples of the Union of Soviet Socialist Republics, will always and steadfastly follow the Leninist traditions of active solidarity with their comrades-in-arms in the struggle for great and noble aims, and will always be faithful to proletarian internationalism.   □

12

LEONID BREZHNEV

Concluding Remarks

Summing Up the Debate on the Report

March 1, 1976

Comrade delegates,

There is no doubt that the new Central Committee which we are to elect will make a careful study of the views and opinions expressed here and will take account of them in its work. We must remark on the exceptionally constructive, businesslike and principled character of the debate.

A serious analysis of the results of the past five-year period; thoughts on the present and the future of the Party and the country; meaningful and interesting proposals concerning many problems of our development; a critical and exacting approach to one's own activity—that I would say, is the principal characteristic of the speeches delivered here.

A creative style of work worthy of Communists prevails at the Congress as in the whole Party. Expressions of devotion to proletarian internationalism, words about the friendship of the peoples and the struggle for peace rang out loud and unanimous. This is our policy and we shall not depart from it.

I must note the tremendous optimism of those who spoke here, their confident and purposeful tone. This is the result of the feasibility of our plans, a result of their understanding that when the Party charts its goals relying on its collective wisdom, and sets itself and the whole country tasks, these goals will be attained, these tasks will be fulfilled.

I am grateful to all the comrades who have given a high assessment of the Report. Kind words have also been spoken here by our foreign friends about our Central Committee, our Political Bureau and about myself. However, we shall be doing the right thing in regarding the successes achieved as the result of collective work, of the joint efforts of the Party's governing bodies and of all the Party committees and organizations.

We shall be doing the right thing, acting in a Leninist manner, if, in acknowledging what has been achieved, we concentrate our attention on the shortcomings which we still have, on tasks still to be carried out.

I think the delegates to the Congress will agree that that is the kind of approach which will best promote the growth of the political activity and creative energy of the Communists and our whole people.

At the Closing of the Congress

Comrade delegates,
    The members of the newly elected Central Committee of the Party have asked me to express their wholehearted gratitude for the trust placed in them. Allow me to assure you that the Central Committee as a whole, and the Political Bureau and Secretariat which it has elected, will do their utmost to measure up to their responsibilities.

Quite naturally, we believe that our main task is to ensure implementation of the decisions of the 25th Party Congress, which means ensuring the achievement of new major victories for the cause of communism and the cause of peace.

Dear comrades, the 25th Congress has come to a close. The Congress has discussed the results of the past five-year period, attentively and objectively analyzed the experience acquired, and examined our plans for the future. We now have a better realization of where the new sources, new reserves for further growth lie, and a clearer understanding of the tasks facing the Party.

The Congress has determined the Party's principled political line for the coming years. Our 25th Congress has outlined new horizons in the struggle for further developing the country's strength, for raising the Soviet people's living standards, and for bettering our entire social life. It has also put forward new concrete tasks in the sphere of foreign policy, in the struggle for peace and international cooperation, for the freedom and independence of the nations.

The plans approved by the Congress are challenging and not easy to fulfill. The tasks which it has set are very serious tasks. But we are quite sure that these plans will be realized, that these tasks will be fulfilled. After all, since their purpose is to bring about greater prosperity for our socialist homeland, and secure a happy life in peace for the Soviet people they will, without doubt, have the support of all the Soviet people.

The work of the Congress has gone far beyond the limits of this hall. It has reached out to all the Party organizations, to the factories and the scientific institutes, to the collective and state farms and fields, across the whole of our vast country. Millions of Soviet people marked the 25th Congress with good deeds and by getting the very best results in their work. The number of these remarkable achievements is immense. Let me recall a few.

The atomic ice-breaker Sibir has been launched ahead of schedule. The family of Soviet passenger cars has been increased by the new Moskvich and VAZ models. An important stage in the assembly of the giant 350-passenger IL-86 airliner has been completed ahead of schedule, and test flights of the new Yak-42 plane have been started. The working people of Leningrad have built the country's most powerful turbine generator with a capacity of 1.2 million kw, while the Zeya Hydroelectric Power Plant, the first such plant in the Far

East, at the other end of the country, has been made operational. In the south, the main operations in building the first, 400-kilometer section of the North Crimea Canal have been completed, while new deposits of polymetallic ores, iron ore and apatites have been discovered in the Northeast of the country. The USSR Academy of Sciences has received and started to operate the world's largest optical telescope.

These splendid achievements are a most powerful and most effective demonstration of the unity of purpose, thought and deed of the Party and the people in our society. Every participant whether a member of the Communist Party or not, has, in effect, made a contribution to the work of our Congress.

The Party highly appreciates this contribution as a remarkable expression of Soviet patriotism and concern for our common great cause of communist construction.

Or take another thing—the endless stream of thousands upon thousands of letters and telegrams addressed to our Congress, arriving daily and hourly and still coming in. They cannot be read without emotion and pride for our Soviet people—the politically mature and active citizens of the Land of the Soviets— ardent patriots and internationalists.

Allow me, comrade delegates, to express sincere gratitude on your behalf, to all those who have addressed the Party forum expressing their feelings and thoughts.

Allow me also to express profound gratitude to our foreign comrades, friends and people of good will in the socialist and capitalist countries, and in the newly liberated countries who on the eve of and during the Congress sent in tens of thousands of letters with warm greetings and best wishes for our Party, our country and the Soviet people.

More than 100 delegations of Communist and Workers' Parties, national democratic parties and movements have taken part in the work of our Congress.

Here, from this rostrum, and also at numerous meetings and rallies in various cities of our country, our brothers by class from other countries have expressed many warm feelings for the Communist Party of the Soviet Union, for our country and our people. They spoke of the CPSU's historic mission in blazing the trail for the peoples to socialism and communism. They spoke of our country's role in the struggle for peace for all nations.

We are grateful for these expressions and, for our part, assure the Communists, workers and all fighters for national and social freedom in all countries that the Communists and all the people of the Soviet Union will continue to be equal to their internationalist tasks in the future as well!

Allow me, on behalf of the Congress, to convey our ardent militant greetings to all the Communists of our country, and to wish them success in their undertakings, in their plans, in their life.

We are well aware that all of us will have to work long and hard to reach the planned objectives. Every Communist, every Party organization, every Party committee must contribute to fulfilling the Congress decisions. They must be translated into concrete targets and plans. We must consolidate and sustain the spirit, the working rhythm generated by the pre-Congress emulation. The Central Committee is sure that this will be done.

Comrades, comments in the international press about our Congress, including bourgeois press comments, note the cohesion and optimism of the Soviet Communists, and the peaceable, stable and confident character of the CPSU's policy. I think that we can all agree with this appraisal.

The history of our Leninist Party has been marked by a remarkable constellation of congresses. Each of them has been an important milestone in the life of the Party and the country. There is no doubt that the 25th Congress will rank among them as a special and unique congress, as a congress of great accomplishments, which has been keynoted by realism and efficiency, calm confidence in our strength, confidence in fresh victories for our great cause of communist construction, our struggle for a just and lasting peace in the world!   □

Part Six: United States Opinion

13

Statements of Prominent Americans

The editors solicited reactions to the Congress from a variety of people–trade unionists, peace and political activists, journalists, scholars. The respondents are listed immediately below; their statements follow.

Frank L. Batterson
Phillip Bonosky
Harry Bridges
David DeGrood
Hugo Gellert
Joe Harris
Cliff and Chris Herness
Joshua Kunitz
Edward Lamb
John Howard Lawson
Carolyn F. Lobban
Richard Lobban
Richard Morford
George B. Murphy, Jr.
Joseph North
Howard L. Parsons
William L. Patterson
Art Shields
Jack Spiegel
James Steele
Dorothy Steffens
Augusta Strong
Jarvis Tyner
•
Antar Sudan Katara Mberi

To me, a member of the American working class, the 25th Congress of the CPSU stands out primarily as a historical milestone on the road to world peace. In its program of "immediate objectives," the Congress has charted the road to world peace for the Soviet people, and humanity as a whole. Regardless of the Reagans, Wallaces, Jacksons and their multinational backers, detente is sinking deeper and deeper roots in the ever-changing realities of our times.

The confidence and trust which the 25th Congress has inspired is simply the spiritual reflection, in the minds of millions of people throughout the world, of the concrete achievements and total record of the Soviet Union, since the October 1917 socialist revolution.

Peace is an imperative condition placed on humankind, on pain of destruction, by its present attainments in scientific and technological knowhow. For it is doubtful civilization itself could survive another world war. Therefore, not only the Soviet people, but struggling, economically backward nations, and progressives everywhere feel heartened by these words of General Secretary L. I. Brezhnev: "The Soviet Union's foreign policy enjoys the respect and support of many millions of people all over the world. And we shall continue this policy with redoubled energy, working to bridle the forces of war and aggression, to consolidate world peace and assure the people's right to freedom, independence and social progress."

FRANK L. BATTERSON
Washington State Council, American-Soviet
Friendship

People of the finest motives, noble people, people inspired with the love of mankind, for centuries have cried in vain against the scourge of war, and war always walked over them with its bloody boots. Why, if all good men hated war, did war in fact fall upon the world year after bloody year from the very beginning of recorded time?

War was never a moral question alone, to be solved by moral suasion. No Pope ever stopped a war, no King or President. Only in our times, only now when war has grown so monstrous that it eats up not only people but the land itself, trees, cows and chickens, water and air, has the power come on earth that can not only stop war now but can truly raise the prospect of eliminating it altogether from the affairs of men. That power is embodied in the man in overalls, carrying a hammer and a sickle.

We know why wars take place. War is not born in our evil hearts. It is born in the social necessity of history. But it has become like the monster of Frankenstein grown now so powerful and anarchic in its lust that it has overtaken history and threatens to engulf it.

Only now, as we behold the possibility of annihilation, can we also see the possibility of salvation. This possibility was hailed and celebrated in the 25th Congress of the Communist Party of the USSR. And it is because this Congress took steps to ensure that the world will survive in peace, or at least will avoid all-destructive war, that it was of enormous importance to all Americans. Beyond all divisions stands the need to survive for mankind. And more acutely than ever before in history millions are aware of both the incredible danger that faces them and of the tremendous power that exists in their own hands to save themselves, to save humanity.

The threat of war today comes only from one main source: American imperialism.

The assurance for peace comes from all working mankind, backed up by the organized might of the international working class and, above all, of the working class organized into a state, the Soviet working class.

It's not in the Pentagon that an American should look for peace. It's in the promises that come out of congresses like the congress in Moscow that peace can be assured. It is, therefore, in the profoundest sense of the word, an act of patriotism to support the decisions of the congress, throwing into the winds all accusations that to do so is to belie one's own love of country and dedication to its best interests.

PHILLIP BONOSKY
Author

The achievements of the Soviet people, as highlighted in the proceedings of the 25th Congress of the Communist Party of the USSR, are exemplary.

In a little over a half-century, they have completely remade their own country. They have created a society in which unemployment and inflation do not exist, and in which the individual citizen can develop his or her own potential to the fullest. They have set a new standard for what can be accomplished by and for the working class.

Second, the Congress highlights and reaffirms the commitment of the Soviet people to world peace and detente. The point is correctly made that there is no alternative. The Congress reaffirms that the Soviet people and the Soviet Government will never permit thermonuclear war.

Finally, the reaffirmation of the USSR's unselfish willingness to assist in the struggle of the colonial nations for real independence is also a key achievement of the Congress. Again, the existence of the Soviet Union guarantees that the people of Africa, Asia, and Latin America will have the opportunity to work out their own destiny without interference by their former masters. The success of socialism in the USSR has given people all over the world tremendous hope that they can control their own destinies.

The American people should be aware of the resolutions and proceedings of the 25th Congress. I support and salute the efforts of NEW WORLD REVIEW to bring them the full story.

HARRY BRIDGES
President, International Longshoremen's &
Warehousemen's Union

The 25th Congress of the CPSU is a symbol of the vast changes that are occurring in the world. Imperialism has been forced to retreat from many areas of our planet, and the world's first socialist state has made steady, unprecedented progress on all levels. The policy of detente has shown itself to promote peace, disarmament, economic prosperity and new jobs (in the US, for example), international cultural and tourist exchange, acceleration of scientific-technological progress. The CP Congress in the Soviet Union and its results and plans show what humans can do working cooperatively, without exploitation, unemployment, crisis, bourgeois decadence, and preparation for aggressive war. Detente undergirds its foreign policy. Objectively and humanistically the American people have the same needs and interests. It is up to them and not "their" bourgeois politicians to realize them.

DAVID DEGROOD
Professor of Philosophy

Millions prepared the 25th Congress of the CPSU, and Brezhnev told the Congress that a total of more than a million proposals and suggestions had been received. A special commission will consider and take them into account in the final drafting of the five year plan. "Democracy" said Brezhnev, "is an empty word if it does not embrace the places where people work and where their talents and abilities are unfolded. The USSR attaches special importance to the strengthening of democratic principles at the point of production."

Genuine democracy is determined by who owns the material wealth—the land, banks and factories; the few or the entire society. Socialism in the USSR means owning collectively, working collectively and ruling collectively.

There is no inflation in the USSR, nor unemployment, nor racism—the three curses that plague the capitalist world. There is steady growth in the living standards of the people instead.

In my opinion, it is our good fortune that there is a Soviet Union—safe and sane—the protector of peoples large and small wherever they dwell on this earth.

HUGO GELLERT
Artist

The tremendous achievements of the Soviet people, recorded in the 25th Congress of the CPSU, show conclusively that only socialism has "an answer to the requirements of social and economic progress" (Kosygin).

Half a century ago Lenin urged the young Soviet republic to enter into economic competition with the capitalist nations. He called upon the Soviet people to overcome their legacy of economic backwardness and to overtake and surpass the heights of imperialist production.

Today Lenin's behest to the Soviet people is on the verge of completion. In 1975, industrial production in the USSR reached 95 per cent of the US level. In many important industrial products, the USSR has already surpassed the USA. For example, by 1970 the USSR produced "more pig iron, iron, manganese and chromium ore, coal and coking coal, cement, potassium salts, phosphate primary materials, tractors, diesel and electric locomotives, cotton, wool, flax and some other items than any other country (Kosygin—25th Congress). By 1975, the list expanded to include crude oil and steel!

The technological gap is also being bridged, and in many industries the USSR is a net exporter of technology. In the next few years, we should expect to see the gap in computer and chemical technology overcome as well.

By 1980 the Soviet Union will be far ahead of the USA in total industrial production, and its per capita industrial production may very well exceed that of the USA. This will lay the foundation for living standards, including consumer goods usage, to also surpass US levels. *The ideological struggle between socialism and capitalism will be profoundly affected by these economic developments.*

Progressive Americans must bring the USSR's message of peace and detente to the American people. We must tell the American people that the USSR is using its increasing power for the benefit of the working people of the world, for opposing imperialism's efforts to start wars, to reinforce racism and colonialism. We must convince workers, students, intellectuals, small businessmen—the vast majority of

Americans—that Soviet power does not threaten our vital interests; instead it is the best guarantee for a world without wars, colonial oppression, racism, and fascism.

JOE HARRIS
Research Director, Labor Research Association

We must agree with Pauline Frederick's comment on a recent radio program to the effect that most Americans are too misinformed to participate appropriately in international affairs. As an indication of how little we know of the Soviet Union, for instance, what percentage of our electorate has read the report of the Central Committee to the 25th CPSU Congress? How many of our libraries or newsstands have that extremely important report available for those who would like to read it in order to learn at first hand what the Soviets see as their main accomplishments of the past five years and their main goals for the next five?

Many US citizens would be surprised at the thoughtfulness of that report, its strong emphasis on the need for lasting peace and the means for achieving it; for good-neighborly relations with all countries; for mutually beneficial trade (which would help to increase jobs in the US); for the increased well-being of all Soviet citizens and a steady effort to ensure full participation by the working people in running all the affairs of the country.

For that matter, how many Americans realize that the Soviet Union has had no unemployment since 1930; that it provides really free education from kindergarten through University and even gives the students living-expense stipends; that excellent health care is free to all; and that crime has been reduced to a minimum so that one can walk the streets alone in Moscow, Leningrad, Tashkent or any other Soviet city at any hour of the day or night without fear?

We hear much about "freedom of information" but the Soviet Union publishes more books than any other country; the average Soviet family subscribes to four periodicals and the 25th Congress is recommending expansion to meet the rapidly growing demand for more. Soviet citizens are well informed.

The Report to the 25th Congress rightly concludes that in the six decades since the October Revolution (less than one life-time) a new society has been created, a society with a crisis-free, steadily growing economy; a society that has firm confidence in the future based on the solid successes of the past.

CLIFF AND CHRIS HERNESS
Minnesota Council of American-Soviet Friendship

An octogenarian does not easily spark into a festive mood. But the reports from the 25th Congress of the CPSU have produced just this happy effect. I am elated with the sense of past achievement and confidence in the future that breathes from the speeches of Brezhnev, Kosygin and others. I am happy with the stress on the historic imperatives of detente; with the evidence of unanimity in the struggle for peace, and with the unyielding adherence to Marxist-Leninist principles.

Despite the huffing and puffing by Kissinger, Ford and Jackson; despite their threats, warnings, hesitations, twists and turns, any alternative is impossible for them to advocate.

For nearly sixty years American correspondents in Moscow and *The New York Times* (that tireless cold warrior) have orchestrated the dire prophecies of either the imminent collapse of the first socialist state or its failure to serve the needs of its people. During that time I have watched the USSR complete nine consecutive five-year plans; build a great, modern industrial plant; great institutions of learning and a unique multinational culture. In short, a society which has ended exploitation of man by man.

I lived to see all this. It is easy to be elated.

JOSHUA KUNITZ
Writer

The 25th Congress of the Communist Party has ended and the people of the Soviet Union are now enthusiastically embarked upon their Tenth Five-Year Plan. At the same time, the American people, choosing a Chief Executive, not fully informed about the accomplishments of a socialist or planned society, will themselves be involved in discussions of their many problems, domestic and international. It may be that we're disillusioned with our leadership and that actual citizenship participation in the process of deciding who will be our President is low. Everyone should recognize that the basis for internationalism and togetherness in the World Community will not occur without disarmament and detente. But there are few suggestions by the candidates for solving problems of unemployment, inflation and the quality of life. There will even be attempts by various candidates to snow-job us and it behooves each of us to individually and collectively stand up and speak the truth about our relationships with other countries.

The United States must face up to the fact that it is rapidly becoming a have-not nation, devoid of surpluses and now required to import vast resources from nations with differing political systems. Inflation, as we know, means the shortage of goods and services. Nor will we solve the problems of inflation by turning on the printing presses or "increasing the supply of money." Productivity and not monetary manipulation is the solution. In this connection it is wise to remind ourselves that we're piling up deficits of seventy billions of dollars a year. I join others who suggest that this debt under present planning will never be repaid.

Planning? There is widespread discussion of getting planning into our American public sector, even under our so-called mixed economy, where we have enterprises, public and private. To even mention planning requires America to look to the world's first planned economy. No unemployment, no inflation, increasing attention to the social needs of its people—and increasing productivity. And most of all, a policy of peaceful coexistence with all of mankind working within an international organization. Indeed, what could be a better objective for Americans than that we turn our eyes to the future with an awareness of our need for friendship and love between the two great peoples of the USSR and the USA?

EDWARD LAMB
Industrialist, Banker and Attorney

We are living in a great period of historic change. The people of the United States begin to see the breakdown of American policy based on imperialism and aggression. But Americans have heard so many lies that the truth is obscured. The role of the Soviet

Union is clear to all thinking people but so many Americans have no means of knowing the truth. Peace and detente must be explained. We must reach our people. We must spread the word.

JOHN HOWARD LAWSON
Playwright, Author

We are living in an exciting time, a time that is witnessing the growing strength of the socialist world with the parallel decline of imperialism. Socialism is no longer an experiment; it is no longer just another alternative to monopoly capitalism; it is the dominant historical trend of the twentieth century. Nowhere was this made more apparent than in the recent 25th Congress of the CPSU, a great achievement for the Soviet people and for working and progressive people the world over. The leading role of the Soviet Union in international solidarity with socialist countries, the solidarity expressed with the communist movements in the capitalist countries and the support given by the Soviet Union to national liberation struggles *underscores* the critical role of the CPSU in formulating a world policy that means peace and progress for all peoples. As the bourgeois electoral farce in the US gets under way we recognize that the two capitalist parties do not represent the future of our class, but that the international working class movements and the anti-imperialist forces are our greatest allies.

It was for me a happy occasion that the 25th Congress of the CPSU met at a time soon after the People's Republic of Angola was fresh from victories against western imperialism and racism. The decade-long Soviet support for the MPLA proved that making class and political distinctions between MPLA, FNLA and UNITA was critical to a correct appraisal of the Angolan situation. Angola's victory was not a fluke or an accident, nor were the victories in Guinea-Bissau or Mozambique, nor the triumph of the NLF in Vietnam. These successes were the result of correct political theory and practice within these movements harnessed to the international support of the socialist countries led by the Soviet Union. Angola has been the final international lesson in the Maoist school of counter-revolution. The opportunism and bankruptcy of Chinese support for the CIA agents of the FNLA and the allies of South African racism, UNITA, expose the essence of Maoism. That essence is anti-Sovietism. Still in the report of the General Secretary at the 25th Congress the Soviet Union extends itself once again to normalize relations with China under the principles of peaceful coexistence. Here in the American progressive movement, it is our profoundest wish that the Chinese leadership will recover from its period of error and join with the socialist nations of the world in the struggle against imperialism, monopoly capitalism in the US and western Europe, and finally give support to the legitimate national liberation movements representing the best interests of their people.

Viewing the change which has occurred since the last Party Congress five years ago, especially the international victories, we look forward with confidence and optimism to the progressive change the next period will bring.

CAROLYN F. LOBBAN
Assistant Professor of Anthropology

Peace in the world today is no longer just desirable, it is necessary. For this very important reason I consider the 25th Congress of the Communist Party of the Soviet Union to be another stepping stone in the long walk to peace in the world. Insecurity, instability, and the threat of war are constant burdens in a world filled with class antagonisms and a neocolonial division of the great wealth of this planet. Every step toward the ultimate elimination of class and national inequalities is a step toward peace for mankind. Never before in the history of the human race have we had such strong reasons for optimism coexisting with the gravest threat of nuclear war. All peace-loving Americans rejoice that the internationally beneficial policy of detente has become almost irreversible. While the commercial and governmental news media seldom make note of the origin of detente, Secretary of State Kissinger has confided that the policy was conceived by the Soviet Union.

My special professional and personal interest is African Studies, and I can say that the foreign policy outlined by the 25th Congress has been of particular merit and success on the African continent. The long-standing and principled support by the Soviet Union for national liberation movements has achieved profound victories in the struggle against colonialism, imperialism, and racism. Part of the beauty of these great transformations in social and political relations is that the world has not been thrown into a bloody nuclear confrontation, yet the freedom-loving people of Angola, Cape Verde, Guinea Bissau, Mozambique, and Sao Tome and Principe have won their historic battles and the struggles in Zimbabwe, Namibia, and South Africa are making rapid, very rapid gains.

The unique combination of a correct foreign policy linked to a planned domestic economy in the Soviet Union shows a nation with greater strength and firmer resolve than ever before. With the American working class facing heavy hardships of unemployment and inflation, the example of the Soviet Union shines through the fog of confusion which clouds the vision of the working people in America. The capitalist and the "Maoist" alternatives are nearing the end of their credibility for millions of workers who see that international socialism is the only answer for global peace and an end of exploitation of man by man.

DR. RICHARD LOBBAN
*Assistant Professor of African
Studies and Anthropology*

Why do we not take Mr. Brezhnev at his word? "To make the danger of war recede . . . and to create favorable conditions for progress towards disarmament," Mr. Brezhnev declared in his report to the 25th Congress of the CPSU, "we now offer to conclude a world treaty on the non-use of force in international relations." The unfriendly may say he does not mean it. I believe the people of the Soviet Union would back this offer. Etched indelibly in memory and burned in their hearts are the 20 million lives lost in World War II. A people contributing millions of rubles annually to the Soviet Peace Fund will support their leaders in every reasonable effort to achieve international agreement to safeguard the peace.

Mr. Brezhnev's statement is not rhetoric; it is the sober expression of a consistent historical peace policy. One goes back to 1922 when the old League of Nations Association was challenged by the representative of the Soviet Union, Mr. Maxim Litvinov, to undertake a plan for world-wide disarmament. Follow through the years. In 1955 the Soviet Union introduced a proposal in the United Nations outlining a plan for general and complete universal disarmament to be accomplished in four years. No one challenged the good faith of the Soviets then. World opinion compelled the United States to offer a general disarmament plan in the United Nations in 1962, a plan replete with escape clauses; the United States itself never chose to push it. The Soviet Union has made proposals frequently for the outlawing of nuclear weapons. When these proposals have fallen on deaf ears, the Soviet Union has said it was willing to negotiate a reduction in conventional arms. Before the United Nations for two years has been a Soviet proposal for a ten per cent across the board reduction of military budgets of the major countries.

True enough, in the light of this history of reluctance on the part of the USA to consider disarmament seriously, in the light of open and covert increase in the sophistication and quantity of USA armament, the Soviet Union matches us step by step in the creation of new weaponry. I understand the determination of the Soviet defense establishment in this connection, while I do not acquiesce in it. Nor do I acquiesce in what the USA is doing. My job is at home putting effort into the mobilization of demands for a drastic curtailment in USA arms expenditures which we are told by competent authorities is possible without endangering our national security. The National Council of American-Soviet Friendship of which I am the director is prepared to join in this effort.

Were our people able to prevail upon the Congress, I dare to say this action would not be lost upon the Soviet Union. Their earnest desire is to put a stop to the arms race. Mr. Brezhnev does not say that an agreement for the non-use of force in international relations will solve all problems. He says such agreement would create favorable conditions for progress towards disarmament. To meet this Soviet challenge squarely would serve the best interests of the USA; it would be realism of the highest order; it would mark a major advance on the road to peace.

RICHARD MORFORD
Executive Director, National Council of
American-Soviet Friendship

The historic twenty-fifth CPSU Congress of the Soviet Union, first socialist country on earth, and the leading force among nations for world peace, has just ended.

The Congress gave an accurate demonstration of the democratically arrived at unity of the entire Soviet people, comprising fifteen republics and representing more than 100 different nationalities, in support of the government's Leninist peace policy, while setting new goals for a continuing, steady improvement in the material, social, cultural and spiritual well-being of 250 million people engaged in building a communist society.

Fully conscious of the USSR's internationalist responsibilities to the international working class, the national liberation movements in Africa, Asia, Latin America and the

Middle East, in concert with all progressive humankind, the 5,000 Congress members and 1,000 fraternal representatives from more than 100 countries gave a resounding standing approval in support of the Soviet Union's reaffirmation of detente and the Leninist principles of peaceful coexistence between nations of different social systems.

The historic decisions arrived at during the 25th CPSU Congress, representing sixty years of Marxist-Leninist working-class science operating in a planned economy, will be given sober and thoughtful attention by progressive-minded people in all countries of the world, who are now convinced that detente and the principles of peaceful coexistence are the only alternative to nuclear death and destruction for the human race.

All of this augurs well for the hopes and aspirations of Black Americans, all other minorities, Black and white working people, and all progressives in our country, daily engaged in sharp struggles against genocidal racism, for jobs, equality, justice and democracy and peace.

The world's peoples must never be allowed to forget that the Soviet people gave the life blood of twenty million of its finest sons and daughters, of all nationalities, in the defeat of Hitler racist fascism. This is the concrete fact that illuminates the work of this Soviet Congress. It is the concrete fact that must illuminate our struggles to abolish racism, under conditions of democracy and peace, in our country.

GEORGE B. MURPHY, JR.
Staff member, Afro-American Newspapers
Editorial Consultant, New World Review

A statue stands on the banks of the East River in Manhattan which is, to me, a symbol of what the 25th Congress charted. The monument is by the Soviet sculptor Vuchetich, and shows the heroic figure of humanity beating swords into plowshares. I saw crowds of New Yorkers gather around it these spring days to ponder its message. So humanity is reflecting on the results of the 25th Congress of the world's most dedicated men and women—the CPSU. The Congress took place at a point in history when the world fervently strives for irreversible guarantees against war in this nuclear age. And simultaneously humanity was seeking some measure of social progress in a day when capitalist crisis engulfs millions in the mire of unemployment.

Five years have passed since mankind welcomed the declaration of an all-out offensive against war at the 24th Congress. By the time of this Congress they were reaping the results of policies that achieved a heartening advance in detente. Hundreds of thousands of US workers and many millions worldwide exulted in detente agreements which mean jobs. They know many millions more could go to work if detente, peaceful coexistence, and reduction in arms, are furthered. Those were Leonid Brezhnev's proposals on behalf of his Party and the Soviet People at this Congress which registered unprecedented gains in peaceful production and consequent standards in living.

Peace has been the salient point in each CPSU Congress since the first working day of the Revolution in 1917 when Lenin called on the nations to lay down arms. These Congresses have taught humanity that war is not a natural cataclysm like an earthquake. We have reached a point today where ending war is a practical possibility. World War III has been staved off due to the surging dynamic of the peoples' anti-war resistance led by the Soviet people and their CPSU. And the plain people of mankind have come to realize their own power to intervene to halt war forever. Humanity—observing the mighty advances in production, living standards and in the quality of life in the USSR—tenders its heartfelt thanks to those selfless men and women of factory, farm and laboratory who met at their Congress in February and March. It was a monument to the invincible human spirit.

JOSEPH NORTH
Author and Journalist

The reports at the CPSU Congress are new confirmation of the close connection between the health of the Soviet people's economy and the vital Soviet contribution to world peace in the past five years.

Soon after the Bolshevik Revolution, an American reporter, Lincoln Steffens, who had been in the Soviet Union, said: "I have been over into the future, and it works." That was more than fifty years ago. Anyone who doubts that it is still working and is working well should read the Congress reports concerning the greatly increased productivity of the Soviet people. A planned economy free of inflation, unemployment, run-away military spending, a crumbling monetary-fiscal-currency system, and an energy crisis is indeed incredible from a capitalist perspective. But such an economy does exist in the Soviet Union, providing through collective labor and reason rising income and benefits for all. It is a challenging alternative for all humanistically minded people in capitalist countries to behold.

A progressive, democratic nation is bound to strive for relations of peaceful coexistence with nations of different social systems, securing the conditions for avoiding war and for guaranteeing the progress of peoples. Consistent with Lenin's policies and the inherent necessity of socialism, the Soviet Union has negotiated the US-USSR agreements of 1972, the agreement of 1973 on the prevention of nuclear war, and the SALT agreements, as well as the Helsinki accords. The Congress has demonstrated once more that the Soviet government and people are serious about peaceful coexistence and detente and their extension, and about ending the arms race, reducing arms, and disarmament. They understand that progress, democracy, and peace are indivisible.

Some people in capitalist countries say that these Soviet policies are tricks and intrigues. Such a view comes from either ignorance or malice. These policies derive from self-interest, to be sure. But it is a self-interest that recognizes that no social system can be safe and no people can freely develop materially and spiritually in a world of arms and war. It is a self-interest that wills the life and the welfare of all peoples.

The great imperative of our time for every person and government is the democratic development of all peoples through detente, peaceful coexistence, and disarmament.

HOWARD L. PARSONS
Professor of Philosophy

The report presented by Leonid I. Brezhnev, General Secretary of the Communist Party of the Union of Soviet Socialist Republics to the 25th Congress of that party is not alone the property of that Party. It is not alone the property of the millions of heroic men, women and youth who live within the confines of that "family of nations," that once was the empire of the Russian Tsars.

That historic report and the resolutions flowing from it which those heroic Soviet citizens have sworn to implement are also of vital concern to the untold millions of the world at large who stand unqualifiedly for the peaceful coexistence of sovereign states differing fundamentally in their economic, political and cultural structure. It is also of great value to those who from their own lives see the absolute necessity for world peace and national security, those who cannot live with racism and bigotry in any of their varied forms.

For the millions of Africa, Asia, Latin America, the Caribbean Basin, that report is a massive stimulant and inspiration. It records in no uncertain terms that the decisive spiritual and material aid extended to their desperate liberation struggles will not cease, as in the case of Angola and other nations. For those who live under the crisis-wracked racist democracy of monopoly capitalism in the United States their role in the process of change and its direction looms infinitely clearer through this report.

History has intervened favorably. The 25th Congress with its report on the magnificent growth and development of Soviet economy and politics, the unprecedented advancement of the standard of living under socialist democracy appeared upon the stage at the moment when the American bourgeoisie is celebrating the two hundredth anniversary of this nation's birth in slavery.

What an amazing contrast in the economic, political and cultural status of the two worlds history presents!

The first picture reveals a unified people, formulating a program that reflects the vital interests of industrial workers, collective farmers, scientists, literary men and women and art workers, alike. It reveals a people creating a new world, a people struggling to prevent a third imperialist world war, a people supporting the liberation movements of all oppressed and exploited humanity. The course of social development is scientifically analyzed and the perspectives embued with optimism. There is neither unemployment nor inflation. The voice one hears is that of a people fully aware of its responsibility to progressive humanity.

The US Bicentennial celebration comes in an atmosphere of millions of unemployed and destitute people, victims of the "benign neglect" of a ruling class whose racist crimes crowned by the myth of white superiority have become a way of life pitting the white oppressed masses against their class brothers and sisters of color. The interim between the birth of the nation and the 1970s is characterized by the growth of racist terror, inspired by the ruling class.

The report of Leonid Brezhnev to the 25th Congress of the Party and Soviet peoples is of tremendous significance to the people fighting for peace and against racism the world over.

WILLIAM L. PATTERSON
Co-Chairman, Black Liberation
Commission, CPUSA

One feels the beauty and strength of socialism as he reads the reports of Leonid I. Brezhnev and Alexey I. Kosygin to the 25th Congress of the Communist Party of the Soviet Union. I felt this beauty and power when I sat in the press gallery of the Palace of Congresses at the 23rd Congress ten years ago. This beauty and power is still richer today. And my mind goes back to my first glimpse of the Soviet land 58 years ago. I was visiting the Eskimo school at Cape Prince of Wales, the far western tip of Alaska. It was early evening. The fog, that hid the horizon, had just lifted. The sun was setting, and the hills of Chukhotka were bathed in purple and gold on the western side of Bering Strait not far away.

That was in April 1918, six months after the October Revolution. Soviet power had not yet reached the Eskimo villages in Chukhotka. But I felt the promise of the future, and this promise is being gloriously fulfilled. In 1964 I talked to two young Eskimo women from Chukhotka at a medical institute in Khabarovsk on the Amur River. Their once isolated villages have been transformed by the collective way of life with good schools, medical clinics, cooperative fur farms, fisheries and hunting collectives, and they were looking forward to a happy and useful life.

It is people like these two women who were represented at the 25th Congress. They are members of the coalition of socialist peoples, who are leading the peoples of the entire world to a happy and useful future.

ART SHIELDS
Veteran Labor Journalist

Despite all the pressures from the right wing and militarists of our country to scrap detente and to push through the over $113 billion military budget, the majority of people in our country surely, in our own interests, want normal and peaceful relations with the Soviet Union. It was a delight and encouragement to read about the 25th Congress of the CPSU, to feel the complete dedication of General Secretary Leonid Brezhnev and the rest of the Soviet leadership to a continued course of detente and world peace, and the emphasis on this course by all the delegates. There is no question of the complete sincerity of Soviet leaders and people in their calls to rid the world of war as an instrument of international policy.

Our job here is to keep on fighting for detente, for easing world tensions that could lead to a new world war. Of first priority in this is the struggle to reduce our huge military budget. The very act of reducing the scale of investment in areas like the B-1, the Trident submarine, and the cruise missiles and other terror weapons, will ease the atmosphere, making it possible to revive the drive for peaceful trade with the USSR, creating hundreds of thousands of jobs for US workers.

Funds saved from slashing the budget can be turned to increasing expenditures for health, education, housing and the people's welfare and numerous projects that will ease our continuing unemployment crisis.

Let us join with the Soviet Union and other peace-loving nations in the fight for curbing the arms race, above all in the call for a world disarmament conference that will be a great step forward to a peaceful world.

JACK SPIEGEL
Lake States Director, United Shoe Workers' Union

I would like to briefly consider the significance of the 25th Congress from the standpoint of the special victims of the present US economic crisis—the young generation, especially Black and other oppressed national minority youth. In this context, I also strongly suggest that all young people read the documents of the Congress, particularly the report delivered by Leonid I. Brezhnev, and compare the Soviet emphasis on peace and the people's needs with the State of the Union and budgetary messages of President Ford.

It is a tremendous inspiration to hear a country's leadership say that *the most important thing is to ensure* that the "Soviet people are better off materially and richer spiritually." "Inflation," "cut-backs," etc. are totally absent from Soviet life. Think of what confidence, security and enthusiasm this gives to young Soviet workers and their families.

Mr. Brezhnev underlined the role of youth when he noted that youth, led by the Young Communist League or Komsomol, are building the Baikal-Amur Railway, one of the most important and ambitious construction projects in the USSR's history. The YCL also took responsibility for 670 construction and 1,200 land-improvement projects over the past five years. Imagine the creative contribution this nation's unemployed youth could be making if it had Soviet socialist society's confidence in young people.

Another feature of the Congress, even more important to American youth, is the fight for peaceful coexistence and detente, especially in relation to the United States. Without peace there can be neither the building of communism in the USSR nor democratic advance and economic well-being of the people in the USA.

The struggles of US youth for jobs, education, equal rights, sports and cultural facilities are intimately tied to this question. We will not end unemployment with a cruise missile, or be educated in a B-1 bomber, or housed in a Trident submarine. Youth should demand that President Ford and every candidate in the November elections give a positive answer to the specific Soviet initiatives for peaceful cooperation and expanded trade which would create tens of thousands of jobs for US workers. If they are not for detente, vote against them because they are not really for jobs, good education and a better life for this country's youth.

JAMES STEELE
National Chairman, Young Workers
Liberation League

The recent Congress of the Communist Party, USSR, took place during the US primary elections. The contrast between these two major events provides interesting insight into democracy, as this word is interpreted in the two countries.

In the US, we have become familiar with the hope, springing anew every four years, that people can significantly alter government policies through the electoral process. Many of us put money, time and organizing skills into one or another of the two major political parties, hoping against hope, flying in the face of past experience, to make our constitutional democracy work—to elect a government which will provide jobs; decent housing; day care; free, superior education; a safe environment; security in our old age; and all the other guarantees which are subsumed under the phrase "life, liberty and the pursuit of happiness."

In 1976, as in 1972, '68, '64 and all the way back as far as my own memory carries me, this hope has been doomed to failure—by our capitalist economic system which has subverted and distorted the Constitutional guarantees and turned our government into a government of the military-industrial complex, serving the insatiable maw of the military machine and the faceless owners of the multinational corporations who reap profit from it.

The current noise and posturing of this year's primaries clearly show the dichotomy between the ideals of democracy as originally conceived in the Declaration of Independence and the Bill of Rights—documents which shook and continue to shake the world—and the reality of bought elections, TV demagoguery, manipulation and obscuring of issues, and contrived renewal of the Cold War.

The contrast between this "sound and fury signifying nothing" and the reality of the CPSU's 25th Congress sharply delineates what "socialist democracy" is all about. The Congress itself, with its sober evaluation of past successes and weaknesses, serious consideration of grassroots programs and proposals, and realistic, yet forward-looking establishment of future goals was an exercise in participatory democracy. The people were involved in the process from the initial publication of the proposals through two and one-half months of debate involving tens of millions of citizens in trade unions, women's, youth, cultural and other organizations, as well as in the press. In fact, Brezhnev told the Congress that more than one million proposals and suggestions had been received for consideration in the final drafting of the five-year plan. Of the 4,998 delegates elected to represent their peers, 73.5 per cent were attending a Party Congress for the first time; 77 per cent were from the working class (more than 1300 coming directly from big industrial centers, open-hearth furnaces, coal mines and factories); 25 per cent were women; and over 70 per cent under 50 years of age (12.5 per cent of them under 35).

The people at the 25th Party Congress defined their major concerns as increasing worker participation in the management of production and extending the powers of the Soviets (national, regional and local governmental bodies).

It is not easy for US citizens, reared in a tradition of primaries, elections and two-party politics, to understand how participatory democracy works in a socialist society where the meaningful involvement precedes the voting, and the ballot box merely confirms the input people have already had.

The Women's International League for Peace and Freedom has engaged in seminars with representatives from the Soviet Women's Committee since 1961, the first US women's organization to breach the Cold War curtain for a face-to-face seminar. These 15 years of "detente" with our Soviet sisters have enabled us to ask questions, probe answers, and witness first-hand during our visits to their country what grassroots democracy means and how it works to improve the quality of people's lives.

The juxtaposition of the US primary elections and the USSR Party Congress made the differences very clear indeed.

DOROTHY STEFFENS
Women's Leader for
for Peace and Freedom

Returning here recently after three years in the Soviet Union, I have been asked many times, "What is it like to live under socialism?"

Contrast is easier than comparison. I came home to find in my native city that public housing programs have been dropped, social welfare curtailed, essential workers excised from the public payrolls. Unemployment is rife, medical costs incredibly high, and pessimism about the future widespread. On the other hand, in the great cities of the USSR, new housing for workers is continually being constructed; education, culture and social welfare are expanding; and workers not jobs are at a premium.

The dynamic heart of this society is the Communist Party of the Soviet Union whose 25th Congress has just concluded. The Congress was an oasis of harmony and sanity in the midst of a world of imperialist domination of smaller nations by the capitalist states, abrasive relationships spurred by the financial and military maneuvers of the capitalist world, and the nuclear arms buildup.

One can only contrast our national Republican and Democratic Party conventions, held every four years, and the frenetic wheeling and dealing that goes into the selection of a Party platform and a candidate for office, with the five-year Congresses of the Soviet Union. The first is concerned primarily with maintaining land, national resources, and all means of production as a private preserve and the United States as the dominant factor in world economy. The other is dedicated to planning for the progress of the entire people, based upon collective ownership of land and property and on peaceful coopera-tion, rather than rivalry among nations.

The 25th Congress was a gathering of the sanest, most responsible and far-sighted people on earth. While we here have yet to found a society of peace and progress, the Congress of the Soviet people has made one more giant stride in strengthening theirs.

AUGUSTA STRONG
Writer and Editor

Though the capitalist press did its best to misrepresent the historic 25th Congress of the CPSU, they were hard-pressed to distort and conceal the spirit of this tremendously successful congress, or the facts reported there.

The bourgeois media clamors constantly about the "cumbersome Soviet economy"—let's see what that economy has done. During the last five years industrial production rose at an annual rate of 7.4 per cent, as compared to 1.2 per cent for the US and Common Market countries. There is no unemployment. The Soviets aren't aban-doning housing and evicting tenants; they have the world's fastest growing housing industry and some of the world's lowest rents. They aren't closing hospitals and schools, but building more and more. Prices are steady, and real income will continue to rise by a sixth to a quarter during the Tenth Five-Year Plan. The Soviet Union provides for its people because the working class is in charge.

That leadership causes the USSR to maintain its active concern for the rest of the world. Besides assistance to the other socialist states, thousands of Soviet projects throughout the developing world aid the achievement of economic and political inde-pendence. Soviet aid to the national liberation movements has made possible the victories of the people of Vietnam, and of Guinea-Bissau, Mozambique and Angola, which are helping speed the final collapse of colonialism in Africa.

All this is in full harmony with the Soviet initiatives for detente and peaceful coexistence. The 25th Congress charted the next phase in this historic struggle. In the words of Leonid Brezhnev, "Socialism and peace are indissoluble."

JARVIS TYNER
Chairman, Communist Party of New York State

ANTAR SUDAN KATARA MBERI

Solar Salute to the 25th Congress
(Excerpt)

Song of Lenin,
25th Congressional song,
you rise
from stone, from steel
you rise
from seminal soil,
the germinative soul
of all people,
your people,
my people,
our peoples,

you came up from subterranean parents
long years ago,
blazing coal you came up,
to dazzle the earth and sun
with your fiery diamond of sacrifice,

so woman and man,
girl and boy, could forever
wring war and soldiers
blood from the earth's linen
spirit;

ANTAR SUDAN KATARA MBERI taught literature and history at Ohio University. He is now Director of the W.E.B. Du Bois Harlem Community Center, and a leader of the Young Workers Liberation League.

so a planetary patriotism
could flower, you meet:
congress of victors,
guardians of light and song,
planetary patriots,
who watered the earth with your blood,
your precious blood,

so spring might be born again,
so the rose could undress
and discard the thorn
in its side,
so the child could release
the lethal hand of hunger
bullets and bombs.

You met: the 25th Congress
of victors, the 25th Congress
of guardians, the 25th Congress
of light, and song,

Planetary
Patriots
who watered the earth with your blood,
delivered the sun from its grave,
and now deliver the world
from the prison walls
and firing squads
with your sweat;

My voice remains one
among four billion;
and more:
communist voices,
raised in a solar salute,
a lunar tribute of love,
to you.